Missouri
Marriages
in the News

1851-1865

by
Lois Stanley
George F. Wilson
Maryhelen Wilson

Please direct all correspondence and orders to:

www.southernhistoricalpress.com
or
SOUTHERN HISTORICAL PRESS, Inc.
PO BOX 1267
375 West Broad Street
Greenville, SC   29601
southernhistoricalpress@gmail.com

ISBN #0-89308-438-7

Printed in the United States of America

Newsworthy for genealogists, the approximately 2100 records here
provide a wealth of detail not found in Missouri's courthouses.
Virtually all identify the bride's father. Several hundred report
marriages which took place outside of the state. Some are from
"burned" counties, notably Montgomery and Chariton. Some show place
of birth, maiden names of "Mrs." remarrying, occupations, actual
location of the ceremony ("at the home of the bride's uncle"), and
similar interesting details.

While the newspapers represented here did not cover the whole state --
some areas had no newspapers -- the marriages recorded here include
residents of 73 counties. A bride's index starts on page 74; and
the hundreds of surnames in the two lists may help researchers
pinpoint a family during the period when published marriage records
are scarce.

NEWSPAPER CODES

BOBS	Boonville Observer	Cooper Co.
BOL	Bolivar Courier	Polk Co.
BRUNS	Brunswicker	Chariton Co.
CANE	Canton Reporter	Lewis Co.
CANP	Canton Press	"
CAWN	California Weekly News	Moniteau Co.
CECB	Central City & Brunswicker	Chariton Co.
CHAC	Charleston Courier	Mississippi Co.
COSE	Columbia Sentinel	Boone Co.
COWS	Missouri Statesman, Columbia	"
FULT	Fulton Telegraph	Callaway Co.
GAL	Northwest Missourian, Gallatin	Daviess Co.
GLWT	Glasgow Weekly Times	Howard Co.
HAM	Hannibal Messenger	Marion Co.
HANT	" Tri-Weekly	"
HANJ	Hannibal Journal	"
HAWU	Hannibal Western Union	"
HIM	Huntsville Independent Missourian	Randolph Co.
HOLS	Holt County Sentinel (Oregon)	Holt Co.
HOLT	Holt Co. News "	"
JEX	Jefferson Examiner (Jefferson	Cole Co.
JINQ	Jefferson Inquirer City)	"
KCJC	Kansas City Journal of Commerce	Jackson Co.
LADB	Louisiana Democrat-Banner	Pike Co.
LAJ	Louisiana Journal	"
LANA	LaGrange National American	Lewis Co.
LEXC	Lexington Citizen	Lafayette Co.
LEXP	Lexington Express	"
LIT	Liberty Tribune	Clay Co.
MAG	Macon Gazette	Macon Co.
MARD	Marshall Democrat	Saline Co.
MORE	Missouri Republican, St. Louis	St. Louis Co.
OVAS	Osage Valley Star, Osceola	St. Clair Co.
PALS	Palmyra Spectator	Marion Co.
PWH	Palmyra Whig	"
RANC	Randolph Citizen	Randolph Co.
RICE	Richfield Enterprise	Clay Co.
RICON	Northwest Conservator, Richmond	Ray Co.
RIF	Richfield Monitor	Clay Co.
SAND	Savannah Northwest Democrat	Andrew Co.
SAS	Savannah Sentinel	"
SEDA	Sedalia Advertiser	Pettis Co.
SJH	St. Joseph Herald	Buchanan Co.
SJWW	St. Joseph Weekly West	"
SLMD	Missouri Democrat, St. Louis	St. Louis Co.
SPRIM	Springfield Mirror	Greene Co.
SPRIP	Springfield Patriot	"
STGAZ	St. Joseph Gazette	Buchanan Co.
SteGPD	Ste. Genevieve Plain Dealer	Ste. Genevieve Co.
WARS	Warrensburg Standard	Johnson Co.
WAVE	Waverly & St. Thomas Visitor	Lafayette Co.
WEBS	Weston Border Star	Jackson Co.

These newspapers are generally available in the Newspaper Library of the State Historical Society of Missouri, Columbia. MORE is also available at the Missouri Historical Society, St. Louis.

ABBOTT, Lucius of St. Louis   22 Nov   MORE 23 Nov 1855
CHAMBERLIN, Flora B. (late Rev. of Alton)   Rev. William Homes

ABRAHAMS, Michael   19 Nov   MORE 20 Nov 1851
LEWIS, Rebecca of New York   Edward Meyers, Pastor   United Hebrew

ABRAMS, P.H.   20 Nov   MORE 22 Nov 1862
TUTTLE, Mary E. (E.G.) at the home of her father by H.A. Nelson, D.D.

ACKERLY, M.W. late of New York   6 Aug   MORE 12 Aug 1856
PURCELL, Frances of Knox Co. IN at the home of her father

ADAIR, John   25 Mar   COWS 9 Apr 1858
SINCLAIR, Eliza (James) of Callaway Co.   Thomas P. Stephens

ADAMS, Carter   28 Oct   MORE 17 Nov 1855
BOON, Ann   in Montgomery Co.

ADAMS, Daniel   1 Apr   (all of St. L.)   SLMD 9 Apr 1861
KLINEFELTER, Josephine (2nd dau Capt. John) Rev. H.E. Niles

ADAMS, James S. of St. Louis   21 Nov in Philadelphia   MORE 29 &
BUCKINS (BUCKIUS?), Annie (William) of Frankford PA   Rev Thomas Murphy   30 Nov '59

ADAMS, John of St. Louis   16 May, Rev. Calhoun, at home of br's father   SLMD 19 Jun 1858
RICE, Mary Ellen (eldest dau/Dr. C.) of St. Charles, MO

ADAMS, Samuel T. of Franklin Co.   18 Oct   MORE 20 Oct 1859
NORTH, Elizabeth (3rd dau/William and Nancy)   of Franklin Co., at home

ADAMS, W.H. of the Platte Argus   both of Weston 20 Jan, Rev. Z.N. Roberts   LIT 7 Feb 1851
GIST, Harriet A. (G.W.)

ADKINS, J.C.   (see next item)   26 Nov   KCJC 12 Dec 1857
FISHER, Annie (Merritt R.) of Liberty   Rev. R.C. Morton

ADKINS, John C. of Kansas City (see above)   26 Nov   LIT 27 Nov 1857
FISHER, Fannie (M.R.) of Liberty   Elder R.C. Moreton

ADKINS, Joseph C. of Boone Co.   11 Dec   MORE 8 Jan 1856
EDWARDS, Malinda (Frazier)   I. Winfrey

AFFLECK, Charles D. of St. Louis   27 Jun Rev. Sunderland   MORE 12 Jul 1859
CHITTENDEN, Julia M. (William E.) of-at Niagara, Canada West

AKERS, Thomas P.   3 May in Lexington   COWS 20 May 1859
ANDERSON, Kate (Col. Oliver)   Rev. B.M. Hobson

ALBRIGHT, William A.)of St. Louis   28 May in Chicago   MORE 30 May 1863
DONAHOE, Mrs. Kate)   Fr. Converse

ALEXANDER, Charles T., Surgeon U.S. Army   4 Dec in St. Louis   MORE 5 Dec 1863
BARRET, Julia (late Dr. Richard F.)   Rev. Montgomery Schuyler

ALEXANDER, Fitzhugh   all of, and at, Lexington MO 9 Feb   MORE 29 Feb 1864
RUSSELL, Fannie E. (William H.)   Rev. J.H. Warder

ALEXANDER, G. Chapman   in St. Louis at the home of the bride's brother, J.M.
GARDINER, Mary J. (William)   23 Feb   Rev. J.H. Brooks   MORE 1 Mar 1865
            (Bride and groom both of Lexington MO)

ALEXANDER, Ira   26 Dec in Greene Co.   MORE 8 Jan 1856
PAYNE, Mrs. Sarah A. (Kindred Rose)   S. Bedford

ALLEN, E.D. of Kidder   9 Nov, Rev. P.B. Smith   MORE 25 Nov 1865
FOREE, Miriam (H.S.) of-at Breckenridge

ALLEN, Ethan, Editor of the Platte City Herald 20 Sep in Lexington   COWS 9 Oct 1857
MUSGROVE, Ann M. (late William)   Rev. M.M. Hobson

ALLEN, T.T. of Liberty   21 May   COWS 24 May 1861
DUNCAN, Margaret A. (W.H.) of Columbia   Rev. J.T. Williams
            (Rev. Williams was president of the Baptist Female College)

ALLEN, William of Lexington   at the home of the bride's father, 7 May, in   WAVE 19 May 1860
BRIDGES, Mary L. (James)   Syracuse MO Rev. S.B.H. Wooldridge

ALLEN, William L. of Audrain Co.   17 Jan   HANT 5 Feb 1856
BOYCE, Catherine (William) of Callaway Co.

ALLEYNE, Dr. J.S.D. of St. Louis   30 Nov   Rev. Orville Dewey   MORE 7 Dec 1858
STEDMAN, Henrietta (Josiah) of - at Boston MA

ALLGAIER, M.S. of Weston   3 May   MORE 24 May 1859
WILLIAMS, Amanda (A.G.) of Platte Co.   Rev. Thomas

                                        1

ALTHOUSE, H.A. of St. Louis   22 Dec   MORE 24 Dec 1864
GORDON, Julia   of - in Cairo IL   Rev. Olmstead

ANDERSON, Rev. G., pastor of 2nd Baptist Church 23 Apr in Alton   MORE 24 Apr 1861
ROBERTS, Mary E. (E.G., at his home) formerly of New York   Rev. Jameson

ANDERSON, James of Montgomery Co.   5 Dec   COWS 20 Dec 1861
WOODSON, Anne E. (David) of Audrain Co.   Rev. S. Scott

ANDERSON, Samuel W.   17 Nov   RANC 25 Nov 1859
REED, Mollie (Henry J.)   Elder James Williams
                        "all of Randolph Co."

ANDERSON, Dr. S.H. of Hannibal   13 Feb in Palmyra   MORE 26 Feb 1856
TATLOW, Anna Mary (Thomas M.)   Rev. Leighton

ANDERSON, Rufus   18 Jan   SLMD 27 Jan 1854
THOMPSON, Cornelia (Thomas E.)   Rev. Mayhurst
                        "all of Palmyra"

ANDREWS, J.T. Jr. of St. Louis   1 Aug at Cottage Hill   MORE 6 Aug 1857
PEMBERTON, Georgia "ward and adopted daughter of C.L. Pemberton"
                        Ceremony performed by Rev. Edmonds of Chicago

ANGELL, James H.   10 Sep   COWS 18 Sep 1857
FOUNTAIN, Hannah (late Absolem)   Elder James Barns
                        "all of Boone Co."

APPLEGATE, James L. of Brunswick   29 Jul in Chariton Co.   MORE 21 Aug 1858
HAWKINS, Amanda A. (Harrison) of Keytesville   Rev. J.S.M. Beebe

APPLETON, Edward of St. Louis   5 Oct in Beloit WI   MORE 10 Oct 1854
STEWART, Helen (Alanson) of Chicago   Rev. Eddy

ARCHER, William   20 Dec in Montgomery Co.   MORE 8 Jan 1856
HENSLEY, Amanda

ARMSTRONG, Charles   27 Jan   COSE 10 Feb 1853
ARMSTRONG, Mary (Benjamin)   Rev. D. Doyle
                        "all of Boone Co."

ARNOLD, John W. of Montgomery Co.   28 Jun Rev Wm. Douglas   SLMD 30 Jul 1860
LAIL, Mollie (Elijah, at his home) of Callaway Co.

ARNOLD, R.R. of Boone Co. in Audrain Co. 10 Jun   COWS 26 Jun 1863
MORRIS, E.O. (Judge John B.) of Audrain Co.   Rev. James Dudly

ARNOLD, Thomas T. of Boone Co.   28 Mar   Rev. John Rogers   COWS 7 Apr 1865
BALDWIN, Mrs. Nannie (John Throckmorton)   of Nicholas Co. KY

ARNOT, A. of St. Louis   27 Oct in St. Louis   GLWT 10 Nov 1853
WILDER, Harriet E. (Spencer) of Rutland MA   Rev. William Crowell

ASHBURY, John H.   17 Feb   COWS 22 Feb 1861
WATERS, Lizzie (Jo.)   Elder J.T.M. Johnson
                        "all of Boone Co."

ASHBY, T.T. of the Missouri Conference   MORE 3 Apr 1860
TEST, Mrs. E. of Tennessee

ATKINS, Granville   16 Dec   GLWT 8 Jan 1857
PATTERSON, Adaline M. (Professor A.) "all of Platte City"

AUSTIN, A.A. of Boonville   29 Nov near Arrow Rock   BOBS 3 Dec 1859
BROWNLEE, Sarah J. (James)   Rev. P.G. Rea

AUSTIN, Andrew J.   27 Nov   Rev. Wiley Clark   GLWT 1 Dec 1853
WALLACE, Martha P.E. (A.)   "all of Livingston Co."

AUSTIN, Calvin J.   23 Apr Elder T.M. Allen   COWS 31 May 1861
DUNCAN, Pamelia (James)   "all of Columbia"

AVERY, James W.   6 May Rev. W.A. Gray   COWS 26 May 1865
WOOLFORK, Sallie (Charles T.) at the home of the bride's mother
                        "all of Henry Co."

BACON, J.L.   Immaculate Conception Church, 10 Nov
GROVER, Kibbie M. (G.M. and Elinora J.)   Rev. Feehan   MORE 15 Nov 1859
                        "all of St. Louis"

BAGBY, Julian   24 Jun   MORE 27 Jun 1857
BRIDGES, Mary E. (Andrew)   Rev. J.N.W. Springer
                        "all of Franklin Co."

2

BAILEY, Frank formerly of Cincinnati   8 Dec   MORE 11 Dec 1855
JOHNSON, Kate (only dau/Col. A.H.) Washington Co. Rev. William Hopkins

BAILEY, Robert late of Callaway Co., now of San Jose 18 Oct in Fulton   COSE 28 Oct 1852
JAMISON, Mary Ellen (late Judge) of Monroe Co.   Elder T.M. Allen

BAILEY, Dr. J.T. of Howard Co.   1 Feb   COWS 5 Feb 1858
NICHOLS, May (James) of Boone Co.   Rev. L.B. Wilken

BAKER, George A.   29 Jul in Lexington   MORE 21 Aug 1858
STREET, Sarah Eleanor (late Gen. Joseph M.) Rev. R.A. Young

BAKER, Levin N. of St. Louis   in Sugar Grove WI 7 Sep   MORE 17 Sep 1853
BEALE, Clara (Bazil) of Brooks Co. VA   Rev. Nesbit

BAKER, Napoleon   16 Jun in Callaway Co.   MORE 3 Jul 1857
FREEMAN, Sarah Ann (William)   Rev. J.F. Smith

BAKER, Reinhard   3 Nov in Lexington   WAVE 5 Nov 1859
CURRIE, Mary E. (S.F.)

BAKER, T.J.   1 Mar   MORE 8 Mar 1865
WEST, Ann (Alvin)   Rev. W.W. Robertson
                        "all of Callaway Co."

BAKER, Thomas F. of Shelbina   11 Nov   COWS 28 Nov 1862
THOMAS, Lydia A. (Elder H.) of Boone Co.   Elder Alfred Wilson

BALDWIN, Jamuel   15 Aug   COWS 24 Aug 1855
TIPTON, Sarah (Maj. L.D.)   Rev. M. Payne

BALDWIN, Oscar P. of St. Louis   8 Jun Rev. W.D. Shumate   MORE 10 Jun 1865
AXTELL, Addie E. (eldest dau/Thomas R.) of Central Twp., St. Louis Co.

BALLARD, Patrick   in Lexington, no date   MORE 9 Dec 1856
McCLURE, Cynthia (H.S.)   Rev. Hobson

BALLENGER, George W.   6 Dec 1853   GLWT 23 Feb 1854
GWYNN, Fanny   at Stafford's Ranch, California
                        "both of Saline Co."

BALLEW, Irving of Howard Co.   15 Jan   Rev. John Y. Porter MORE 22 Jan 1861
WOLFSKILL, Martha (John) of Livingston Co.

BANKHEAD, Arthur   Rev. Worthington, on 10 Jun at Oakland, near   MORE 13 Jun 1857
CHAMBERS, Mary (late Col. A.B.) of St. Louis   Bowling Green

BANKS, Marvin R. of Lafayette Co.   12 Oct   COWS 24 Oct 1856
McAFEE, Mary R. (Rev. R.L.) of Boone Co.

BANTZ, Peter Sowers, of St. Louis (formerly of Frederick MD) 30 Oct   MORE 3 Nov 1861
MURPHY, Sarah A. of Dublin

BARBOUR, Thomas P. of Pike Co.   22 Dec 1859   LAJ 5 Jan 1860
GAMBLE, Jennie R. (John W.) of Audrain Co.   Rev. Eli B. Smith

BARCLAY, D. Robert of St. Louis   in Van Buren AR 24 Dec 1851   MORE 6 Feb 1852
WATSON, Sallie Virginia (William A.)   Rev. Marshall

BARD, William E. of Sedalia   26 Sep at Boonville   SEDA 1 Oct 1864
TALBOT, Sallie E. (eldest dau/Levi) of Boonville Rev. M.M. Pugh

BARKSDALE, William H. of St. Louis   15 Mar at Louisville KY   LEXP 23 Mar 1853
TRABUE, Mary E. (James) of Louisville   Rev. Breckinridge

BARLOW, Charles   1 Nov   MARD 21 Nov 1860
CATT, Sarah (Solomon)   Rufus Bingham
                        "all of Saline Co."

BARLOW, J.C. of St. Louis   11 Nov in New York   COWS 3 Dec 1858
CLARKE, Mrs. C.M.   Rev. Stryker
          "at the residence of the bride's brother, Henry A. Morgan"

BARNARD, John H. of St. Louis   6 Sep in Princeton IL   MORE 11 Sep 1864
FRARY, Ellen M. formerly of Deerfield MA   Elder Willing

BARNARD, L.H.   1 Sep   MORE 2 Sep 1864
WATSON, Emma (Robert J.) at her father's residence

BARNES, Abraham   7 Dec   GLWT 28 Dec 1854
BARNES, Sarah (Richard per Glwt, Richardson per Bruns)   BRUNS 23 "

BARNES, Cyrenius   31 Oct   COWS 9 Nov 1855
BAKER, Sallie P. (John)   "all of Boone Co."

3

BARNES, D.W. of Boone Co.   25 Jun Elder J.M. Robinson   COWS 7 Jul 1865
GLASGOW, Susan C. (Nathan) of Millersburg, Callaway Co.

BARNES, F.   9 Dec   Rev. Henry Hill   LIT 17 Dec 1852
NULL, Henriette (William) "all of Clay Co."

BARNES, Dr. J.H. of Columbia   8 Mar   COWS 16 Mar 1855
HASTON, M.A. (Jesse) of Howard Co.   Rev. William W. Rush

BARNHILL, William   9 Feb near Edina   MORE 23 Feb 1860
HAINES, Ellen (eldest dau/Simpson)   Rev. W.H. Hicks

BARNS, Thomas   17 Aug   MORE 30 Aug 1854
DAVENPORT, Susan (John) of Boone Co.   Rev. Green Carey

BARNUM, L. of St. Louis   18 Oct in Springfield IL   MORE 19 Oct 1854
CLARK, Mary D. (Samuel)   Rev. Wilson

BARR, Boyd   26 Feb   SAS 28 Feb 1852
JENKINS, Mary J. (Joseph)   Rev. E.A. Carson
                              "all of Andrew Co."

BARR, Edwin W., M.D. of St. Louis   25 Aug in Lexington MA   MORE 4 Sep 1859
BLASDEL, Mary (John)   Rev. C.H. Leonard

BARRET, Arthur B.   "Thursday last" in Christ Church (Episc.)   MORE 19 Jun 1859
SWERINGEN, Annie E. (J.T.)   Bishop Hawks

BARRETT, Henry W.   2 Nov Rev. James Craik   MORE 8 Nov 1865
TYLER, Emma (Mrs. Robert)   "all of St. Louis"

BARRET, J.R. of St. Louis   14 Dec in Louisville KY   MORE 21 Dec 1864
NICHOLAS, Matilda (S.S.)   Rev. Edward Humphrey

BARRON, J.A.   4 Oct in Springdale, Bates Co.   MORE 21 Oct 1859
ELLISTON, Sallie Ann (T.T.)   Rev. G.W. Geyer

BARTH, Alex of Columbia at Sapson St. Hall, Philadelphia   COWS 6 Sep 1861
JACOBS, Pauline (Israel) of Philadelphia   Rev. Isador Frankel

BARTH, Moses of Fayette   21 Mar in Philadelphia   GLWT 12 Apr 1855
ARNOLD, Minna of Philadelphia

BARTHOLOW, Theodore   5 Sep   GLWT 7 Sep 1854
ROPER, Edmonia J. (William)

BARTHOLOW, Thomas J. in Deposit, Delaware Co. NY 23 Aug   GLWT 2 Sep 1852
SPRAGUE, Laura T.   Rev. Allen

BARTLETT, Dr. J.W. of Brunswick   11 May   MORE 22 May 1859
RANDOLPH, Kate (late Capt. W.S.) of St. Louis   Rev. William G. Eliot

BARTON, William   25 Oct in Roanoke   GLWT 1 Nov 1860
BULL, Julia (Dr. John) of Chariton Co.   Rev. William G. Caples

BASS, Robert L. of Boone Co.   16 Feb at Glasgow   MORE 21 Feb 1864
McCOY, Juliet (J.C.) of Glasgow   Rev. J.A. Quarles

BASS, William H. of Boone Co.   11 Sep in Paris KY   COWS 26 Sep 1856
HICKMAN, Irene of Paris KY   Rev. Carrier

BASSETT, Gen. J.M. of St. Joseph   Tuesday   JINQ 7 Jun 1851
DIXON, Nancy (Henry) of Cole Co.   Rev. R.H. Weller

BASSETT, Dr. S.T.   15 Feb in Kingston MO   LIT 2 Mar 1855
ARDINGER, Carrie D. (eldest dau/John H.)   Rev. Canfield

BASSETT, Thomas E.   at Grand River College, St. Louis, 20 Feb   MORE 22 Feb 1861
WETHERGREEN, Mrs. Nina "youngest daughter of Christian Hirsch of
                      Christiana Norway"   Rev. Edward F. Berkeley

BATES, Edward R. of St. Louis   11 Jul at Utica NY   MORE 15 Jul 1865
COREY, Mary Ella (Rev. D.G., who officiated)   Bleecker St. Baptist Church

BATES, Fleming of St. Louis   5 May at Solitude, St. Charles Co.   MORE 14 May 1857
WILSON, Nannie (Dr. B.F.)

BATES, John M. Editor of the Kansas City Metropolitan 26 Oct   COWS 29 Oct 1858
PREWITT, Mattie (Moss)   Rev. X.X. Buckner

BATTERTON, W.W.   31 Aug   COWS 3 Sep 1858
WINN, Mollie (Charles)   "all of Boone Co."   Rev. P. Kemper

BATTLE, Maj. John   24 Jul   GLWT 31 Jul 1851
McCARTY, Elizabeth (Daniel)   Rev. Samuel C. Davis
                              "all of Randolph Co."

```
BAXTER, William                            13 Nov                          MORE 21 Nov 1858
BRYAN, Sallie (late Samuel, of Marion Co.)    Rev. Morton
          "at the home of his brother-in-law, S.T. Finley"

BAXTER, William of St. Louis               5 Nov                           SLMD 12 Nov 1861
SAPPINGTON, Mary Emily (Tyrie) of Oak Ridge   Rev. E.J. Foote

BAY, W.V.N. of St. Louis                    20 Oct at Tremont IL            JINQ 30 Oct 1852
WRIGHT, Maria Elizabeth (only dau/Nathaniel) of Tremont  Rev. W. Andrews

BEAN, John of Cass Co.                      1 Feb in Richmond               COWS 4 Mar 1859
YANTIS, Kate (Rev. J.L.)                     Rev. J.T. Lapsley

BEARD, E.J. of St. Louis                    25 Oct in Milford CT            MORE 4 Nov 1864
CARRINGTON, Martha J. of Milford            Rev. James Hubbel

BEARD, George E. of St. Louis               26 Oct, St. George's Church     MORE 27 Oct 1861
PERKINS, Abby L. (Capt. T.P.)               Rev. Berkeley

BEARD, James C.                             9 Nov in St. Francois Co.        MORE 22 Nov 1854
WILLIAMS, Sarah Jane (Gardner)              Rev. Alvin Rucker

BEARDSLEE, R. of St. Louis                  5 Dec in Collinsville IL        MORE 7 Dec 1859
WICKLIFFE, Annie E. (2nd dau/William decd)    Rev. G.C. Clarke

BEAZLEY, Thomas of Brunswick                12 Oct                          MORE 11 Nov 1858
WITT, Sallie (Highter) of Howard Co.        Rev. B.T.F. Coke

BEAUMONT, J.G. of St. Louis                 21 Jul in Green Bay WI          MORE 22 Aug 1853
PELTON, Julia

BEAUVAIS, John B.                           20 Feb                          MORE 22 Feb 1865
WRIGHT, Julia (J.C.)    "all of St. Louis"   Fr. Frehan

BEAZLEY, Richard E.                         5 Mar                           COWS 13 Mar 1863
McCONATHY, Alice T. (James)                 Elder J.K. Rogers
          "all of Boone Co."    Louisville & Memphis pc

BECK, Dr. James P. late of New Mexico       17 Dec 1861  in Boonville       COWS 10 Jan 1862
BROADDUS, Helen L. (Mrs. B.F.) of Howard Co.  Rev. Parister
          (Rev. Parister was from Cooper Co.)

BECKER, W.H.R. of St. Louis at Frederick City MD 8 Feb                      MORE 17 Feb 1865
HYATT, Mary E. of Harper's Ferry VA          Rev. Downs

BECKER, William G.H.                                                        MORE 9 Feb 1855
JACOBS, Maria Louisa F. (J.M.)              Rev. William G. Eliot
              "all of St. Louis"    Baltimore pc

BEDSWORTH, T.M.L. of Callaway Co.           24 Nov                          COWS 3 Dec 1858
CURRIE, Margaret (Samuel) of Lexington      Rev. W.W. Suddath

BEEBEE, Rev. Samuel J.M.      24 Nov at Pilgrim's Church, Brooklyn NY       GLWT 8 Dec 1853
WEST, Sarah L. (Frederick)                  Rev. S.M. Cox

BELL, J.G.                  17 Dec at Central Presbyterian Church           MORE 22 Dec 1863
SIMONDS, Laura (late Capt. John) of St. Louis  Rev. Anderson

BELL, Dr. John B.                           13 Jul                          MORE 20 Jul 1853
CASTLEMAN, Catherine (Lewis decd)           Rev. Cowan

BELL, Col. T.P.                             22 Jun  in Saline Co.           BOBS 4 Jul 1856
CATHRAE, Bettie McDowell (eldest dau/late Lewis)   Rev. W.M. Bell

BELLAMA, George W.                          13 Sep in Fulton                COWS 18 Nov 1864
THOMAS, Sallie F. (Solomon) all of Callaway Co.  Rev. Steerbargen

BELLES, Gilleve                            14 Oct in Lexington             COWS 22 Oct 1858
MOREHEAD, Fannie (Charles B.)               Rev. F.S. Dulin

BENEDICT, R.A.                             5 Dec in Boonville              MORE 8 Jan 1856
PIERCE, Josephine (Peter D.)                Rev. H.M. Painter

BENEPE, H.X.                               16 Sep                          COWS 24 Sep 1858
COPPER, Mrs. (Levi Bishop) of Callaway Co.  Rev. X.X. Buckner

BENNETT, James of Iowa                      19 Jul                          COWS 24 Jul 1857
HARRIS, Cornelia (James) of Boone Co.       Rev. N.H. Hall

BENIGHT, B.W.                              3 Apr                           MORE 25 Apr 1860
DAILEY, Malissa J. (Capt. S.G.) of Platte Co.  Rev. F.M. Miller

BENTON, William H. of St. Louis             18 Jun in Chicago               MORE 22 Jun 1863
STURGES, Kate (youngest dau/Solomon, at his home)  Rev. Z.M. Humphrey
```

BERNOUDY, Edward A.   Immaculate Conception Chapel, 2 Feb   MORE 5 Feb 1859
TAYLOR, Ellen A. (late John A.)   Fr. Feehan
                    Louisville & New Orleans pc

BERRY, Samuel G.   11 Feb Elder T.M. Allen   COWS 23 Feb 1855
HOBAN or HULEN, Mary Jane (John) "all of Boone Co."

BERRYMAN, James R.   "last Tuesday in the vicinity of Marshall"   MARD 24 Oct 1860
O'BANNON, Virginia (Minor W.)   Rev. J.W. Clark

BESEL, John   16 Aug Charles R. Moller   JINQ 21 Aug 1852
FUBRODT, Mrs. Anna Maria formerly wife of Ronimus
                    "both of Jefferson City"

BIDWELL, Thomas S.   "last Wednesday"   HANT 14 Nov 1854
HUBBARD, Mary Jane (William) of Marion Co.   Dr. T.D. Morton

BIGBEE, John S. of Springfield   in Robertson Co. TN 2 Oct   SPRIP 19 Oct 1865
KRISEL, Mrs. Lucinda of Robertson Co.   Rev. William Etherly

BIGGERS, David A. of St. Louis   in Cincinnati   MORE 18 Jun 1857
LOWRY, Rebecca (Samuel)   Rev. William Scott

BIGGERS, Joseph R.   27 May   HAWU 5 Jun 1851
LIPP, Caroline (Thomas) of Ralls Co.   Elder A.G. Galliher

BIGGS, William H. of Canton   19 Mar   LANA 26 Mar 1859
ELLIS, Martha E. (Judge William) of Canton   Rev. Henry Mayhew

BIGGS, William K.   16 Feb 1865   LAJ 25 Feb 1865
HAWKINS, Mattie Ann (2nd dau/Wm. G.) of Pike Co. Elder M.M. Mollisett

BILLINGS, James A. 7 June at the home of the bride's mother, Cote Brilliante MORE 8 Jun 1859
KIENLEN, Adaline (Mrs. Maria M.)   Rev. Fr. Van Hulst

BILLINGSLEY, R.H. of St. Louis   Wednesday at the Methodist Church   PALS 22 Jul 1864
LANSING, Fannie G. (A.B.)   Rev. Berkeley of St. Louis

BILLINGTON, J. of Kirksville   24 Nov   HANT 10 Dec 1853
LONG, Permelia Jane (John) of Monroe Co.   Rev. J.F. Young

BIRCH, Charles C. of Plattsburg   25 Oct   LIT 16 Nov 1855
YOUNG, Mollie (Willis W.) of Buchanan Co.   Rev. Middleton Jones

BIRCH, Hon. James H. 8 Oct at Mountain View, Fairfax Co. VA   GLWT 3 Nov 1853
FROST, Mrs. Elizabeth C. (late William Fitzhugh Carter)

BIRCH, James H. Jr. of Missouri   26 Jun Episcopal Church   MORE 2 Jul 1855
BASSETT, Mary B. (J.V.) of Harrison Co. KY   Rev. Carter Page

BISHOP, Benjamin   31 Dec in Weston   MORE 24 Jan 1855
HOLLAND, Eliza M. (James)   Rev. Frederick Starr

BISHOP, William T. of Hannibal   29 Jul   HAM 15 Aug 1861
BRIGHT, Maggie A. (Joseph) at his home in Clay Co. Rev. W.C. McPheters

BIXBY, E.   Rev. James Montgomery, in Georgetown MO   COWS 3 Dec 1858
DUNCAN, E.T.   at the home of her uncle, John Henderson

BIXBY, William L. of Daviess Co.   16 Jan   GLWT 27 Jan 1853
ALLEGA, Nancy (John) of Chariton Co.   Esq. Hampton

BLACK, John   31 Mar Rev. Anderson   MORE 4 Apr 1863
NORAY, Catherine S.J. (A. & Rebecca Russell Noray) of Glasgow, Scot.

BLACK, T.G.   26 Apr   MORE 27 Apr 1865
LEVI, Lizzie (2nd dau/S.J.) "all of St. Louis" Justice Levi Block

BLAKESLEY, Henry of St. Louis in New Orleans 22 Jan by Rev. Leacock   MORE 1 Feb 1861
LEARY, Mrs. Virginia of Ocean Springs LA

BLAKELY, R.W. of Marion Co.   9 Feb   HANJ 17 Feb 1853
LAMB, Mrs. Sarah R. of Louisville KY   Rev. Dines

BLANCHARD, Eleazer of St. Louis at St. Patrick's Cathedral, New York 19 Jul MORE 1 Aug 1853
VASQUEZ, Rosalie Mignault of Canada

BLAND, Richard E. of Bridgeton   at the home of George Lackland   MORE 20 Aug 1856
EDWARDS, Laura P. of Virginia   in St. Louis Co.

BLAND, William W.   23 Mar   SLMD 7 Apr 1854
PAYNE, Anna (Elder A.H.F.)   in Clay Co.

BLANKS, Andrew   28 Sep by David Ray Esq.   COSE 14 Oct 1852
WEARALL, Minerva (John) of Cole Co. (JINQ shows her name as WEAR)   JINQ 2 "

                                    6

BLOCK, Hyman of St. Louis   17 Jan   MORE 18 Jan 1856
BINGHAM, Virginia (John) of St. Louis Co.   Rev. Parsons (Methodist)

BOARDMAN, Charles
STEVENS, Jennie (T.B.)   of Marion Co.   23 Dec   HANT 25 Dec 1855

BOFINGER, John N.   13 Jul   MORE 13 Jul 1854
STILWELL, Mary E. (adopted dau/Samuel)   St. Paul's Church

BOGIE, T.D. of Huntsville   8 Dec   COWS 15 Jan 1864
MAUGHAS, Jennie (Dr. M.M.) of Callaway Co.   Elder E.J. Lampton

BOGUE, Henry C.   27 Oct   COWS 29 Nov 1861
CONGER, Margaret E. (eldest dau/William) of Audrain Co. Rev James Martin

BOGY, Ben I. of St. Louis   25 Jul in Galena   StGEPD 13 Aug '53
MACKAY, Charlotte (late A., qtrmaster US Army) F. Masterson

BONEY, W.J.   8 Mar   RANC 16 Mar 1860
CAMPBELL, Emily (Samuel L.)   Rev. James Dysart

BONNEL, Mason S.   Rev. Jesse Terriell   GLWT 11 Mar 1852
EVANS, Lucy A. (late John) of Howard Co.

BONNER, Samuel of St. Louis   30 Aug in Rochester   MORE 14 Sep 1853
GARRISON, Cordelia   Rev. W.H. Douglass

BOOGHER, Simon L.   17 Sep   MORE 28 Sep 1864
HOGAN, Sophia (John, at his home)   Rev. D.R. McAnally

BOONE, T.P. of Rocheport   17 Jul   COWS 1 Aug 1862
BOWER, Laurs S. (Dr. G.M.) of Monroe Co.   Elder S.A. Beauchamp

BOSWELL, J.H. of Cooper Co.   17 Dec   BOBS 26 Feb 1859
RUCKER, Sallie J. (J.W.) of - in Dover   Rev. McGarvey

BOTELER, Thomas P.   26 Feb   HANT 15 Mar 1856
BUCKNER, Sallie (Col. R.R.)   Rev. Robertson
                 "all of Callaway Co."

BOTTS, Joshua A.   9 Jun in Livingston Co.   MORE 14 Jun 1864
WILEY, Mary E. (eldest dau/W.)   Rev. W.W. Walden

BOTTS, Thomas H.   8 Mar in Linn Co.   GLWT 17 Mar 1853
HARVEY, Mary C. (Charles) "late of Linn Co." E.D. Harvey

BOULWARE, I.W.   15 Jan in Fulton   MORE 29 Jan 1856
LACK, Anna M. (eldest dau/John A.) of Washington, MO Rev John S. Cowan

BOUVIER, Leopold   1 Dec   MORE 14 Dec 1858
BENNETT, Emma (2nd dau/Willism)   Rev. Schuyler

BOVARD, R.D. of St. Louis   5 Jul   SLMD 20 Jul 1864
McLIN, Maggie   at the home of her father in New Orleans   Rev. Beatie

BOVER, Henry Jr. of Marshall   29 Nov in Alton IL   MARD 5 Dec 1860
FALL, Hettie O. (only dau/Dr. James S. of New Orleans) Rev. Melville Jameson
           "at the residence of Mrs. Adams"

BOYCE, Upton Lawrence   Rev. J. Boyle   COWS 19 Feb 1858
WRIGHT, Melinda Frances (Maj. Uriel) of St. Louis

BRADBURN, Isaac   18 May at Elm Narrows   CANE 2 Jun 1853
BLOID, Ruth Ann (only dau/Jackson)   John C. Bass

BRADFORD, George A. of Boone Co.   28 Jan   COWS 5 Feb 1858
SMITH, Annie (Joel) of Randolph Co.   Elder T.M. Gaines

BRADFORD, James R. of Moniteau Co.   1 Jan Rev. W.A. Taylor   CAWN 17 Jan 1863
ROBINSON, Eliza M. of Montgomery Co., at her mother's home

BRADLEY, Henry C.
SUGGETT, Eliza P. (John P.) both of Boone Co. 27 Sep by Elder Crisman   COWS 30 Sep 1859

BRADLEY, Prof. J.B.   29 Jun near Liberty   LIT 2 Jul 1858
WYMORE, Mary (William H.)   Elder A.M. Jones

BRADLEY, James   4 Oct? Rev. Fle-- Shaver?   LEXP 19 Oct 1853
McCANBY, Martha M. (T.A.J.) "all of this county"

BRADLEY, James W.   16 Sep   HANT 20 Sep 1856
LEAR, Jane V. (William) of Marion Co.   Elder Green

BRADLEY, L.K.   20 Nov   GLWT 1 Dec 1853
HUNT, Mary (J.) of - in Huntsville   Rev. Green Cary

BRADLEY, Thomas of Bloomfield, Callaway Co., age 80 in May   GLWT 10 Jun 1852
CRAIG, Mrs. (daughter of Richard Swan) age 25

BRAGG, Oliver T. (A.G.) of St. Louis   5 Sep in Quebec   MORE 17 Sep 1855
AHERN, Eleanor Elizabeth (late John) of Quebec Rev. John Cook D.D.

BRANCH, Joseph W. of St. Louis at the Parish Church, Sprotbro near   MORE 3 Mar 1857
                      Doncaster, Yorkshire, 3 Feb by Rev. Scott F. Stirtees
CLARK, Annie (Matthew) of Cotsworth

BRASHEARS, James   13 Jun   HANJ 17 Jun 1852
BROWN, Clarinda (eldest dau/Col. William) of Pike Co. Elder J.M. Johnson

BRAWNER, T.E., editor of the Milan Farmer 7 Apr in Lexington   SLMD 17 Apr 1858
NEET, Lizzie R. (late Jacob)   Rev. C.A. Davis

BRECK, Edward C. of Sacannah   in Columbia   COWS 16 Nov 1855
TODD, Letitia (Hon. David)

BRENNAN, John   6 Jan   MORE 11 Jan 1861
CONWAY, Sarah Magdalen Gayle (John) "all of St. Louis"

BRENT, F.E.   8 Apr at Christ Church   BOBS 12 Apr 1856
COOPER, Sallie (John)   Rev. Terry

BREWSTER, George W.   20 Sep   MORE 22 Sep 1860
MURPHY, Theresa (Thomas)   Rev. W.D. Shumate

BRIGHT, Edward F.   27 Mar in Palmyra   HAM 10 Apr 1862
REDD, Annie E. (Judge John T.   Rev. Jacob Creath

BRIGHT, William F.   Rev. Hodges   LIT 19 Nov 1852
THOMPSON, Virginia A. (Robert C.)   "all of Clay Co."

BRINKERHOFF, David W.   4 Oct, Baptist Church   SJH 8 Oct 1865
LYON, Mary Evelyn (eldest dau/Capt. Thomas) of - in Utica MO Rev T.B. Bratton

BRINKMEYER, H.N.   of St. Louis   18 Oct   MORE 22 Oct k860
SCHAUFFELBERGER, Lena of Baltimore   Rev. Hugo Krebs

BRITTINGHAM, Dr. I. Byron   Rev. S.W. Capes   MORE 23 Jun 1855
LEAGUE, Mary June (Judge W.R. of the Hannibal Messenger)

BRITTON, Alfred M. of St. Louis   13 Dec in Georgetown KY   MORE 16 Dec 1864
McHATTON, Annie of Baton Rouge   Rev. John Ganor
                      "at the residence of her uncle Dr. Kenry Craig"

BROADUS, Elijah G.   21 Jan
BASSET, Jane R. (William N.)   Elder Alfred Wilson   COWS 5 Feb 1864
                "all of Monroe Co."

BROCH, Ferdinand   14 Mar at Carondelet   SLMD 19 Mar 1861
BLUMENTHAL, Caroline E.(eldest dau/Augustus A.) Rev. G.W. Wall
 see also PLASS

BROCKMAN, Louis   12 May   MORE 14 May 1864
COLLINS, Annette Isabel (James) of St. Louis Rev. Fr. Henry

BROOKE, Edward G. of St. Louis   31 Dec in St. Ferdinand Twp.   MORE 4 Jan 1858
WOOLVERTON, Rachel (Charles and Mary) of St. Louis Co. Rev. Funney

BROOKS, John B. of Hannibal   21 Sep   MORE 1 Oct 1854
BALE, Catherine, lately of Ft. Madison IA   John L. Lacy

BROTHER, Howard   St. Paul's Episcopal Ch.   MORE 30 May 1861
WILSON, Annie (late John)

BROTHERTON, Lyne S. of St. Louis   3 Oct   MORE 7 Oct 1865
MOORE, Lizzie (Enoch) of Wilmington DE   Rev. Joseph Mason

BROUGHTON, H.W. formerly of Boone Co.   15 Jan   MORE 4 Feb 1856
FRAZIER, Ann H. (James) of Ray Co.

BROWN, F.W.   13 Apr   MARD 23 May 1860
HAYS, Marvann (eldest dau/William decd)   Rufus Bigelow JP

BROWN, Hayden   last Thursday   COSE 8 Apr 1852
FOWLER, Telitha (Joe) of Pettis Co.   Rev. Peter Kemper

BROWN, J.B. of Franklin Co.   17 Nov   COWS 27 Nov 1857
BAKER, Kitty (Capt. John) of Danville   Rev. McNeilly

BROWN, J.W.   6 Feb   GLWT 10 Feb 1853
MARKLAND, Nancy (Levi) "all of Howard Co."   Rev. W.B. Watts

BROWN, James   Thursday   MORE 7 Jun 1861
HART, Maria Church (Henry)   Rev. E. Carter Hutchinson

8

BROWN, James M.	11 Oct in Charleston MO	CHAC 5 Oct 1860
SAYERS, Laura Agnes (late William)	Rev. J.C. Maple, Baptist	
BROWN, John D. of Clinton Co.	15 Mar	MORE 4 Apr 1860
SMITH, Mary Ann (Peter M.) of Richmond KY	Rev. E. Forman	
BROWN, John H. of Shelby Co.	26 Jan Elder A.B. Jones	MORE 23 Feb 1860
SAMUEL, Alice (stepdaughter of Lewis Brown) of - in Clay Co.		
BROWN, Joseph Thomas 19 Feb, St. Paul's Church, St. Louis		
GUNN, Ellen Eliza Griggs 6th dau/Thomas Smith of Buckingham Eng.		MORE 3 Apr 1856
BROWN, Presley		COWS 9 Feb 1855
OLIVER, Ann (Isaac)	13 Jan	
BROWN, Samuel H.	11 Feb in Marine IL	MORE 17 Feb 1863
BLAKEMAN, Kittie (Curtis) at her father's home Rev. Mitchell		
BROWN, Thomas formerly of Polk Co.	5 Aug	SPRIM 14 Aug 1856
KELTNER, Sarah E. (George) of Greene Co.	Esq. Sanders	
BROWN, Walter T.	19 Nov in Jasper Co.	COWS 18 Dec 1857
JENKINS, Margaret (late William) formerly	Rev. Samuel Patterson	
of Alabama		
BROWN, William B. late of Lexington KY		GLWT 17 Feb 1853
THOMSON, Leona V. (Rev. Robert) of Saline Co. Rev. Thomas Fristoe		
BROWN, Wray of Keokuk IA		HANT 14 Mar 1857
FUQUA, Sarah (M.M.) of Marion Co.	12 Mar	
BROWNING, Joseph A. of St. Louis	20 May in Platte City	LIT 23 May 1856
DORRIS, Martha (eldest dau/Hon. George P. of St. Louis)		
BRYAN, Charles S. in Otterville, Cooper Co., 25 Nov		MORE 27 Nov 1863
WEAR, Mildred Y. (William G.) of Otterville Rev. William J. Garrett		
BRYANT, David W.	in Cottage Grove, Jefferson Co. 3 Oct	MORE 10 Oct 1855
HOW, Eliza (Judge William C.)	Rev. Myers	
BUCHANAN, A.H., MD	23 May	MORE 3 Jun 1861
HUGHES, Laura (youngest dau/Dr. Berry)		
"all of Ray Co."		
BUCHANAN, Charles W.	31 May	
WATSON, Laura Kate (Mrs. Sarah A.)	Rev. Anthony	MORE 4 Jun 1864
"all of the town of New Madrid"		
BUCHANAN, George W.	9 May in Boonville	MORE 18 May 1855
TERRY, Emily (Col. Joseph B.) of Lexington	Rev. A.V.C. Schenck	
BUCHANAN, R.S. of LaGrange	30 Jan in Quincy IL	HANT 3 Feb 1855
HARRISON, Mattie J. of Quincy IL		
BUCHANAN, Robert of St. Louis	Rev. William Newland	MORE 25 Jun 1865
ROWE, Mary Willie (Joseph) at her father's home, Oakland Green, Marion Co.		
BUCKNER, Rev. X.X.	3 Sep, Baptist Church	COWS 4 Sep 1857
PREWITT, Clara (Moss) of Columbia	Elder J.M. Johnson	
BUFFINGTON, William H., auditor of Public Accounts, MO 28 Jun, Cabell Co. VA		JINQ 16 Jul 1853
NICHOLS, Georgella of Cabell Co. VA Rev. Joseph Creighton, Methodist Church		
BUNNELL, J.W. of Howard Co.	23 Sep	
PATTERSON, Kate A. of Georgetown KY	Rev. Joshua Terrill	GLWT 2 Oct 1851
"at the residence of Hiram S. Moffett"		
BURBACH, Anthony	5 Nov	MORE 8 Nov 1863
McGUFFIN, Mollie E. (James M.) "all of St. Louis" Rev John Robison		
BURGESS, James of Sulphur Springs, Jefferson Co.		MORE 13 Dec 1857
SMITH, Phebe Ellen (Joshua) late of Shelby Co. Rev. Robert Kay		
"at the residence of Washington Manning, Lewis Co."		
BURGESS, William J. of Liberty	6 May in Mayslick KY	MORE 14 Jun 1856
RUNYAN, Mary R. (2nd dau/Asa R.)	Elder James Henshall	
"at the residence of Maj. R.J. Burgess"		
BURKLIN, Charles H.)both of St. Louis	30 Aug in Leavenworth City	MORE 6 Sep 1859
CLOSE, Christina L.	Mr. Pitcher	
BURLINGAME, J.F.S.	18 Nov	MORE 2 Dec 1856
CUSTER, Emma (Joseph) "all of Danville"	Rev. William Taylor	
BURNES, Calvin F.	27 Sep	COWS 7 Oct 1859
HUGHES, Kate (James M.) of - in St. Louis	Rev. E.M. Marvin	

BURNES, Hon. D.D.   13 May in Platte City   LIT 23 May 1851
WINN, Virginia (Mrs. Emily) late of Tennessee   Rev. Z.N. Roberts (M.E. Ch South)

BURNESON, John C. of St. Louis   24 Apr   MORE 27 Apr 1861
HAUK, Lizzie (Capt. William)   Rev. H. Morris

BURNETT, Frank   in Louisiana, MO   5 Dec   HAM 19 Dec 1861
PETTIBONE, Mattie L. (Levi)   Rev. James W. Campbell
          "at the home of the bride's brother-in-law, Edwin Draper"

BURNETT, P.S. formerly of Clay Co.   8 Aug in San Jose   LIT 11 Aug 1854
TOONEY, Mrs. Elizabeth Jane formerly of Jackson Co.   Rev. Graham

BURNHAM, Erastus   7 Feb   COWS 16 Feb 1855
FORBIS, Nancy (Robert B. "all of Boone Co."   Rev. D. Doyle

BURNS, Patrick (of Burns, Degnan & Co., St. Louis) 31 Oct in Boonville   MORE 10 Nov 1865
McCUBBIN, Ann (George W.) of Cooper Co.   Rev. Fr. Hilner
                Nashville & Baltimore pc

BURROUGHS, C.M. of Howard Co.   9 Jun   GLWT 23 Jun 1853
HARRIS, Mary (Tyre) of Boone Co.   Rev. Noah Flood

BURTON, John O. lately of Shelby Co.   13 Jan   MORE 19 Jan 1859
YANCY, Elizabeth (L., at his home)of Howard Co. Rev. F.A. Savage

BURTON, Samuel J.   1 Dec by Elder T.M. Allen   COSE 8 Dec 1853
HICKS, Elizabeth dau/Willis, formerly of Boone Co., now of New Mexico

BUSH, Porter late of Kentucky   15 Nov   MORE 24 Dec 1860
GENTRY, Ann Eliza (Col. Joshua) "now all of Marion Co."

BUSKETT, James L.
EVANS, Theresa (eldest dau/late Augustus H.)   31 Aug   Rev. James H. Brooks MORE 2 Sep 1865
          "all of St. Louis"   ceremony at the 16th St. Presbyterian Ch.

BUST, Robert   in Washington Co. 27 Jul   MORE 28 Jul 1865
McGREADY, Lucy "only daughter of the late Dr. James Hardege."

BUSTER, Charles W.   23 Dec Rev. E.S. Dulin   LIT 26 Dec 1851
MINTER, George Ann (John)   "all of Clay Co."

BUTLER, Henry M. of St. Louis   at Sherman House, Chicago, 23 Apr   MORE 27 Apr 1863
STUART, Anna of Sherman CT   Dr. T.M. Post

BUTLER, John Wesley of St. Louis   4 Nov   MORE 11 Nov 1860
REED, Frances (Logan) of Louisville KY   Rev. J.R. Anderson

BUTLER, W.C.   13 Apr   MORE 15 Apr 1859
CLENDENIN, Julia (late James M.)   Rev. Anderson

BYRNE, Mark of St. Louis
SHIELDS, Sophia (John)   Rev. Higginbotham   MORE 5 Aug 1854

BYRNE, Peter O.D.   (both of St. Louis) 28 Feb   MORE 2 Mar 1854
FITZPATRICK, Kate (Edward)   Archbishop Kenrick

BYRNES, Richard A.   6 Dec   COWS 18 Dec 1857
THOMAS, Mary J. (Jackson) "all of Audrain Co." Rev. Stephen Scott

CABANNE, J.S.   10 Oct   SLMD 15 Oct 1861
CHENIE, Julia (A.L.)   Fr. Capezzute

CABLE, Ransom R. of Rock Island IL   16 (18?) Feb   MORE 19 Feb 1865
STICKNEY, Josephine (Benjamin) of St. Louis   Rev. James H. Brooke

CALDWELL, James R. of Boone Co.   13 Dec   HANT 29 Dec 1855
OWENS, Mary A. (Elder B.F.) of Audrain Co.

CALHOUN, V.B.   13 Apr   COWS 22 Apr 1864
SCHAEFER, Jennie (J.C.) "all of Randolph Co."   W.R. Rothwell
       (MORE 25 Apr shows Calhoun's initials as W.B.)

CAMDEN, John B. of St. Louis   27 Mar in New Orleans   MORE 9 Apr 1851
MUSGRIVE, Jane W. of New Orleans "at the residence of Henry Richardson"

CAMPBELL, John   22 Feb in Bolivar   SPRIM 5 Mar 1857
GILL, Mary B. (D.C.)   Seth Walker

CAMPBELL, J.T.   19 May
ROGERS, S.A. (Stephen) "all of Marion Co."   Rev. H. Louthan   MORE 27 May 1859

CAMPBELL, L.D.   5 Aug
BERRY, Elizabeth (eldest dau/Maj. D.D.)   Rev. David Ross   MORE 17 Aug 1851

10

CAMPLIN, Edward G.   29 Sep Rev. W.F. Bell   COWS 2 Oct 1863
QUISENBERRY, Molie E. (William B.)   "all of Columbia"

CANDLER, John   St. John's Episcopal Church   MORE 29 Nov 1856
JACKSON, Ann (Samuel)   Rev. Clere
                        Louisville pc

CANDY, Oliver J. formerly of Pittsburgh   17 Jan   MORE 22 Jan 1856
HERBERT, Nancy A. formerly of Cumberland MD   Rev. Read

CANNON, J. William M.D. of Jackson, MO at Cape Girardeau 15 Dec   MORE 30 Dec 1865
STOCKTON, Elizabeth (Robert G., M.D.)

CANNON, James K.   19 Jul in St. Joseph   SLMD 23 Jul 1860
MARTIN, Charlotte Rebecca (Henry) at the home of Dr. Sydnor Rev. N.G. Berryman
                        "all of Lincoln Co."

CANTRELL, David G. late of New York   9 Nov in Potosi   MORE 15 Nov 1857
JONES, Mary Emily (Gen. Augustus of Texas)   Rev. Laird

CANTWELL, John J.   11 Jul
HUNT, Helen L. (2nd dau/C.R.)   Rev. J.V. Schofield   MORE 16 Jul 1865
                        New York and Brooklyn pc

CANTWELL, William J.   St. John's Church, 13 Jun   MORE 15 Jun 1865
CLINTON, Maggie (John) "all of St. Louis" Fr. Ring

CAPEN, Henry   9 Aug   MORE 10 Aug 1864
JENNINGS, Lizzie (Mrs. George Hall)   Rev. Hickman
     "at the home of the bride's mother near Bridgeport, St. Louis Co."

CARE, F.C.   14 Aug   MORE 20 Aug 1855
MYERS, Mary E. (late George) of St. Charles   Elder T.J. McKnight

CARKENER, Hudson C.   4 Oct   MORE 8 Oct 1859
BATES, Emma C. (M.L.) at her father's home   Rev. Samuel Huffman

CARLETON, George, formerly of St. Louis, in Clackamas Co. O.T. 1 Dec   SLMD 17 Jan 1854
BALDWIN, J. Ann formerly of Cincinnati

CARLILE, John W. of Columbia   22 Oct   COWS 25 Oct 1861
EVANS, Annie A. (Willis G.) of Boone Co.   Rev. Jordon

CARR, Maj. Gen. Eugene A.   12 Oct   MORE 18 Oct 1865
MAGWIRE, Mary P. (John) of St. Louis   Rev. P.J. Ryan

CARROLL, James of Mexico MO   1 Jun   Rev. E. Engle   MORE 5 Jun 1859
WARDWELL, Georgie M. (eldest dau/S.W.) of-in Frankville MD

CARTER, J.E. late of Alton   in Jefferson City 19 Mar   COWS 5 Apr 1861
MATTHEWS, Roxana (Dr. Tenessee)   "at the home of the bride's father"

CARTER, James M.   21 Sep Elder Wren   MORE 10 Oct 1854
CARTER, Mary Ann Elizabeth (William)   "all of Boone Co."

CARTER, John F. of St. Louis in Rutherford Co. TX 26 Dec   MORE 1 Jan 1861
JAMISON, Sallie

CARTER, John W.   22 Dec   COSE 30 Dec 1852
HAYDEN, Margaret (Joel) "all of Boone Co."   Elder T.M. Allen

CARTER, Stewart   14 Dec   MORE 20 Dec 1854
RHODES, Mary C. (Lieut. H.H., US Navy)   Bishop Hawks

CARTER, W.W. of St. Louis   7 Jan   MORE 10 Jan 1858
JONES, Emily M. (W.H.) of Cheltenham   Rev. S.J.P. Anderson

CARTWRIGHT, Dr. Matthew W.   27 Apr Elder A. Rice   COSE 12 May 1853
BRYANT, Mary (Joseph) "all of Callaway Co."

CARVELL, George F.   24 Dec Rev. F.A. Morris   MORE 26 Dec 1863
ROBIRDS, Isabella (Capt. Oby)   New Orleans pc

CARVER, William H.   near Spencersburg, Pike Co. 12 Jan   LAJ 19 Jan 1860
OGLE, Emily (Adrian)   Elder A.P. Rogers

CASE, Dr. George S. near Lexington, at the home of Mrs. Martin   LEXC 29 Oct 1856
CAMDEN, Sallie Ann (adopted dau/P.G. & Ann B.)   Rev. Joseph Warden
                        "all of St. Louis"

CASEY, Charles of St. Louis   at the Parish Church, St. Alanes, Dublin 15 Nov MORE 26 Jan '63
LETT, Nessy (2nd dau/William of Tomsallah, Ferns, Co. Wexford)
                        (residence of bride's father very hard to read)

CASEY, Frank T. of Washington Co.   St. Malachi's Church 26 Oct   MORE 29 Oct 1864
TATUM, Sophie (late David)   Fr. Tobin

11

CASEY, Lawrence W. of Potosi   at Old Mines by Rev. James Fox MORE 22 Feb '60
ROUSSIN, Sophia (youngest dau/Stephen decd) at the residence of Dr. Taylor
                Sacramento CA & Fredericktown MO pc

CASON, Henry   1 Apr   GLWT 3 Apr 1856
EARICKSON, Martha (P.) "both of this vicinity" Rev. Thomas Fristoe

CASEY, George M.   in Henry Co. 13 Sep   COWS 11 Sep 1857
CROSSWHITE, Lucy Ann (Thomas)   William Paul

CASTARPHEN, Ezra of Ralls Co.   (16?) or (18?) Jun   HAM 27 Jun 1861
BROWN, Christiana (2nd dau/Col. William) of Pike Co. Elder John M. Johnson

CASTERLINE, Edward F. of St. Louis   in Pittsburgh 30 Jun Rev. George Chase MORE 8 Jul 1863
DAKE, Julia E. (Dr. D.M., at his residence)

CASTLEMAN, David of Fayette Co. KY   17 Jan   MORE 31 Jan 1856
HARRISON, Sarah A. (Robert C.) of Cooper Co.   Rev. R.E. Terry

CASTLEMAN, John A.   29 Mar L.G. Berry, Esq.   COWS 15 Apr 1864
CARTER, Lizzie (Peter F.) "all of Boone Co."

CASTLEMAN, Capt. Thomas D. of Potosi 28 Nov, Church of the Messiah MORE 29 Nov 1865
McILVAINE, Sallie B. (Col. J.H.) of Carondelet   Rev. Elliott

CAUGHLIN, Ad C.   13 Feb   MORE 15 Feb 1859
WAITE, Mary M. (Liberty)   Rev. Richard Thornton
                    San Francisco pc

CAVE, Justinian   8 Nov   HANT 22 Nov 1855
GATRIGHT, Mary E. (M.W.) of Marion Co.   in Callaway Co.

CAVENDER, R.S. of St. Louis at Middletown near Alton IL 9 Aug MORE 12 Aug 1853
ATWOOD, Carrie M. of Middletown

CAZE, A.S.   18 Nov   MORE 20 Nov 1856
HARRIS, Martha (late William G.) Central Twp.   Rev. T.M. Post

CHAMBERLAIN, G.T. of St. Louis   22 Feb at Kalamazoo MI   MORE 6 Mar 1865
RICHARDSON, Mrs. N.P. of Ausable Forks, NY   Rev. (Peedson?)

CHAMBERLAIN, John   8 Sep   GLWT 11 Sep 1851
FISHER, Sarah M. (Elijah) "all of Howard Co." Rev. R.P. Holt

CHAMBERLAIN, John F. of St. Louis 13 Aug at St. Stephen's Church, New York City
MERCILLIOTT, Elizabeth of New York City   Archbishop Hughes   MORE 19 Aug 1861

CHAMBERS, B. Maziere   10 Oct at St. Malachy's Church MORE 15 Oct 1865
WALSH, Marie C. (Edward) "all of St. Louis" Fr. Tobin

CHAMBERS, Dr. J.A. of St. Joseph   27 Jun   STGAZ 12 Jul '54
GINGRY, Helen (J.) of the St. Joseph vicinity   Rev. Reeve

CHANCY, Benjamin   5 Apr in Carroll Co. Arkansas   SPRIM 16 Apr '57
ALCARN, Celia (James W.) of Stone Co.   Rev. William Steel

CHANDLER, Dr. Charles Quarles of Rocheport in Paris, Monroe Co. 10 Oct COWS 18 Oct 1861
WOODS, Annie (late James) of Columbia   Rev. Robert H. Harris

CHANSLOR, George A.   Rev. William H. Price   LIT 3 Dec 1852
SUBLETTE, Margaret (Littleberry) "all of Clay Co."

CHAPMAN, Dr. A.J. of Richfield   7 Feb   Elder M.E. Lard   RICE 9 Feb 1855
MOSEBY, Mildred F. (Walter, per LIT; Wade, per RICE) of Clay   LIT 16 "

CHAPMAN, Charles E. of St. Louis   Co. I 4th OH Vol Cav. 3 Nov SLMD 26 Nov 1861
DEARTH, T.A. (youngest dau/Absalom, Supt. Comm. Hosp. and Grand Master
            Free Masons) at Maineville OH   Rev L. Whitcomb

CHAPMAN, Walter F. of St. Louis   10 Nov in Caroline Co. VA   More 19 Nov 1859
CONDUIT, Virginia   Rev. Robert Cole

CHASE, George H. of St. Louis   Rev. Marvin 31 Jan   SLMD 7 Feb 1854
OFFUTT, Frances A. (Eli) of Callaway Co.

CHATARD, Pierre F.   29 Oct, St. John's Church   MORE 31 Oct 1861
ELDER, Eliza Key (only dau/Joseph E.)   Rev. Bannon
                "all late of Baltimore"

CHEYNE, Robert   15 Nov in St. Louis   MORE 20 Nov 1858
GASPER, Josephine (John of Fulton, Oswego Co. NY)
        "at the residence of F.C. Berkeley near St. George's"

CHICK, P.W.   24 Dec   KCJC 2 Jan 1858
GILHAM, Mary C. (Capt. Alex) "all of Kansas City" Rev. J.T. Peery

CHILD, A.A. of St. Louis   in Nashuah NH   6 Sep   MORE 11 Sep 1859
PAIGE, Frank L.   Rev. M.W. Willis

CHILD, Jacob T., junior editor of the St. Joseph Journal 24 Apr   COWS 17 May 1861
McROBERTS, Lizzie R. (Maj. Andrew) of Buchanan Co.   Rev. J.G. Fackler

CHILD, Orange W. of St. Louis   in Boonville NY 6 Aug   MORE 19 Aug 1851
STICKNEY, Susan   Rev. Gillet

CHILES, Elijah of Jackson Co.   in Boyle Co. KY 27 Sep   MORE 30 Oct 1855
WALKER, Mary H. (John)   Rev. D. Buckner

CHILES, William H. of Callaway Co.   21 Apr   COWS 29 Apr 1859
DAVIS, Delila Ann (James)   Elder B. Wren

CHILTON, James T. of Randolph Co.   18 Apr   COWS 6 May 1859
McQUITTY, Harriet (George W.) of Boone Co.   Rev. Green Cary

CHINN, Cornelius, late of Mason Co. KY at Greenton Valley Thursday last   LEXP 27 Apr 1853
McHATTON, Sallie A. (J.A.) of this county   Elder Allen Wright

CHIPMAN, Col. N.P., US War Dept., Washington 30 Jan   MORE 1 Feb 1865
HOLMES, Nelly (late Robert) at her mother's home by Rev. Nicolls of
                    2nd Presbyterian

CHORN, James W. of Montgomery Co.   17 May   MORE 4 Jul 1864
BRANHAM, Mary W. (Major) of - at Bourbon Co. KY Elder Thomas P. Dudley

CHRISMAN, Joseph Jr.   29 Dec   LIT 13 Jan 1854
LAFFOON, Mary E. (William Henry)   Rev. Joseph Prather

CHRISTIAN, Joseph, of and at Huntsville 29 Oct by Rev. W.R. Rothwell   MORE 6 Nov 1865
MAUGHAS, Eliza P. (late Dr. M.M. of Callaway Co.)

CLAPP, Dr. Fayette   5 Mar   COWS 13 Mar 1857
LYNCH, Kate (John H.)   Presbyterian Church

CLARDY, Dr. J. Bowen   31 Mar in Fredericktown, St. Francois Co.   MORE 6 Apr 1863
FLEMING, Lizzie M. (Dr. N.L.)   Rev. J.C. Farmer

CLARK, Dr. Bennett H. of Bourbonton   5 May   (COSE says 6 May)   GLWT 20 May 1852
WINN, Elizabeth Jane (Charles) of Boone Co. Elder T.M. Allen   COSE 13 "

CLARK, Charles S. of St. Louis   in Chicago 8 Feb   SLMD 13 Feb 1858
BEARDSLEY, Flora Amelia (H.H.) of Chicago   Rev. Patterson

CLARK, D.A. of St. Louis Co.   1 Dec in Cincinnati   MORE 4 Dec 1864
POOR, Ella at the home of her brother H.W.   Rev. W.T. Moore

CLARK, Francis of Perry Co.   3 Nov by Rev. Alvin Rucker   MORE 8 Nov 1854
SMITH, Drucilla Frances (William H.) of St. Francois Co.

CLARK, H.F. of St. Louis in Newburyport MA 23 Jul by Rev. Muzzy   MORE 3 Sep 1858
JOHNSON, H.G.P. (Dr. J.G.) of Newburyport

CLARK, Henry of Montgomery Co.   4 Feb Rev. E.C. Hutchinson   MORE 8 Feb 1863
MITCHELL, Fannie B. (late Col. D.D.) of St. Louis   Kentucky pc

CLARK, John S.   14 Jun   MORE 19 Jun 1859
BASS, Mary (Col. Eli E.)   Rev. J.T.M. Johnson

CLARK, Robert of DeKalb Co.   21 Jun   MORE 25 Jun 1855
GENTRY, Mary (late Gen. Richard) of Columbia Rev. N.H. Hall

CLARKSON, Arthur of Boone Co.   26 Apr   COWS 13 May 1859
BRAND, Emily Austin (H.W.) of Boonville   Rev. Samuel Southard

CLARKSON, James of Charleston MO   24 Mar in Henderson KY   CHAC 3 Apr 1863
ROUSE, Mary Frances of Henderson

CLASBY, Thomas W. of the town of DeKalb   in Savannah   MORE 1 May 1861
SELECMAN, Jennie (Henry)   Rev. W.S. Cope

CLAY, James M.   16 Oct   LIT 24 Oct 1851
GORDON, Mary (Thomas C.) "all of Clay Co." Elder A.H.F. Payne

CLAYTON, James R. of Rocheport   3 Jan   COWS 14 Jan 1859
JONES, Hattie (R.R.) of Union, Franklin Co. Rev. J.H. Thompson

CLAYCOMB, Jonathan D.   11 Oct   MARD 14 Oct 1859
WASHBURN, Georgia Augusta (E.M.) "all of Saline Co." Rev. M. Compton

CLAYTON, T.E. of Harrisonville   5 Jun   MORE 16 Jun 1855
DAVIS, Eliza J. (William) of Cass Co.   Rev. J. Farmer

CLEMENTS, H.W.G., D.C.(?)   6 Oct   MORE 8 Oct 1863
RUTHERFORD, Mary Isabelle (eldest dau/T.S.) Rev. E.C. Hutchinson

COADY, Richard of St. Louis   in San Francisco (9 Sep?)   LEXP 1 Dec 1852
ROBINSON, Charlotte of Honolulu   Rev. T.E. Taylor

COALE, Samuel J. of St. Louis   in Guyandotte VA 22 Nov   MORE 30 Nov 1859
BORDERBY, Bettie

COBB, Capt. John of Farmington   in Potosi WI 6 Oct   MORE 12 Oct 1861
WILSON, Mrs. Mary E. of Potosi WI   Rev. George W. Wells

COBB, William   13 Feb   PWH 15 Feb 1855
ELGIN, Sarah Catherine (Walter W.)   Dr. W.H. Hopson

COCHRAN, George P.   16 Nov   Rev. J.H. Brookes   MORE 22 Nov 1859
POSTAL, Theda (William)   "all of St. Louis"

COCKERILL, Christopher   in Manchester MO 5 Apr   MORE 10 Apr 1855
TRIPLET, Mary Angeline (eldest dau/William)   Rev. Gilbreath (Presbyterian)

COCKERILL, H. Clay, formerly of Glasgow   2 May   Rev. John Fackler   MORE 18 May 1855
ASMOND, Lallie Esther (eldest dau/Hon. William B. of Platte City

COCKERILL, James   7 Apr   Rev Samuel Davis   RANC 29 Apr 1859
BOULWARE, Fannie (Alex)   COWS "
        (not clear whether this couple was from Randolph or Boone)

CODY, Charles F. of St. Louis   in New York 5 Mar   MORE 18 Mar 1856
McGREGOR, Julia O. of New York   Bishop Bangs

COGSWELL, Clay   5 Sep in Bates Co.   MORE 22 Sep 1855
DOUGLASS, Maria (Col. George)   Rev. A. Jones

COLE, Frank of Cooper Co.   27 Sep in Saline Co.   MARD 3 Oct 1860
DYSART, Mollie F. (Judge Robert) of Saline Co.

COLEMAN, John R.   10 Nov   MORE 12 Nov 1862
ORNDORFF, Lizzie C. (J.)   Rev. Fr. O'Brien

COLLIER, John   20 Sep in Bates Co.   WAVE 6 Oct 1860
COGSWELL, Anna M. (late Col. James M.) recently of Jackson Co.

COLLIER, Luther of Chillicothe MO near Russellville   BRUNS 28 Jun 1856
FUQUA, Lizzie A. (Sam) of Logan Co. KY

COLLIER, Samuel B.   22 May   FULT 23 May 1851
NICHOLAS, Susan (William)   Elder Absalom Rice

COLLINS, J.R. of Waverly   GLWT 6 Nov 1856
HALLEY, Susan L. (P.W.) of Howard Co.   Rev. F.A. Savage

COLLINS, John B. of St. Louis at Prairie Park, home of W.B. Sappington   MARD 22 Apr 1859
PRICE, Eleonora Jane (William M.D.) of Saline Co.   Rev. H.M. Painer   14 Apr

COLLINS, Morris   2 May   MORE 3 May 1865
ADAMS, Hannah A. (J.S. of Fitzwilliam NH)   Rev. T.M. Post
        "at the home of the bride's uncle Curtis Coolidge"

COLLINS, P.J.   24 Oct   MORE 27 Oct 1855
OWENS, Annie (M.N.) "all of Platte City"   Rev. J.C. Davis

COLLINS, Dr. W.A., US Navy, of St. Louis   at Helena AR   Rev. Baracute   MORE 19 Oct 1863
NIXON, Dora (T.J.) of Helena   Indianapolis & Louisville pc

COLMAN, B.   24 Nov Rev. E.M. Marvin   MORE 28 Nov 1858
KEYES, Mary Frances (eldest dau/Thomas) all of St. Louis Co.

COMSTOCK, James A.   4 Jul   MORE 21 Jul 1861
LADD, Alice K. (C.G.)   "all of St. Louis"   Rev. J.J. Porter

COMSTOCK, William W. of St. Louis   1 Jan in Longmeadow MA   MORE 12 Jan 1861
COLTON, Julia M. (youngest dau/Jacob)   Rev. J.W. Harding

CONE, Joseph W. of St. Louis   18 Aug in Hartford CT   MORE 28 Aug 1864
BUCKLAND, Juliaette C. (only dau/William)   Rev. M.N. Morris
        "at the residence of her parents"

CONLEY, James   11 Nov   COWS 12 Nov 1858
SPRINKLE, Jane (Charles) "all of Boone Co."   Rev. J.T.M. Johnston

CONNELLY, James C.   29 Jun in Linnaeus   GLWT 10 Jul 1851
WILKERSON, Milly Ann (Judge Henry) of Linnaeus   T.T. Easely Esq.

CONSTABLE, D.A., an iron merchant of St. Joseph   11 Feb   MORE 25 Feb 1862
WORD, Sophie (Samuel) of Buchanan Co., late of Knox Co. KY   Rev. John P. Bruce

CONWAY, F.R. of the Columbia vicinity in Baton Rouge LA   COWS 29 Apr 1859
JARVIS, Mrs. E.A.

COOK, Charles   26 Oct in Oregon City   MORE 12 Jan 1852
BREWSTER, Susan   "both of Marion Co."

COOK, James H.   15 Jul   COWS 30 Jul 1858
GOSLIN, Charlotte (late Reuben)   Judge Daly

COON, Theodore   in Clay Co.   LIT 20 Feb 1857
MILLER, Elizabeth (William)   Elder W.C. Barrett

COONS, Dr. J.N.   13 Oct in Shelbyville   COWS 29 Oct 1858
CONNER, Annie (William) of Shelby Co.   Rev. Livy Hatchett

COONTZ, Thomas B.   at the Methodist Church, 27 Nov   HAM 5 Dec 1861
BREWINGTON, Mary B. (R.D.)   Rev. F.A. Savage

CORBY, Eben of Brunswick   14 Sep 1865   SJH 26 Sep 1865
SMOOT, Hattie (only dau/William) of Fulton, formerly of Warsaw W.B. Tucker, Esq.

CORBY, John of St. Joseph   30 May in Florissant, St. Louis Co.   COSE 24 Jun 1852
MUSICK, Amanda (late Joel)   Rev. Van Ash

CORDELL, P. Dick   8 Oct Rev. J.S. Nichols   MORE 19 Oct 1865
WRIGHT, Mrs. Carrie E. (Henry L. and Emily C. Ellis) at her father's home
               "all of St. Louis"

CORDER, Jackson of Lafayette Co.   5 Jul in Henry Co.   WAVE 16 Jul 1859
WALL, Elizabeth (Major) of High Point Tebo(?)

CORDER, James A.   28 Mar   HANT 7 Apr 1855
FORMAN, Lizzie (Vincent)   Henry Louthan

CORDER, John F. of Waverly   20 Dec 1860   MORE 1 Jan 1861
HENTON, Rebecca C. (Col.) of Lafayette Co. Rev. W.J. Brown

CORWIN, C.J.   in St. Charles (4 Sep?)   CANE 2 Oct 1856
BASYE, Sarah F. (oldest dau/Dr. A.J.)   Rev. Anderson

COWEN, Eustace W.   27 Oct at St. Malachy's   MORE 30 Oct 1863
McENTIRE, Mary E. Wells (Joseph)   Fr. Cummings

CRAFT, E.F. of St. Louis   25 Jun in Ste. Genevieve   MORE 27 Jun 1855
DETCHEMENDY, Mary (youngest dau/Col. D.) Fr. St. Cyr

CRAIG, Alex C. of St. Joseph   27 Mar   STGAZ 2 Apr 1851
CHRISTOPHER, Ellen J. (Thomas H.) of Buchanan Co. Rev. Henry Henderson

CRAIG, Alonzo   "aboard the Consignee at Point Pleasant 23 Aug"   MORE 6 Sep 1854
KEY, Martha   J.J. Cre(?)

CRAIG, James A.   14 Jan in Scott Co.   COWS 23 Fb 1855
GRAVES, F. Ellen (Jefferson)

CRAIN, William H.   Esq. I. Winfrey   COWS 27 Mar 1857
CALVIN, Sarah (Elijah) of Boone Co.

CRANE, H.W. of Lecon IL   9 Jan   SJH 12 Jan 1865
PARSONS, Arabella, 2nd dau/Rev. B.B., who officiated

CRAVENS, Maj. Jure C. of Gallatin, Daviess Co. in Batesville, Independence
                               Co. AR 11 Aug   MORE 23 Oct 1864
SMITH, C. Annie D. at the home of her father

CRESSON, J. Clarence of Philadelphia   1 Feb   MORE 3 Feb 1865
DRAKE, Ella B. oldest dau/Rev. Charles D. Rev. Nicolls, 2nd Presbyterian

CREST, Jonathan of Independence   8 Sep   MORE 9 Sep 1859
BENNETT, Brook   Rev. Marvin

CREWS, James F.   5 Aug   COWS 4 Sep 1857
WALTON, Mat A. (John W.) "all of Boone Co." Rev. James B. Watson

CREWS, John F. of Boone Co.   20 Aug   COWS 29 Aug 1856
BAKER, Louisa (Thomas) of Callaway Co.   Elder Wigginton

CREWS, Thomas B. of Saline Co.   14 May Rev. T.M. Finney   MORE 16 May 1857
JEFFRIES, Virginia (C.J.) of - in Franklin Co.

CROMWELL, H.T. of Audrain Co.   12 May   MORE 24 May 1859
DAVIS, Adda V. (Capt. B.F.) of Monroe Co. Elder J.D. Wilmot

CROMWELL, Stephen A. of St. Louis in Washington DC 14 May   MORE 31 May 1857
CLUSKEY, Mary E. (Charles B.) of Washington   Rev. Bern. McGuire

CRONK, Andrew D.   SLMD 14 Feb 1854
KELLY, Sarah Ann (youngest dau/William)   1 Feb in Monroe Co.

CROSS, George   14 Feb in Randolph Co.   MORE 28 Feb 1856
BURTS, Martha Ann (Rev. James)   Rev. William Shores   RANC 28 "
  (name shown as Burts in More & Ranc, Burks in Cows)   COWS 22 "

CROOKS, Joseph of St. Louis   16 May in Grace Church   MORE 7 Jun 1854
BRANCH, Eliza (only dau/Richard of Long Island NY) Rev. W.H. Woodward

CROSBY, Dexter S.   12 Feb   MORE 16 Feb 1863
BULLITT, Ada (Alfred N.) of Louisville KY   in St. Charles Co.
  "at the residence of A. Chouteau Smith, Portage des Sioux"

CROSBY, Henry T. of New York   Rev. E.C. Hutchinson   MORE 14 Jan 1859
BUCHANAN, Julia (late George) at her father's home

CROW, Clinton P.   Elder T. Ford   COWS 30 Oct 1857
STEWART, Margaret (Gen. David) of Lincoln Co.

CROWDER, A.N. of St. Louis   in Montgomery MD 11 Dec   MORE 19 Dec 1860
WARFIELD, Debbie J. of Montgomery   Rev. Orlando Hutton

CROYSDALE, William   19 March   LIT 28 Mar 1856
SKINNER, Emily (Phineas) "all of Platte Co."

CRUIKSHANK, John J.   2 May   HAM 4 May 1859
BACON, Mary E. (George) "all of Hannibal"

CRUMP, Anderson Jr.   9 Aug   MORE 20 Aug 1855
WREN, Elizabeth (Charles) "all of Boone Co."   Elder B. Wren

CRUMP, John H.   10 Dec   COWS 15 Dec 1865
NICHOLS, Fannie T. (Maj. James B.)   Elder T.M. Allen

CRUMP, Josiah   18 Oct in Boone Co.   MORE 30 Oct 1855
HARMON, Martha Ann (John)   Elder B. Wren

CRUTCHER, W. of Ashley, Pike Co.   16 Aug   MORE 21 Aug 1859
CRUTCHER, Sallie (Thomas) of St. Louis   Elder Alfred Wilson

CUMMINGS, A.L.   11 Oct in St. Louis   MORE 17 Oct 1858
COCHRAN, Anna (Maj. James)   Rev. Porter

CUMMINGS, James A. of St. Louis Co.   1 May in Belvien OH   MORE 6 May 1856
STEVENS, Charlotte E. of Belvien   Rev. Barbour

CUNDIFF, W.H.H. of Kentucky   21 Nov in Jackson Co.   MORE 19 Dec 1854
MADDOX, Ann Elizabeth (Larkin) formerly of Callaway Co.

CUNNINGHAM, Capt. G.W.   14 Jul   COWS 22 Jul 1864
MOBERLY, Josephine   "all of Brunswick"   Rev. Sterling Price, Jr.
                       "at the residence of Col. William E. Moberly"

CUNNINGHAM, W.A.   14 Apr   SLMD 29 Apr 1858
BOYD, Anna B. (J.W.)   "all of St. Joseph"   Rev. John G. Fackler

CURTIS, William H.   20 Apr   MORE 26 Apr 1864
FANT, Hattie A. (A.B.) "all of Callaway Co."   Elder T.J. Marlow

CUSHMAN, Edwin Charles of Boston   3 Apr at the Church of the Messiah   SLMD 9 Apr 1861
CROW, Emma Conn 2nd dau/Wayman   Rev. William Eliot

CUTLER, Dr. S.P. of Warrensburg   21 Nov at Louisville KY   WARS 1 Dec 1865
TALBOT, Mrs. Cordelia A.

DAMERON, W.M. of College Mound, Randolph Co.   3 Jun   RANC 11 Jun 1857
DYSART, S.A. (Robert) of Saline Co.

DANIEL, John   11 Dec   COWS 8 Jan 1858
PULLIS, Sallie (Reuben) of Audrain Co.   Rev. R.W. Wigginton

DARR, John F.   26 Apr   HIM 3 May 1855
CHRISTIAN, Sarah E. (N.B.)

DAUGHERTY, John A. of Carroll Co.   18 Aug   GLWT 15 Sep 1853
LOCK, Elizabeth A. (Rev. Isaac A.) of Livingston Co.   James L. Austin

DAVENPORT, George   6 Mar   COWS 18 Mar 1859
WREN, Martha Frances (David)   Elder B. Wren

DAVIDSON, Blind   18 Nov   MORE 2 Dec 1856
HUNTER, Mary A.   "all of Montgomery Co."   (Rev. William Taylor?)

DAVIDSON, John C. of Adair Co.   5 Oct   MORE 3 Nov 1854
LANDSBERRY, Matilda (Levi) of Knox Co.

DAVIS, Carey B.H.   "at the residence of Capt. Owings"   MORE 17 Jun 1853
FERGUSON, Mrs. Eliza of Alton

16

DAVIS, Franklin, merchant of Milton   13 Jan   GLWT 20 Jan 1853
PATTON, Sarah A.D. (Richard)   Elder T.N. Gaines

DAVIS, George W.   10 Nov in Canton MO   MORE 21 Nov 1863
ELLISON, Isabelle (eldest dau/Hon. James) of Canton

DAVIS, H.R.   2 Feb   LIT 18 Feb 1853
McKISSICK, Martha Ann (John) "all of Clay Co."   Rev. Jacob S. Faubian

DAVIS, John M., clerk of the Chariton Co. Court 13 Feb   GLWT 24 Feb 1853
WALLACE, Maria Ann (late John S.)   Rev. Eads

DAVIS, John T.   Rev. J.T. Williams   PWH 15 Feb 1855
DINGALE, Susan Ella (W.C.)

DAVIS, Joseph B.   17 Feb   COSE 4 Mar 1852
MARTIN, Sarah A. (late Samuel) "all of Randolph Co." Elder Henry Thomas

DAVIS, Richard F.   4 Sep   COWS 20 Sep 1861
CARRINGTON, Julian (Judge W.) "all of Callaway Co."

DAVIS, W.C.   26 Feb   MORE 1 Mar 1859
JOHNSTONE, Emily M. (late Rev.)   Rev. Williams Louisville pc

DAWKINS, Levi Jr. of Randolph Co.   15 Mar in Boone Co.   RANC 25 Mar 1859
TOMPKINS, Lucy Mildred (William decd)   Elder Butts

DAY, Thomas D. of St. Louis   13 Dec   MORE 31 Dec 1859
HELM, Fannie (John M.) of Beverly Place near Natchez Rev. J.B. Stratton

DEAN, David of Marion Co.   24 Sep   Elder D.T. Moreton   HANJ 25 Sep 1851
GARNETT, Mariah (eldest dau/James of Ralls Co., at his residence)

DEAN, Henry A. of St. Louis   8 Jan Rev. E.M. Marvin   MORE 10 Jan 1862
McDUMOTT, Rosa M. formerly of Frederick City MD
                "at the residence of the bride'e mother"

DEAN, J.B.   9 Sep in St. Louis   MORE 11 Sep 1858
CONRADT, Emily (C.G. of Baltimore MD)   Rev. Montgomery Schuyler
                "at the residence of J. Sylvester"

DEAN, J.J. formerly of Carroll Co. MO (10 Nov?) Lakeport CA   MORE 31 Jan 1865
DAVIS, Mary A. late of Williamsburg, Callaway Co. R.H. Larrance JP
                "at the residence of the bride's father"

DeLISLE, Leon J.   9 Mar   MORE 23 Mar 1864
SHEBLE, Miriam (Capt. D.C.) "all of St. Louis" Indiana & Philadelphia pc

DELIME, Dr. Lewis A.   10 Mar   Rev. John Coleman   MORE 12 Mar 1859
JACKSON, Margaret (youngest dau/late Thomas, niece of M.C.)

DENISON, George of St. Louis   3 Feb at Monticello IL   MORE 7 Feb 1864
WEBSTER, Emma A. (B.) of Monticello

DENNIS, James   19 Apr   MARD 12 May 1860
BROWN, Mary C. (William P.) all of Saline Co.   Rufus Bigelow JP

DENNIS, Joseph   9 Feb   Rufus Bigelow Esq.   WAVE 3 Mar 1860
MURPHY, Almarinda (youngest dau/John, soldier war of 1812)
                "all of this county"

DENNY, Alexander   22 Jan   GLWT 29 Jan 1857
SNODDY, Mary Ann (late John)   Rev. Penn

DENNY, Alex Finley of Huntsville   5 Dec   MORE 19 Dec 1855
PITTS, Mattie McDowell (Capt. John A.) of Randolph Co.

DEPEW, Thomas of Maryville CA   2 Aug   MORE 6 Aug 1864
CARDWELL, Sue A. (George Bushey) of St. Louis Co. Rev. W.M. Prottsman?

DERBY, George H. of the US Army   14 Feb in San Francisco   MORE 7 Mar 1854
COONS, Mary A. of St. Louis

DE SPADA, Charles   5 Feb   LIT 20 Feb 1857
BENDLEY, Lydia (Judge John) of Liberty   Rev. John Fackler
                "all of Clay County"

DEXTER, Capt. J.B.   13 Oct in New Orleans   SPRIP 23 Nov 1865
SHACKELFORD, Lizzie "both of Springfield"   Rev. Newman

DEY, John E.   8 Jul   GLWT 22 Jul 1852
FISHER, Eliza E. (Elijah) "all of Howard Co."

DICKENSON, John   12 Apr in Shelbyville   PWH 26 Apr 1855
COTTON, Catherine (Chester K.)   Rev. Newman

DICKSON, George L.   last Wednesday   HAM 25 Sep 1859
BRASHEARS, Zarilda (Thomas) all of Palmyra   Rev. W.H. Hopson

DICKSON, James M. of Palmyra   22 Nov in Nicholas Co. KY   MORE 4 Jan 1865
KENDALL, Mrs. Susa (sic) J. of Nicholas Co. (dau/John Hall) Rev. Holliday
          "at the residence of the bride's father"

DIGGS, William   23 Dec in Montgomery Co.   COWS 16 Jan 1857
MORRIS, Cynthia

DIEHL, Edwin P. of Charleston MO   19 Aug in Canton OH   CHAC 5 Sep 1862
BROWNEWELL, Emma of Canton OH

DILLON, John A.   25 Jan at the Cathedral   MORE 29 Jan 1865
VALLE, Blanch (dau/Neree, goddaughter of Henry Chouteau) Archbishop Kenrick

DINWIDDIE, J.N.   COWS 8 May 1863
MOSELEY, Kate E. (William) "all of Boone Co." Elder J.M. Robinson

DITTMORE, John of Buchanan Co. 27 Aug at Troy Hotel, Troy KS   SJH 2 Sep 1865
MYERS, Mrs. Nancy A. of Doniphan Co.   L. Smith

DITTO, J.L. of Clinton Co.   3 Nov   LIT 11 Nov 1859
ALBRIGHT, Eliza (Daniel) of Clay Co.   Rev. J.W. Luke

DIVINE, William of Clay Co. 18 Nov at Mt. Byrd or Mt. Ryrd, Trimble Co. KY LIT 17 Dec 1852
MOFFETT, Mary E. of the above place   Rev. C.J. Smith

DIX, Eugene W. of Massachusette   last Monday   HANT 15 Dec 1857
REED, Mary B. (Thomas D.) of Hannibal

DOBBINS, John K.   9 Dec in St. Francois Co.   MORE 17 Dec 1863
GALLATIN, Cornelia   Rev. Alvin Rucker
          "at the residence of her uncle William L. Boyce"

DODD, Thomas   24 Dec   COWS 8 Jan 1858
HICKAM, Mariam (Erskine) "all of Boone Co." Rev. J.T.M. Johnson

DONAHOE, Alonzo H.   11 Oct in Howard Co.   MORE 30 Oct 1855
FINKS, Louisa (Capt. J.F.)   Rev. William Thompson

DONALDSON, William B. of Richmond   19 Oct in New York City   RICON 4 Nov 1865
MORRISON, Sallie of NY City   Rev. John Q. Adams

DORSEY, J.S.   Pres. L.B. Wilkes   COWS 11 Sep 1857
WILLIAMS, Mag. (late Samuel) formerly of Nicholas Co. KY

DOUGHERTY, John K.   18 Dec   LIT 26 Dec 1856
REED, Irene F. (A.G.) "all of Liberty"

DOUGHERTY, William D.   5 Nov   MORE 7 Nov 1854
BURKE, Maggie L. (Capt. William)   Rev. Fr Ward

DOUGLASS, George E.   10 Jul   COWS 15 Jul 1859
PENDLETON, Mag (Mrs. B.A.)   Rev. J.A. Hollis

DOUGLAS, William   19 Oct   Bishop Hawks   MORE 23 Oct 1863
BORRON, Florence Willesford (youngest dau/late John Arthur of Woolden Hall,
          Lancashire ENG) "at the residence of J.S.C. Hogan near Boonville"

DOWNEY, James E. of St. Aubert MO   20 Mar   COWS 28 Mar 1862
WILLING, Sallie (W.) of Fulton   Rev. A.H. Bourland

DOWNING, Joseph   10 Dec   LIT 12 Dec 1856
TURNHAM, Louisa (Col. Joel) "all of Clay Co."

DOWNING, J.C.   Presbyterian Church   COWS 27 May 1859
PENDLETON, Mary E. (Mrs. Betsy)   Rev. Mutchmore

DOWNEY, James   18 Jan at Joseph Conway's   HANT 10 Feb 1853
McCREA, Elizabeth Jane (oldest dau/Rev. John)

DOXEY, Thomas F. of Chariton Co.   26 Oct in Chariton Co.   COWS 2 Nov 1860
SALISBURY, Julia E. (late Capt. P.)
          "at the home of the bride's uncle, Hon. L. Salisbury"

DOYLE, James   25 Sep   MORE 2 Oct 1861
BLAISDELL, Mrs. Mary E. (Joseph Brannan)   Rev. W.C. Stewart

DOYLE, Lamber L., late of Evrecourt, Galway, Ire. 11 Oct at St. Patrick's MORE 13 Oct 1864
CALVERT, Locia H. of St. Louis Co.

DOZIER, John   21 Sep   COWS 26 Sep 1856
PHELPS, Nancy Jane (James) of Boone Co.   Elder B. Wren

DOZIER, Richard of St. Louis   Rev. Anderson   MORE 20 Dec 1856
BRUMFIELD, Caroline (Judge R.B.) of St. Charles.

DRAKE, Charles of St. Louis   24 Nov in Christ Church   GLWT 1 Dec 1853
MACK, Adelia M. (N.W.) of Boonville   Rev. R.E. Terry

DRAPER, Gen. Daniel M.   10 Oct in Danville (MO?IL?)   MORE 12 Oct 1865
STEWART, Julia (A.C.)   Rev. Thomas B. King

DRESSLER, George   2 Oct   LIT 3 Oct 1862
MOSEBY, Mrs. Emiline (Samuel Tillery)   Elder Henry Hill

DRUESDAN, Franz Alexander of Hamburg   Rev. J.P. Hogan   25 Nov   MORE 3 Dec 1855
CALLAGHAN, Margaret Catherine (Peter S.) late of Wisconsin

DRYER, Hiram H.   15 Jan   MORE 24 Jan 1857
OSBORN, Sarah J. of Montgomery Co.   Rev. J.C. Kendrick

DRYSDALE, Alexander T.   In Philadelphia   MORE 22 Aug 1851
RITTER, Emma Matilda (late Jacob)   Rev. Walter B. Drysdale

DUDLEY, James R. of Missouri   28 Oct   COWS 12 Nov 1858
RODES, Sarah (Waller) of Fayette Co. KY   Rev. William N. Pratt

DUFFER, Repps O. of St. Louis   13 Mar   HANT 29 Mar 1856
WILLIS, Mildred M. (James C.) of Palmyra

DUHRING, Henry P.   St. James Church, Cheltenham, St. Louis Co.   MORE 5 Sep 1864
RILEY, J. Amanda (James M.)   Rev. Fr Welby
                "all of St. Louis Co."

DUKE, Bazil Esq. of St. Louis   Rev. James Craik   13 Apr in Louisville   MORE 16 Apr 1851
ANDERSON, Adelaide (James)   (this might have been 13 or 18 March)

DUNCAN, James B.F.   20 Apr   LIT 28 Apr 1854
EATON, Mary Ann (John)   Elder A.H.F. Payne

DUNHAM, Daniel   6 Oct   COWS 14 Oct 1859
WREN, Tinetta (David)   Elder B. Wren

DUNHAM, Robert of St. Louis, formerly of Brooklyn NY, 29 Sep in Kalamazoo MI   MORE 3 Oct 1856
NOTTRAM, Alice (William)   Rev. E.B. Palmer

DUNLAP, Rev. G.K. of Christ Church, Lexington   23 Jul, St. John's Church   MORE 24 Jul 1857
COBB, Mary (eldest dau/late Charles of Johnson Co.) Bishop Hawks

DUNN, Rev. J.W., Rector of St. Mary's, Fayette 9 Dec in Boonville   GLWT 30 Dec 1852
HOWARD, Anna Maria (eldest dau/William)   Rev. John A. Harrison

DUNN, Lieut. Col. R.F., 2nd Prov. Reg.   7 May   COWS 22 May 1863
HARRY, Augusta (Nathan) "all of Chillicothe" Rev. T.B. Bratton

DUNNICA, Capt. Theodore W. of New Orleans 8 Dec in Glasgow   RANC 18 Dec 1856
LEWIS, Sallie B. (Rev. A.M.)

DUPONT, Francis of Andennes   31 May   MORE 2 Jun 1856
FOURDRIGNIERS, Jeannette of Antwerp   Justice Herkenrath

DURKAN, John of St. Louis   at the Cathedral in Cincinnati   MORE 5 Aug 1854
McDERMOTT, Mary A.   Rev. E.T. Collins

DURKEE, Dwight of St. Louis   27 May in Cincinnati   MORE 16 Jun 1851
DAVIS, Jane (C.E.R.)   Rev. N. Gholson(?)

DURKEE, Camillus C.   (see below)   12 Jun in Lewis Co.   HANT 24 Jun 1856
SUTTON, Sarah P. (J.M.)   Elder Hatch

DURKER, Camillus C.   12 Jun in DeSoto   CANE 19 Jun 1856
SUTTON, Sarah P. (J.M.)   ? ? ?   Elder S. Hatch

DUTY, William P. of St. Louis   24 Nov in Hannibal   MORE 28 Nov 1858
LEE, Sue (Col. Stephen) of Hannibal

DYER, David, Circuit Attorney in Callaway Co. 15 Nov   MORE 3 Dec 1860
HUNT, Lizzie (late Judge Ezra) of Louisiana MO Rev. Worthington

DYER, Samuel R. of Fulton   "last Tuesday"   COSE 3 Mar 1853
BRYANT, Lizzie L. (late John) of Boone Co. Rev. Tyre Harris

DYSON, Robert C. of Neosho in the Presbyterian Chapel, Columbia 22 Aug   COWS 23 Aug 1861
STARKE, Priscilla (late N.B.) of Boone Co.

EAGEN, John M. (Mail Agent, Hannibal & St. Joe RR) 27 Mar in Shelbina   HAM 31 Mar 1861
NICHOLSON, Lutie G. (Joseph) of Palmyra   J.A. Foster

EARICKSON, John Kirk of St. Louis   17 Dec in Howard Co.   MORE 22 Dec 1863
BOWMAN, Anna Reed (William H.) of Howard Co. Rev. T.W. Gaines

EARICKSON, Richard   "both of the Glasgow vicinity" 25 Oct   GLWT 27 Oct 1853
EARICKSON, Sarah (P.)   Rev. Wm. Perkins

EARLE, James F.   16 Dec in Lexington   WAVE 25 Dec 1858
PERSINGER, Delia Ann (Henry) of Waverly   Rev. R.A. Young

EARLEY, Easton   5 Sep   HAM 13 Sep 1859
BROWN, Lucinda Jane (William and Malvina)   Elder John M. Johnson
                          "all of Pike Co."

EASLEY, Moss of Boone Co.   17 Nov   COSE 1 Dec 1853
PEBLEY, Sarah (George) of Cole Co.   Franklin Jackson Esq.

EATON, John   15 Jan Elder W.C. Boon   GLWT 22 Jan 1852
HARDIN, Ann (Joseph) "all of Howard Co."

EATON, Lucien   27 Mar   SLMD 2 Apr 1861
PARTRIDGE, Emily F. (eldest dau/Hon. George)   Rev. William G. Eliot

EDWARDS, John J.   25 Jan in Boone Co.   COWS 10 Feb 1860
WRIGHT, Amanda (Fletcher)   B. Wren

EDWARDS, John J. of St. Louis in Chicago at the home of H.V.S. Brooks   MORE 28 May 1865
ROGERS, Lottie A. (late Rodney A.) formerly of Chicago   Rev. Charles Cheyney,
                                                  Pastor of Christ Church

EDWARDS, Rufus R. of St. Joseph   25 Dec   MORE 12 Jan 1858
WATERSIN, Nannie (G.W.) of Doniphan Co. KY

EDWARDS, Samuel C.   15 Nov in Mexico MO   COWS 25 Nov 1859
SHRYOCK, Lucy (Samuel)   Rev. Burr

EDWARDS, Thomas S.   Elder G. Brown   MORE 9 Jan 1862
ANDERSON, Amanda Jane (eldest dau/Richard I.) "all of St. Louis"

EASTERLY, Dr. E. of St. Louis   1 Nov   in Janesville WI   MORE 14 Nov 1855
BOSTWICK, Elizabeth B. of Janesville   Rev. Foot

EATON, William L.   29 Apr in Hannibal   HANT 2 May 1857
LEER, Ella G. (William and E.H.) "all of Marion Co."

EDDINS, Benjamin J.   20 Dec   GLWT 28 Dec 1854
TWYMAN, Emma (Joel)   Rev. William Thompson

EDGAR, W.T. of St. Louis   26 Oct   MORE 29 Oct 1854
PALMER, Kate (J.J.)   Rev. Clare

EDWARDS, James   25 Sep   MORE 23 Oct 1859
ENGLISH, Louise (Thomas) "all of Jackson Co." Rev. McGeary

EDWARDS, William B.   2 Feb   COWS 12 Feb 1858
ADKINS, Eliza (William decd)   Israel Winfrey

EGBERT, J.D.   Rev. G. Anderson   MORE 19 Apr 1861
HUME, Mrs. Sue (John F. Long)

ELLINGTON, Rev. William T.   13 May   GLWT 15 May 1851
MONROE, Mary Ann Soule (youngest dau/Rev. Andrew) Rev. Jacob Lanius

ELIOT, Thomas L.   28 Nov   MORE 12 Dec 1865
MACK, Etta R. (Samuel E?)

ELKIN, Tandy   14 Jun in Boone Co.   SLMD 26 Jan 1858
ASHBURY, Angeline (late Rawley)

ELLIOTT, Arthur W. of St. Louis   24 Jul in Louisville   MORE 28 Jul 1851
BLOOM, Mrs. Sarah   Rev. Holman

ELLIOTT, George F.   11 Dec   HANT 19 Dec 1857
HOPKINS, Martha A. (Herod) "at the residence of William Robbins"

ELLIOTT, Dr. G.W. of Randolph Co.   19 Apr   COWS 6 May 1859
McQUITTY, Hattie (Daniel) of Boone Co.   Rev. Green Cary

ELLIOTT, Robert   10 May in Saline Co.   MORE 18 May 1859
ISBELL, Susan (James)   Rev. W. Wharton

ELLIOTT, Stephen T. of Ralls Co.   12 Jan   HANT 23 Jan 1858
MOORE, Matilda C. (James C.) of Monroe Co.

ELLIOTT, William T.   Rev. F. Wilhite   MORE 24 Jan 1855
COCHRAN, Amanda (John G.)   "all of Boone Co."

ELLIS, John of Savannah MO   13 Oct in Sonoma CA   SAS 29 Nov 1851
LEWIS, Sarah (John) of California

ELLIS, Peter   29 May   COWS 7 Jun 1861
MOSELEY, Amanda (William S.) Rev. J.T. Williams, Pres. Baptist Female College

ELLY, Edward G. of Callaway Co.   3 Nov in Callaway Co.   LIT 3 Dec 1852
MAHONEY, Mary Jane (Maj. Leonard) of Clay Co.   Elder T. Boulware

EMMONS, Robert W. of Boston   7 Oct in All Souls Church, New York City   MORE 11 Oct 1863
CROW, Mary Isabella (Wayman) of St. Louis   Rev. O.B. Frothingham

EMORY, James J.   24 Aug in Monroe Co.   MORE 12 Sep 1858
SWINNEY, Mary E. (Joseph D.)   B. Pollard

ENGLISH, James W. of St. Francois Co. at the Mansion House, 14 May   MORE 20 May 1860
DAVIDSON, Angeline B. (Benjamin) of Potosi   Rev. D.A. Wilson

EPERLEIN, Herman   14 Oct   MORE 19 Oct 1865
KETHLINE, Mrs. Annie (widow of Isaac C.) JP Levi Block, 2nd Ward

ERR, Dr. of Jackson Co.   "Thursday week"   GLWT 18 Mar 1852
RYLAND, Clintona (John F.) of Lafayette Co.   Rev. Russell

ESKRIDGE, M.B.   15 May in Bloomington MO   RANC 31 May 1860
McCALL, Martha Susan (A.P.)   Rev. S.B. Caldwell

ESSEX, William T.   at Grace Church, Kirkwood   MORE 6 Nov 1863
BODLEY, Euphemia B. Hensley (Harry J. Bodley)   Bishop Hawks

ESTELL, Jonathan   5 Jul in Callaway Co.   SLMD 16 Jul 1860
BAKER, Clarissa Catherine (E.W.)   W.C. Gilman, Esq.

ESTES, Edward Thomas of St. Louis   7 Sep in Belleville   MORE 10 Sep 1857
WEST, Mary W. of Belleville

ESTILL, Eugene of Howard Co.   26 Mar   COWS 19 Apr 1861
ROBERTSON, Laura A. (N.S.) of Saline Co.   Rev. William Henry Robertson

EVANS, A.P., merchant of Liberty   18 Nov   LIT 26 Nov 1858
BAKER, Eliza (Caleb) of Clay Co.   Pres. Thompson

EVANS, H.W.   15 Aug   MORE 25 Aug 1858
COFFMAN, Sarah (Mathias) "all of Phelps Co."   Hon. John Matlock

EVANS, Rev. W.L.T.   23 Feb   COWS 10 Mar 1865
BULLOCK, Sue M. (N.S.) of Monroe Co.   Rev. George W. Simmeade

EVERETT, G.W.   12 Aug   LIT 29 Aug 1851
WILSON, Caroline (William)   Rev. D. Patton

EVERTS, Charles   29 Dec   MORE 31 Dec 1859
TAMM, Bertha (oldest dau/Jacob)   Rev. Hugo Krebs

EWING, Jackson   9 Oct   HANT 16 Oct 1856
JONES, Sarah E. (Judson C.) "all of Lewis Co."   Rev. Taylor

EWING, Milton   21 Sep   WAVE 8 Oct 1859
GORDON, Lucy (ygst dau/late George)   Elder Haley
      "at the residence of T. Shelby in this county"

EWING, Robertson C. of Clay Co.   21 Jan in Clinton Co.   LIT 29 Jan 1858
DOWNING, Sallie Ann (Charles) formerly of Mason Co. KY   Rev. Edward A. Martin

FAGON, William   13 Apr   MORE 15 Apr 1865
WEST, Annie H. (Richard)   Fr. Tobyn
      "at the residence of John McAlvy"

FAIR, James W.   near Miller's Landing   MORE 27 Dec 1856
THURMAN, Rachel Ann (John T.) of Franklin Co.

FALCONER, W.K. (or W.E.)   23 Nov at Camden Point   MORE 8 Dec 1854
TODD, Mollie W. (Prof. H.B.)   Elder O.C. Steele
      "all of Platte Co."

FALLON, Wesley   9 Nov   MORE 14 Nov 1858
MARTIN, Cora (late Rev. Corbly)   Rev. J. Doyle

FANT, Hamilton G. of Missouri   16 May in Washington City   JINQ 4 Jun 1853
HELLEN, Josephine (only dau/Johnson) of Jefferson City   Rev. Mathias Alig

FARRAR, John H. of St. Louis   4 Apr /6th St. Methodist Church, Cincinnati   MORE 8 Apr 1861
ROSE, Sarah R. of Cincinnati at her father's home /Rev. White/of the /

FARRELL, F.G. of Pleasant Plains   18 Sep   MORE 1 Oct 1855
DUNLAP, Mary J. (Stephen) of Morgan Co.   Rev. Crow

FARRELL, James R.   5 Apr   COWS 21 Apr 1865
McGEE, Cassie A. (James L.) "all of Monroe Co."   Elder Alfred Wilson

FAULHABER, George L.   2 Jan by Rev. J. Rieges (or Bieges?)   JINQ 5 Jan 1861
GRIMSHAW, Lillie (J., express agent)

FAWCETT, A.F.   2 Dec   COWS 17 Dec 1858
FULKERSON, Amanda (James F.) "all of Boone Co." Elder W.R. Wigginton

FAWKNER, James C.   17 Nov   COWS 26 Dec 1862
ANGELL, Julia Anna (Robert) of Boone Co.   Rev. Landis

FERGE, Sebastian   29 Apr   GLWT 7 May 1857
SMITH, Cynthia (William G.)   William G. Brown

FERGUSON, John L. of St. Louis Co.   4 Oct   MORE 6 Oct 1859
ORME, Olivia (late A.E.) of St. Louis   Rev. G. Anderson

FERGUSON, Judge William F.   8 Oct   MORE 10 Oct 1863
NOE, Jennie C. (C.) of Norfolk VA   Rev. S.J. Anderson
                        Baltimore pc

FERREL, James A.   25 Jan   WAVE 4 Feb 1860
GIVENS, Rhoda E. (John S.) all of Cooper Co. Rev. J.W. Lewis

FERRIL, John R. of Audrain Co.   9 May   FULT 12 May 1865
JAMESON, Susie (Samuel) of Callaway Co.   Rev. W.R. Robertson

FIELD, Charles R. of Kansas City   17 Aprat St. James' Church, St. Louis   MORE 18 Apr 1861
BAYLESS, Mary Jane of Warrenton Ohio   Rev. J.J. Corbyn

FIELD, Dr. G.W. of New Madrid   14 Feb in Platte Co.   MORE 27 Feb 1854
DUNCAN, Lucie E. (Judge)   Elder M.E. Lard

FIELD, N.   of Clay Co.   25 Sep near Lexington   LIT 5 Oct 1855
CARTER, Catherine (D.R.) of Lafayette Co.   Elder Allen Wright

FIELD or FILED, Thomas M. of Columbia 17 Sep   COWS 27 Sep 1861
ELLIS, Amanda F. (Gen. John) of Boone Co.   Rev. Smith

FILLEY, Chauncey J. of St. Louis   1st Presbyterian, Lansingburg NY   MORE 9 Jul 1855
ADAMS, Anna E.   Rev. N.S.S. Beeman

FINK, Charles   18 Oct, Christ Church   MORE 22 Oct 1855
BRUMBAUGH,.Marietta (Mrs. Mary Ann Murry)   Rev. Schuyler

FINNEY, Rev. Thomas   3 Mar near Bridgeton   MORE 9 Mar 1864
EDMONSTONE, Lou (late Maj. Benjamin)   Rev. J.W. Lewis
         "all of St. Louis Co." "at the residence of Dr. Edmonstone"

FINNEY, William H. of St. Louis   9 Nov in Boonville   MORE 12 Nov 1855
BUCKNER, Sallie T. (Dr. E.E.)   Rev. R.E. Perry

FISHER, Charles E. (Edward) formerly of Delaware 2 Mar   JINQ 5 Mar 1853
NOLAND, Elizabeth (Rev. M.D.) of Cole Co.   Rev. William M. Kabenson

FISHER, Prof. M.F. of Westminster College   Union Presbyterian Church   MORE 1 Sep 1856
ATWOOD, Anna (Dr. N.B.) of St. Louis   Rev. J.S.P. Anderson

FISHER, Capt. R.   25 Nov in Clay Co.   LIT 3 Dec 1852
CLAY, Mildred (stepdaughter of Capt. Rice E. Davenport) Elder A.H.F. Payne

FISHER, William H.   7 Aug   LIT 8 Aug 1856
MURRAY, Magg Clara (E.D.) "all of Clay Co."

FLEMING, Sam of St. Francois Co.   7 Jun   MORE 11 Jun 1861
NIFONG, Bettie (eldest dau/Col. A.) of Madison Co. Rev. J.C. Farmer

FLESHMAN, Harrison A.   8 May in Callaway Co.   FULT 16 May 1851
CROWSON, Louise Jane (Thomas)   Rev. W.W. Keep

FLETCHER, Frank H.   9 Nov   MORE 10 Nov 1863
CLAPP, Helen (eldest dau/Alfred) of St. Louis   Rev. Dr. Nelson
            "at the Silver Wedding of the bride's parents"

FLETCHER, Patrick   1 Sep, St. Bridget's Church   .MORE 4 Oct 1857
McCARTHY, Ellen (Timothy)

FLETCHER, Thomas Jefferson of St. Thomas in Lexington last Thursday   WAVE 14 Jun 1859
WHITTLESBY, Mary Frances (Dr. P.R.) of Lexington Elder T.P. Haley

FLOURNOY, Frank G. of Carroll Co.   17 Nov   MORE 20 Nov 1859
PEEBLES, Allie M. (Dr. H.E.) of St. Louis   Rev. E.M. Marvin

FLOYD, B.L. of St. Louis   14 May in Louisville   MORE 18 May 1856
HARRISON, Mat M. (James)   Rev. J.T. Halsey

FOGG, Josiah of St. Louis   16 Feb in Rome NY   COWS 26 Feb 1858
BROOKS, Josephine (Merritt) of Rome NY   Rev. N. Barows

FOLBRACHT, Joseph   31 Jan   MORE 3 Feb 1861
OWINGS, Marietta E. (oldest dau/Capt. Sam J.)   Fr. Bannon

FOLEY, John   25 Nov   LIT 3 Dec 1858
GARDNER, Elizabeth (Thomas) "all of Clay Co.   Elder Morton

FORBES, Dr. Charles M. of St. Louis   3 Jan   MORE 5 Jan 1856
EMERSON, Olive (Thomas) of St. Louis Co.   Fr. Kennedy

FORBES, David of St. Louis, formerly of Canada West 16 May, Christ Church   MORE 17 May 1860
NASH, Mary (6th dau/late Samuel of Haslar House, Worcester ENG /Rev. Schuyler

FORBUS, Thomas   6 Oct   COWS 18 Oct 1861
HAMILTON, Angeline Ann (Dudley) "all of Boone Co." Elder B. Wren

FORD, James of Nodaway Co. (Whitecloud Twp)   20 Oct Justice Wm. Ammons   MORE 6 Dec 1854
ALEXANDER, Elizabeth (Joseph) "

FOREMAN, Rev. A.P., Pastor 1st Presbyterian Church
WARDLAW, Virginia (Judge H.H.) all of Hannibal   HANT 17 Nov 1857

FORMAN, W.W. of St. Louis   5 Sep   MORE 20 Sep 1855
KELLY, Helen (Thomas Sr.) of Paris MO   Rev. E. Forman

FORRESTER, Thomas   5 Jan, Trinity Church   MORE 8 Jan 1858
DROUGHT, Annie Frances (only dau/Philip)   Rev. E.C. Hutchinson
          Belfast, Dublin & Kings Co. Ireland pc

FORTNEY, Wherry   14 Jun   COWS 26 Jun 1857
BERRY, Roxana (David C.)   Elder B. Wren

FOSTER, A.   8 Dec   GLWT 18 Dec 1851
DAVIS, Sallie (James) "all of Glasgow"   Elder Proctor

FOWLER, John G. of Pettis Co.   27 Feb   COWS 15 Mar 1861
BRERETON, Janie L. (Benjamin B.) of Cold Neck, Cooper Co. Rev. Josiah Godby

FOX, E. William of St. Louis   at Fredonia NY   MORE 28 Jul 1854
JOHNSON, Eusebia C.   Rev. A.C. Barrett

FOX, Thomas L.   Tuesday in Paris, Monroe Co.   HANT 13 Oct 1855
FOX, Malvina (only dau/J.)

FRALEY, Moses   (A Hebrew wedding by the Grand Rabbi of United   MORE 28 Nov 1865
HARSH, Rosa May (Col. N.)   Hebrew - name illegible - 26 Nov.)
          Cleveland & Baltimore pc

FRANCE, Charles B. of Denver, Colorado Territory in St. Joseph Sep 1   SJH 3 Sep 1864
McDONALD, W. (Dr. Silas)   Rev. T.M. Barrett

FRANCIS, Charles W.   2 Aug   MORE 7 Aug 1860
MAGUIRE, Eulalie (George) "all of St. Louis"

FRAZIER, John G. of Boone Co. 24 April, Walnut Grove Baptist Church   COSE 12 May 1853
BARNETT, Julia (Solomon) of Howard Co.   Rev. Noah Flood

FRAZIER, Lewis M.   9 Oct in New Hope, Lincoln Co.   MORE 17 Oct 1858
P.ALTON, Sallie (Thomas) of near Paintville, / Elder J.J. Everett

FREEMAUN, Sylvester of Weitenung, Groschen-Zogthum, Baden, Germany 28 Feb   MORE 2 Mar 1859
SALER, Augusta of St. Louis   Fr. Welcher of St. Mary's Church

FRENCH, George B., late Major 2nd OH Vols. 19 Jan in Potosi   MORE 24 Jan 1865
PERRY, Mrs. Ann S. (George W. Wallis, at his home) Rev. Love

FRENCH, W.L. of Audrain Co.   26 Oct in Callaway Co.   MORE 30 Oct 1855
BULLARD, Eliza Jane (Richard)

FROST, Fitzhugh Carter   25 Aug at Prairie Park   GLWT 4 Sep 1856
BIRCH, Sarah Catherine (Hon. James H.)   Rev. William Rush

FROST, P.B.   15 Mar, Centenary Church   MORE 15 Mar 1851
CREARY, Mrs. Ann S. formerly of Lynchburgh VA

FULENWIDER, F.B. of Jackson MO   6 Dec   COSE 9 Dec 1852
BARR, Cannie (late Robert) of Boone Co.   Rev. Tyre C. Harris

FULLER, George S.   "Friday last"   MORE 4 Apr 1853
ICENHOWER, Eliza Jane (Andrew)   Rev. Church

FUNK, John A.   31 Aug   LIT 3 Sep 1858
GARTIN, Sarah (A.)   Pres. Thompson

FUNK, Samuel   7 Oct   MORE 13 Oct 1851
SAPPINGTON, Catherine (Joseph decd)   Rev. James Higgins
          Philadelphia pc

FURGUSON, Dr. James G.B.   29 Aug   MORE 31 Aug 1865
HUDGENS, Jennie (Prince) "all of St. Louis"   Rev. Brooks

23

GALBRAITH, H.J., merchant of St. Thomas   WAVE 12 Feb 1859
CARPENTER, Anna E. (Joseph M. and Mary E.) of Randolph Co. Rev. Root

GALLAGHER, Dr. F.R. of St. Charles   26 Jun in Cincinnati   MORE 9 Jul 1855
FINGLAND, Maggie of Cincinnati   Rev. Wilbour

GALLAHER, John T.   23 Apr in Louisville   MORE 1 May 1857
BENEDICT, Mary H. (W.B.) of Louisville   Bishop Spalding

GALLOP, Robert   8 Feb   COWS 19 Feb 1858
ROBERTS, Nancy Elizabeth Jane (Jesse)   Rev. B.S. Woods

GAMBLE, Joseph   St. George's Church   MORE 12 Nov 1861
RAWLINGS, Annie (eldest dau/D.A.)   Rev. Berkeley

GAMBREL, Robert T. of Glasgow   1 Jan in Rough & Ready CA   GLWT 23 Feb 1854
COX, Mrs. Emma of Harmony IN

GAMBRELL, William J. of Glasgow   26 Jul   MORE 6 Aug 1855
BROWN, Ida R. (Judge Bernis) of Glasgow   Rev. C.D. Simpson

GANO, Daniel   20 Jul in Ray Co.   MORE 17 Aug 1858
HUBBELL, Fannie (Capt. William)   Rev. J. Leak
        "at the residence of John F. Hubbell"

GANO, Dr. R.   11 Mar?   COSE 31 Mar 1853
WELCH, Mat (Dr. Thomas of Cumberland KY)   Elder Samuel Hatch

GANT, Henry   8 Dec in Liberty   LIT 11 Dec 1857
THOMPSON, Minerva (J.T.V.)   Rev. John G. Fackler

GANT, L.W. of Mexico, Audrain Co.   26 Jul   MORE 22 Aug 1854
BEATTY, Marie E. (eldest dau/John P. of Audrain Co.) Rev. R.C. Mansfield

GARDENHIRE, James, atty-general elect 25 Sep in Fayette   LIT 15 Oct 1852
MAJORS, Sarah (Samuel C.)   Elder William C. Boon

GARDINER, Samuel of St. Louis at St. Paul's Church, Albany NY   MORE 20 Jul 1851
VAN RENSSELAER, Mary E. (Philip)

GARNETT, Henry of Howard Co.   16 Nov   COWS 10 Dec 1858
HILL, Susan M. (William H.) of Madison Co. VA Rev. James Garnett

++ GARNETT, J.H. of St. Louis   in Marshall   Wednesday last   MORE 22 Jun 1859
   CLARK, Betty (Mrs. D.R. Parsons) of Marshall Rev. W. Wharton

... GARNETT, Lesley of St. Louis   25 Oct in Philadelphia   MORE 6 Nov 1860
CHAMBERLAIN, Maria L. of Philadelphia   Rev. Darling

GARNHART, S.H. of St. Louis   Rev. S.J.P. Anderson   MORE 15 Aug 1857
NOE, Bettie (C.) of Norfolk VA

GARRET, James   12 Oct in Palmyra   PWH 5 Oct 1854
HOOTEN, Elizabeth (Enoch)

++ GARRETT, J.H. of St. Louis Co. in Marshall 15 Jun   WAVE 2 Jul 1859
PARSONS, Betty Clark (Mrs. D.R.)   Rev. W. Wharton

GARRISON, D.E. of St. Louis   20 Feb in Millstone NJ   MORE 26 Feb 1861
BEARDSLEE, Hattie (youngest dau/William) Rev. DeWitt
        "at the home of the bride's father"

GARTH, Henry Harrison   9 Oct   COWS 17 Oct 1862
TURNER, Rhoda Ann (B.) "all of Boone Co." Elder T.M. Allen

GARTH, Samuel of Columbia   17 Nov   COWS 2 Dec 1864
CRAIG, Clara (Gen. James) of St. Joseph

GARTH, William of Columbia   Elder M.E. Lard   LIT 28 Mar 1856
BERRY, Catherine (John) of Liberty

GARTWRIGHT, John T.   29 Apr   SLMD 11 May 1858
DAVIS, Betsy J. (John B.) "all of Callaway Co." Elder A. Rice

GASH, O.P.   21 Nov in Clay Co.   RIF 25 Nov 1855
BALDWIN, Elizabeth (Rev. A.) "both of Clay Co." Rev. Hill

GATCHELL, Lemuel F. of St. Louis 10 Sep in Carrollton IL   MORE 17 Sep 1865
WATKINS, Elvira E. of St. Louis   Rev. William B. Barton
        "at the residence of George B. Price"

GATEWOOD, William L. of Bowling Green   3 May near Williamsburg MORE 3 Jun 1860
WHITE, Fannie A. (youngest dau/Morgan B.) of Callaway Co. Rev. Dr. Campbell
      "at her father's home"   Louisville pc

GEARY, Reuben R.   25 Feb   LAJ 5 Mar 1864
WADDLE, Lucy F. (George R.)   Elder John M. Johnson

GEESTERANUS, P. Mars   8 Mar   JINQ15 Mar 1856
ROBINSON, Bettie (youngest dau/late Henry)   Rev. Hedonburg

GENTRY, James   18 May in Ralls Co.   PWH 22 Jun 1854
FORMAN, Amanda (Judge William)   Rev. A.P. Forman

GENTRY, Richard of Missouri   5 Mar   COWS 23 Mar 1855
GENTRY, Mrs. Julia of Madison Co. KY   Rev. Broaddus

GEORGE, James   21 Apr   COWS 24 Apr 1857
SMITH, Lurinda (George)   Rev. Johnson

GEORGE, John   24 Jul   JINQ 30 Jul 1853
KENNY, Martha (Robert) "all of Cole Co."   Tilman Leach

GERSHON, A. of St. Louis   at the residence of H. Cohen on 24 Oct   MORE 25 Oct 1855
LYON, Maria (oldest dau/Dr. Lemuel of London)

GERTHER, John   2 Oct in St. Louis Co.   MORE 4 Oct 1860
PECK, Mary Ann "at the residence of her uncle Thomas Brannon" Rev Fr Miller

GEST, I.H. of Hannibal at Rose Cottage, Hamilton Co. OH 21 Aug   HANJ 11 Sep 1851
BURDSAL, Mary E. eldest dau/C.S. of Cincinnati

GETTY, Milton C.   20 Sep at Grace Church   MORE 28 Sep 1864
PIEPER, Therese (eldest dau/Henry)   Rev. Philip McKim

GHORHAM, Thomas S.   18 Nov   COWS 3 Dec 1858
VIVION, Hallie (Dr. John B.) of Lafayette Co.   Rev. Robinson

GIBBONS, Isaac N.   (29 Jul?)   HAM 8 Aug 1861
BALDWIN, Sarah S. (Willborn) "all of Marion Co." ___ Jackson, JP

GIBBS, Philip C. late of Morgan Co. VA   15 Oct in Boonville   MORE 27 Oct 1855
MORTON, Matilda (George H.)   Rev. Dunn, Episcopal Church

GIBBS, W.T. formerly of Glasgow 10 Oct 1851 in Georgetown CA   GLWT 22 Jan 1852
TURNER, Mrs. Cynthia, formerly of Carroll Co.   Rev. David Enyart

GIBSON, Andrew R. of Columbia   7 Oct   COSE 14 Oct 1852
ROBINSON, Mary Ellen (late H? R.) Boone Co.   Elder T.M. Allen

GIBSON, Dr. H.G.   27 Jan in Boonville   BOBS 1 Mar 1856
NELSON, Mittie of Fauquier Co. VA   Rev. W. Wharton

GIBSON, J.H.   11 Oct in Hannibal   MORE 19 Oct 1865
ANDERSON, Lizzie (Dr. Robert), formerly of Madison Parish LA Rev R.G. Dun

GIBSON, Dr. James E. of St. Louis   27 Feb in Kingston MS   MORE 12 Mar 1861
KING, Ellen   Rev. William Watkins

GILFILLAN, Dr. William of St. Louis   15 Nov in Westchester NY, St. Peter's   MORE 20 Nov 1859
LADD, Carrie M. of Throg's Neck NY   Church, Rev. C.D. Jackson

GILKEY, Prof. Benjamin T. of Fulton   22 Aug in Glasgow   COWS 8 Sep 1865
HUGHES, Lucy A. (Col. Courtney)   J.A. Quarles
     "both mute; he teaches at the Deaf and Dumb Asylum in Fulton"

GILLESPIE, William L.   4 Mar in Boone Co.   COWS 12 Mar 1858
LLOYD, Elizabeth Jane (Mrs. Rebecca) of Callaway Co.   E.E. Chrisman

GIVENS, Charles of Howard Co.   28 Apr   GLWT 6 May 1852
KRING, Mary A. (H.W.) of Fayette   Rev. W.T. Lucky

GIVENS, N.B.   5 Feb in Waverly   COWS 22 Feb 1861
BELLAMY, Mollie E. (eldest dau/William)   Henry S. Earl

GLANVILLE, Octavius A.   28 Jul at the Clarendon Hotel   MORE 30 Jul 1864
McGEE, Mary E.F. (Thomas S.)   Elder P. Donan
          "all of Franklin Co."

GLASGOW, William S. of St. Louis   6 Dec in Charleston MA   MORE 13 Dec 1860
FALES, Carlotta Nestue (late Barnabas)   Rev. Thomas Lambert
       "of San Juan de las Remedias, Cuba"

GLENN, Thomas M.   18 Apr   JINQ 29 Apr 1854
PRESTON, Caroline V. (Capt. John) "all of Washington MO"

GLOVER, William P. of Knox Co.   12 May near Newark   CANE 26 May 1853
ASHCRAFT, Sallie A. of Meade Co. KY   Rev. E.K. Miller

GOADBY, Henry A. of St. Louis   17 Feb   Bishop Levi Scott   MORE 24 Feb 1863
McCLINTOCK, Martha (Dr. James, City Treasurer of Philadelphia)

GODFERY (sic), John W.   28 Nov   SLMD 3 Dec 1861
CONSTABLE, Jennie (eldest dau/Maj. Nathaniel)   Elder T.M. Allen

GOFF, James B. of St. Louis   18 Oct in Springfield IL   MORE 19 Oct 1854
CHURCH, Sue   Rev. Samuel B. Church

GOLDMAN, M. of Liberty   16 Aug in Cincinnati   LIT 28 Aug 1857
BEATUS, Henrietta   Rev. Isaac M. Wise

GOLDSMITH, John H.   31 Oct in Palmyra   CANP 9 Nov 1865
GUTHRIE, Jennie A. (William)   Rev. Vandusen

GOOCH, Luther P.   3 Nov   HANT 15 Nov 1853
SMITH, Michal Francis (eldest dau/J.F.) of Pike Co. Rev. A.P. Mitchell

GOODALL, Oliver P. late of Cole Co.   16 Oct 1853 in Oregon City   JINQ 18 Feb 1854
BELL, Louisa, late of Jersey Co. IL   Mayor Prescott
                "both of Oregon County"

GOODING, Richard R.   17 Jul   RANC 19 Jul 1860
PHIPPS, Melissa A. (Thomas)   Rev. M.J. Sears

GORD, William P.   "Monday evening"   MORE 6 Apr 1853
LANGWELL, Mariah L. (William P.)   Reverend Church

GORDON, George W.   21 Jan   JINQ 31 Jan 1852
E?ANS (EVANS?), __ dau/W.H. "all of this county" Rev. Martin D. Noland

GORDON, John M.   12 Aug in Mexico, Audrain Co.   COWS 20 Aug 1858
LUCKEY, Bettie (Robert) of Audrain Co.   J.T. Brooks

GORDON, N.D. of Dozier's Landing, St. Charles Co. 28 Oct   MORE 2 Nov 1858
DRYDEN, Lizzie "at the home of her father in Montgomery Co." Rev. Taylor

GORDON, Robert C.   8 Jun Rev. Montgomery Schuyler   MORE 9 Jun 1859
LINDELL, Ann Eliza (late John) at the home of Peter Lindell

GORDON, Urias   22 Jan   JINQ 31 Jan 1852
GORDON, Catherine S. (Alex) "all of Cole Co." Rev. Martin D. Noland

GORDON, William M.   12 Nov   HANJ 20 Nov 1851
McWILLIAMS, Elizabeth L. (James) "all of Marion Co."   Elder D.T. Morton

GORE, Stephen W.   3 Feb in Lancaster PA   MORE 18 Feb 1853
HELFENSTEIN, Anna M.

GOSLIN, William T.   15 Mar   COWS 23 Mar 1855
ROWLAND, Frances E. (David B.)   Rev. Green Cary

GOSSADGE, Joseph of the Enrolled Militia   5 Mar   RICON 12 Mar '63
NANCE, Sarah Frances (Bird) of "this vicinity"   Esq. Snowden

GOTT, John   13 Nov   MORE 17 Nov 1859
LAWTON, Angie (Dr. Edward) "all of St. Louis"   Rev. T.H. Mudge

GOUGH, John, late of New York   17 Nov   COWS 25 Nov 1859
McGEE, Hannah (Harvey) of Audrain Co.   Rev. Scott

GOURLEY, Harrison N. of Pike Co. (Louisiana) 23 Nov near Carrollton IL   LAJ 9 Dec 1865
HALBERT, Julia at her mother's home   Rev. J.R. Armstrong

GRACE, Thomas   15 Sep at St. Francis Xavier   MORE 18 Sep 1864
BRENNAN, Mary Ann (oldest dau/late James)   Fr. Corbet

GRADY, Joseph   11 Mar   HANT 23 Mar 1858
DONERLY, Serelda Ann (Noah) of Marion Co.

GRAHAM, James L.   30 Apr   MORE 2 May 1863
GOODFELLOW, Mrs. Madama (Peter Wiles)   Rev. Thomas M. Finney

GRAHAM, Thomas S. of Macon Co.   18 Nov   WAVE 27 Nov 1858
VIVION, Sallie (eldest dau/John) of Waverly   Rev. Robinson

GRANT, David R. of St. Louis   9 Jan at St. George's Church   MORE 13 Jan 1865
LAWRENCE, Helen L. (Leander)   Rev. Berkeley
                Albany, Troy, and NY pc

GRANT, Francis M.   26 Feb   COWS 1 Mar 1861
NICHOLS, Sarah R. (Maj. J.R.) "all of Boone Co."   Elder J.K. Rogers

GRANT, John S.   10 Jun   COWS 18 Jun 1858
PITTS, Susan (John) "all of Boone Co."   John M. Robinson

GRANT, Thomas   MORE 9 Apr 1851
ROPER, Olive (Capt. William), formerly of London ENG.

GRAVES, Jordan of Missouri   22 Aug in Woodford KY   MORE 30 Aug 1854
WILLIAMS, Sarah Louisa (late John)   Rev. W.O. Combs

GRAVES, William H. of Canton   10 Sep in Bloomington IL   CANP 17 Sep 1863
MONTGOMERY, Jessie F. of Bloomington   Elder T.V. Berry

GRAY, Dr. J. Wellington of Windsor, Henry Co.   21 Sep   COWS 30 Sep 1864
HEAD, Clara Elizabeth (Dr.) of Millersburg, Callaway Co.   Elder J.M. Robinson

GREEK, Alexander G.   11 Jun   MORE 12 Jun 1860
CASTERLINE, Ann Eliza (Calvin L.)   Rev. J.J. Porter
      "all of St. Louis"   Pittsburgh & NY pc

GREEN, Clark H., editor of the Glasgow Times 22 Feb in Fayette   GLWT 24 Feb 1853
SNELSON, Susan (Dr. William R.) of Fayette   Rev. C.D. Simpson

GREEN, George R. of St. Louis, formerly of Hannibal, 31 May in Boyle Co. KY   HANJ 30 Jun 1853
TALBOT, Elizabeth (A.G.) of Boyle Co.   Prof. W.M. Scott

GREENE, Charles C. of St. Louis   5 Feb   MORE 8 Feb 1855
SEDAM, Carrie G. (D.L.) of Cincinnati

GREENE, H.M. of Huntsville   24 Sep   GLWT 15 Oct 1857
HALL, Mrs. Mary A. of N. Middletown, Bourbon Co. KY   Rev. J.R. Edds

GREEN, Dr. J.T. of Marshall   30 Mar in Winchester VA   MARD 16 Apr 1858
MILLER, Lila A. of Winchester

GREEN, Rev. James S. of the Baptist Church, Palmyra 13 Dec   HANT 17 Dec 1853
CLUFF, Mrs. Martha (Capt. William Carson) of Marion Co. Rev. J.T. Williams

GREENABAUM, Alexander of Fayette   12 May in Philadelphia   GLWT 3 Jun 1852
ARHOLD, Marium (Manuel) of Philadelphia

GREENE, Samuel of St. Louis   Muscatine IA, 1st Congregational Church   MORE 10 Oct 1861
MOORE, Sarah Elizabeth (Mrs. M.F.) of Muscatine

GRIFFIN, Robert   Elder B. Wren   COWS 19 Mar 1858
GRIFFIN, Sallie Ann (Patrick)

GRIFFITH, Archie P.   12 Dec   MORE 8 Jan 1861
PRICE, Mary E. (Archie) of Price's Landing, Scott Co.

GRIFFITH, F.G.   19 Nov   MORE 21 Nov 1862
GAMEWELL, M. Anna (late James and M.E.) Rev. E.F. Berkeley
            "at the home of the bride's mother"

GRIFFITH, James S. of St. Louis 17 May, St. James Church, Pittsburgh   MORE 27 May 1859
ROSEWELL, Sarah A. (Thomas) of Pittsburgh   Rev. DeWitt C. Byllesby

GRIFFITH, John "considered advanced in Age"   4 Jan   LAJ 14 Jan 1865
GRIFFITH, Mrs. ___, widow of Noah   Rev. W.J. Campbell

GRIGSBY, William F.B.   19 Nov   LIT 27 Nov 1857
BRIGHT, Mollie (Joseph) "all of Clay Co."   Rev. John G. Fackler

GRIMES, Carlton O.   14 Jul near Lexington   WAVE 23 Jul 1859
PRICE, Talitha (Casby)   Rev. J.W. Warden

GRIMSHAW, William A.   10 Jun in Pike Co.   MORE 14 Jun 1856
GRIMSHAW, Margaret (late John C.)   Rev. Robert Ryall
            "at the residence of J.M. Bush"

GRISWOLD, Oliver H.   2 Apr in Montgomery Co.   MORE 11 Apr 1861
RANDOLPH, Kate, at her mother's home   Rev. S.P. Longhead

GROOMES, Robert M.   in Louisville   MORE 12 Oct 1857
GODWIN, Adeline (late E.V.) of Louisville   Rev. J.H. Heywood

GROPPEL, P.H. of St. Louis   4 Aug in St. Louis   MORE 6 Aug 1859
SCHAUFFELBERGER, Kate of Baltimore   Rev. Hugo Krebs

GROVE, J.B., late of California   6 Oct   MARD 7 Oct 1859
WILSON, Kate (Judge William A.) of Marshall   Rev. J.W. Clark

GUERRANT, Robert H.   17 Mar   GLWT 31 Mar 1853
HILL, Zarilda A. (P.M.) "all of Saline Co."   Rev. Bell

GUERIN, E.T. of Huntsville   25 Sep near Cambridge   MORE 6 Oct 1855
GILLIAM, Bettie (Judge Taylor) of Saline Co.   Rev. N.B. Peterson

GUITAR, David of Columbia   24 Oct   MORE 3 Nov 1854
HERNDON, Harriet (F.) of Boone Co.   Rev. N.H. Hall

GUMM, William of St. Charles   10 Jul in St. Louis /by Rev. Pres   SLMD 11 Jul 1860
BUCKLAND, Mattie of St. Louis, formerly of Sussex ENG /Shank of Lindenwood/

GUTHRIE, Thomas F.   19 Feb   HANT 15 Mar 1856
CLATTERBUCK, Mary Elizabeth (O.) "all of Callaway Co." Rev. Coulter

GUTHRIDGE, Melvin of Livingston Co.   26 Jan at the home of James G. Allen   FULT 29 Jan 1864
JONES, Kate (William A.)   Rev. H.A. Bourland

HADLEY, George C.   17 Feb, St. Francis Xavier   MORE 19 Feb 1862
NOONAN, Gussie (late Thomas)   Fr. Garesche

HAGENS, Joseph   10 Mar   COWS 18 Mar 1859
VANDIVER, Elmira (William H.)   Elder B. Wren

HAGGARD, Lewis C. of Cass Co.   6 Sep in Clark Co. KY   MORE 6 Oct 1855
BROADDUS, Mary A.

HAGGERTY, W.H. at St. Peter & Paul Church, New Orleans, 22 Apr   MORE 10-11 May, 1854
BOYLAN, Anna M. (2nd dau/late Thomas H.)

HALE, George D. of St. Louis   11 Sep in Blythedale, MO   MORE 22 Sep 1860
MILLER, Louisa A. (Edward), formerly of Philadelphia Rev. Wallace

HALE, W. Ben   of St. Louis   19 Apr near Canton, Rev. J. Shanks   MORE 23 Apr 1865
NICHOLSON, Matilda (Joseph), formerly of Palmyra, at her mother's home

HALE, William of St. Joseph   15 Oct   LEXP 29 Oct 1859
LOWRY, Kate (eldest dau/James)   Elder Haley

HALEY, Elder Henry H. last Tuesday near Lexington by Elder McGarvey   WAVE 11 Feb 1860
PORTER, Mary E. (John S., at his home)

HALL, Albert E. of St. Louis 3 May at the home of J. Capen, Rev. C.F. Dowd   MORE 24 Jun 1865
CAPEN, Flavia C. of Fairhaven VT
  (Her death notice, in the same newspaper, gives her father's name as J. Cooper)

HALL, George D. of St. Louis. Identical to George D. HALE, above.   SLMD 22 Sep 1860

HALL, Lee A. of St. Louis   28 Oct   MORE 1 Nov 1856
WATT, Harriet (W.W.) of Pike Co.   Rev. J. Errett

HALL, William A. of Richmond   in Clay Co.   LIT 23 Nov 1855
RINGO, Florence (late Samuel)   Elder M.E. Lard

HAMILL, J. of St. Louis   7 Mar in Pittsburgh   SLMD 22 Mar 1854
LEACH, Eliza Jane Perry (Malcolm)

HAMILTON, J.P. of Daviess Co.   21 Sep in Chillicothe   SJH 24 Sep 1865
DAVIS, Mollie D. (William B?) of Chillicothe   Rev. J.H. Hopkins

HAMILTON, John R.   29 Dec   MORE 2 Jan 1860
DARST, Clara E. (eldest dau/Robert A.) of St. Louis Fr. Samrius

HAMM, C. Lester of St. Louis   13 May   MORE 14 Jun 1860
BOGGS, Fannie L. (Col. Wm. G.) of New York   Rev. Tindell

HAMPSON, William   15 Nov   COWS 23 Nov 1860
WHITAKER, Sarah Ann (Hiram) "all of Andrew Co."   Rev. H.M. Painter

HANCE, Harvey   "this morning"   HANT 6 Oct 1853
CAPLINGER, Mary, recently of Georgetown KY   Rev. G.W. Caples of Weston

HANCOCK, D.J. of St. Louis   3 Aug in Boston   MORE 4 Aug 1854
LEARNED, Mary E. of Boston   Rev. D. Read

HANCOCK, George W. of Springfield   5 Oct in Boone Co.   COSE 13 Oct 1853
STONE, Nannie (Madison) of Boone Co.   Rev. T.G. Harris

HANCOCK, William P. of St. Louis   15 Oct in Godfrey IL   MORE 16 Oct 1860
MASON, Helen of Godfrey   Rev. Albert Smith

HAND, William   25 Apr   SJH 27 Apr 1864
KNAPP, Mary (E.J.)   Fr. Hennessy

HANNAH, Samuel   14 Feb   COWS 24 Feb 1865
KEENE, Marium (Alexander) of Boone Co.

HANNA, James B., M.D., of Florida, Monroe Co. 19 Aug at Prairie House,   COWS 29 Aug 1862
MATTHEWS, Mary (E.P.)   Mexico, MO Rev. James Marton

HANSBROUGH, Dr. G.D. of Harrisonville   3 Jun   MORE 16 Jun 1855
McKINNEY, America (N.H.) of Cass Co.   Rev. R. Symington

HANSBROUGH, H.   26 Oct   MARD 5 Nov 1859
GALBRAITH, Nannie (Hugh P.) "all of Pettis Co."   Rev. W.J. Brown

HANSON, George H.   5 Nov   Rev. S.J.P. Anderson   MORE 7 Nov 1863
MONTGOMERY, Maria (S.J.)

HANSON, J.N.	18 Jan	MORE 19 Jan 1860
BENT, Ellen (Joseph K.) "all of St. Louis"	Rev. Nelson	
HARDCASTLE, Addison	2 Jan	MORE 4 Jan 1851
ALEXANDER, Octavia (R.W. or H.W.)	Bishop Hawks	
	Philadelphia and Baltimore pc	
HARDEN, James Hamilton of Glasgow	11 May in Cynthiana KY	GLWT 27 May 1852
JANUARY, Priscie of Cynthiana	Rev. William Trainer	
HARDIN, Edward of Cambridge MS	1 Nov (Dec?) in Jefferson City	COWS 4 Dec 1857
CORDELL, Llewella (Judge Enos B.)	Rev. Longhead	
HARDIN, Dr. T.J. of St. Louis	14 Oct	COWS 18 Nov 1864
KENAN, M. Fanny (Samuel) of Boone Co.		
HARDING, George M. formerly of New York City 23 Feb Rev. Thomas Lee		MORE 2 Mar 1859
ANDREWS, Caroline M. (youngest dau/Thomas) "all of St. Louis"		
HARDING, James of St. Louis	18 Dec in Jefferson City	MORE 28 Dec 1855
CORDELL, Christine (Dr. L.C. of Charleston VA) Rev. Adderly		
HARDWICK, Samuel	27 Dec	LIT 28 Dec 1860
HALL, Addie (John D.)	Pres. Thompson (of Wm. Jewell College)	
HARDY, James K.	5 Oct, St. George's Church	MORE 7 Oct 1864
SHIELDS, Mississippi (Thomas)	Rev. Edward F. Berkeley	
HARKER, George Mifflin	21 Feb	SLMD 25 Feb 1861
WALLACE, Jennie (James W.)"all of St. Louis" Rev. Carleton A. Staples		
HARKINS, Capt. H. of St. Louis	22 Jul in Louisville	MORE 6 Aug 1853
O'REGAN, Kate M. (Caniel) of Bourbon Co. KY	Rev. John Jones	
HARLAN, William H. of KY	6 Oct, St. George's Church	MORE 11 Oct 1863
MACHETTE, M.E. (late John V. & Mary H.) formerly of NY Bishop Hawk		
	NY, Philadelphia, Trenton pc	
HARLOW, Joseph M. in Montgomery Co. 17 Nov		MORE 24 Nov 1859
CHAPMAN, Catherine		
HARMAN, Eli of Boone Co.	16 Dec	COWS 25 Dec 1857
WATSON, Lucy Missouri (John R.) of Callaway Elder B. Wren		
HARPER, Jefferson of Weston	23 Oct	LIT 31 Oct 1862
KELLER, Pauline (Col. J.M.)	Elder R.C. Morton	
HARRELL, J.F.	8 Oct	LEXC 15 Oct 1856
WADDELL, Sarah Elizabeth (late C.R.)	D.A. Veitch Esq.	
HARRINGTON, Henry F.	2 Feb at St. Patrick's Church	MORE 5 Feb 1865
DUNN, Charlotte Cecelia (John) all of St. Louis Fr. Wheeler		
	California, Boston, St. Joseph pc	
HARRIS, A.S. of Brunswick	12 Jun at Cynthiana KY	MORE 27 Jul 1854
MUSSER, Lizzie	Rev. Carter Page	
HARRIS, J.W., a merchant of Rocheport 27 Feb		MORE 7 Mar 1854
McCLURE, Annie (William) of Boone Co. Rev. T.C. Harris		
HARRIS, O.G.	7 Jun Rev. Green Carey	COWS 22 Jun 1855
HARL, Mrs. Eliza (Maj. Stephen Wilhite) "all of Boone Co."		
HARRIS, Overton M. of Monroe Co.	18 Feb	COWS 6 Mar 1863
WOOD, Amanda (Clinton) of Pettis Co.		
HARRIS, Thomas J. of St. Louis	23 Oct	MORE 26 Oct 1856
MILLER, Georgianna (E.G.) of Quincy IL Rev. Thomas Foot		
HARRIS, Capt. Warren Woodson	12 Dec in Fayette	COWS 22 Dec 1865
DAVIS, Sallie (Judge S.E.)	Squire D.W. Street	
HARRISON, William P., Register in the Land Office, Palmyra 20 Dec		HANT 24 Dec 1853
BULLOCK, Nannie M. (late Winfield) of St. Charles Rev. William Hurley		
HART, George of St. Louis	6 Oct in Milwaukee	MORE 9 Oct 1859
DAVIS, Jennie M. (Capt. D.H.) at her father's home James Pyper D.D.		
HART, James W. of Jefferson City	12 Mar	JINQ 22 Mar 1856
SAYERS, Susan (late Samuel) of Callaway Co. Rev. S.S. Scott		
HART, Jesse L.	14 Jun	COWS 22 Jun 1855
BROWN, Mary (late James) "all of Boone Co." Elder T.M. Allen		
HART, Thomas	20 Dec in Palmyra	MORE 27 Dec 1855
GENTRY, Sarah (Moses) of Marion Co.	Rev. Jacob Creath	

HARVEY, Andrew of St. Louis at Cottage Garden, Reading Road, Hamilton Co. OH   MORE 17 Sep 1854
BROOKS, Emma E.   12 Sep by Rev. M.A. Sackett

HARVEY, J.E.   21 Aug   MORE 7 Sep 1856
JACKS, Mary E. (Thomas) "all of Platte Co."   Rev. Woodward

HARVEY, N.A.   1 Feb in Lincoln Co.   SLMD 13 Feb 1854
REID, Amy Jane (James)   Rev. S.S. Ralston

HARVEY, Dr. P.O. of Cooper Co.   22 May   BOBS 27 May 1851
SCOTT, Martha Jane (youngest dau/James) of Pettis Co.   Rev. F. Landrin

HATCH, W.H. of Hannibal   4 Apr   HAM 6 Apr 1861
HAWKINS, Thetis C. (J.F.) of Marion Co.   Elder William Hatch

HATCHER, Thaddeus B. of Palmyra   11 Feb in Paris, Monroe Co.   PALS 18 Feb 1857
CLARKE, Sarah J. (youngest dau/late Dr. David) of Paris Rev. J.P. Finley
             "at the residence of Dr. A.E. Gore"

HAVENS, James   25 Feb   MORE 10 Mar 1859
RIGS, Mrs. Sophia (widow of John) "all of Franklin Co." Rev. Wash Stephens
       "at the residence of John Wyner"   Cincinnati pc

HAWK, Edwin A. formerly of Madison WI   30 Sep   MORE 2 Oct 1857
MARTIN, Mary F. formerly of Richmond VA   Rev. Nelson

HAWKINS, Allen W. of Knox Co.   25 Jun in Palmyra   MORE 2 Jul 1861
BOWER, Annie M. of Palmyra (dau/M.R.)   Elder James S. Greene

HAWKINS, Dr. Edwin J. of Hannibal   HANT 5 Feb 1857
BATES, Martha E. (youngest dau/M.D.)   29 Jan

HAWKINS, George W. of Hannibal   13 May in Ralls Co.   LADB 21 May 1851
PRIEST, Ann E. (Thomas) of Ralls Co.   Rev. J.H. Lorance

HAWKINS, Oscar   31 Mar   GLWT 1 Apr 1852
MARTYR, Fannie (Robert)   Rev. William Perkins

HAWKINS, Stephen G.   9 Jun   William Harris J.P.   HAM 13 Jun 1861
SMEAD, Mrs. Eliza J. (J.F. Lancaster, at his residence)

HAWKS, Rev. C.S., D.D. 1 Feb at Oakwood, Howard Co.   MORE 4 Feb 1864
LEONARD, Ada (late Abiel)   Rev. John F. Fish

HAYDEN, Emmet R. of Boonville   6 Nov in Jefferson City   COWS 4 Dec 1857
SCOTT, Alice (Hon. William)   Rev. William Leftwich

HAYDEN, Henry C. of Fulton   17 Nov in Cambridge MO   COWS 4 Dec 1857
GROVE, Binnie C. (Samuel) of Cambridge   Rev. Charles Simpson

HAYES, Thomas S. of St. Louis   24 Oct in Newark NJ   MORE 30 Oct 1860
WILDE, Amelia (eldest dau/Henry)   Rev. R.L. Dashiel

HAYNES, George W.   13 Nov   COWS 16 Nov 1855
TUTTLE, Elizabeth M. (Judge Gilpin E.)

HAYS, Dr. J.M. of Roanoke   23 Mar   GLWT 26 Mar 1857
HALLEY, Lizzie (P.W.) of Howard Co.

HAYS, William   Tuesday   GLWT 31 Mar 1853
HUME, Susan (Joel) "all of Howard Co."   Rev. N.W. Miller

HAYSE, William Hamilton of Ralls Co. 9 Nov Elder M.M. Modisett (Baptist) HANT 13 Nov 1852
PARSONS, Mrs. Miriam (Samuel Bentley) of Boone Co.

HAZZARD, George H. of St. Louis 15 Aug in Springfield IL   JINQ 8 Sep 1855
OGLE, Frances C. of Springfield

HEAD, Prof. L.S. of the State University   Elder James A. Berry   COWS 16 Jul 1858
SNELL, Amanda (John A.) of Monroe Co.

HEAD, Dr. Thomas B. formerly of Huntsville   1 Sep in Randolph Co.   RANC 2 Sep 1859
PATTERSON, Bettie H. (Rice) of Howard Co.

HEADMAN, C.C.   19 May in Danville, Montgomery Co. MORE 22 May 1852
FULKERSON, Rebecca   Rev. Bower

HEARSUM, Frederick of St. Louis   8 Jan in Grayville IL   MORE 11 Jan 1861
CLARK, Hattie C. (L.B.) formerly of St. Louis   Rev. Benjamin Hutchison

HEARSUM, Fred H. of St. Louis   23 Oct in Boston   MORE 30 Oct 1864
CLARK, Sophia (L.B.) of St. Louis   Rev. Rufus Ellis

HEATH, Lieut. Col. William G.   25 Aug   MORE 27 Aug 1863
FORTUNE, Mary Adelaide (Walker? Walter?) "all of St. Louis" Fr. Ring

HEELAN, P.B.   23 Feb at St. Vincent's   MORE 27 Feb 1859
WYANT, Sarah E., niece of the late Capt. John Ashton   Rev. Thomas Burke

HELFRICH, Henry   8 Nov   BOBS 17 Nov 1860
HAAS, Eliza (William)   Rev. Greiner

HELMUTH, Dr. William T.   10 Feb   MORE 12 Feb 1859
PRITCHARD, Fannie (John N.)   Rev. Montgomery Schuyler
                        Philadelphia pc

HENDERSON, Ferdinand   14 Oct at Central Church parsonage   MORE 15 Oct 1863
MUSICK, Cornelia (James C. and late Phoebe J.) Rev. S.J.P. Anderson

HENDERSON, James A. of St. Louis   20 Apr   COWS 22 Apr 1859
ROYALL, Virginia (late Capt. John B.)   Rev. Samuel Mutchmore

HENDERSON, James M.   3 Aug   MORE 4 Aug 1854
JAMES, Kate (John) "both of St. Louis"   Rev. W.G. Eliot

HENDERSON, Dr. William W.   17 Jun in Bridgeton   MORE 19 Jun 1857
EVANS, Martha E. (late John)   Rev. Gilbreath

HENDRON, Marshall   6 Jan   COWS 15 Jan 1858
ANGELL, Catherine (Robert)   Rev. B.S. Woods

HENESY, F.G. of St. Louis   in Rosedale, IL   MORE 25 Feb 1857
SWALES, Sallie (eldest dau/Thomas)   Rev. McMaster, Episcopal Church

HENNINGER, Robinson   20 Mar   HANT 29 Mar 1856
LEWIS, Sarah (Luke)   "all of Monroe Co."

HENRY, E. Dunham formerly of NY   11 Jun   MORE 13 Jun 1863
LEARNED, Clara (Henry)   Rev. Montgomery Schuyler

HENRY, Edward D.   7 Jul   COSE 15 Jul 1852
PARKER, Susan (Gabriel) "all of Boone Co."   Rev. N.H. Hall

HERNDON, Dr. J.H.   4 Mar in Randolph Co. Rev. C.D. Simpson   GLWT 11 Mar 1852
CLEVELAND, Juliet M. (Capt. John T.) of the Glasgow vicinity

HEYDON, Kenzie   18 Jan in Polk Co.   MORE 27 Jan 1860
BROWN, Selina (Rev. William)   Rev. Callaway

HEYWOOD, Charles P. Jr.   27 Apr in Hannibal   HANT 29 Apr 1858
SHOOT, Kitty (William Sr.)

HICKAM, Lysander   24 Dec   "all of Boone Co."   COWS 8 Jan 1858
WHITE, Margaret (Allen)

HICKAM, Sardis   6 Jan   Elder B. Wren   COWS 14 Jan 1859
GRIFFIN, Susan (Patrick) "all of Boone Co."

HICKMAN, David H., President of the Columbia Exchange Bank, 15 Sep in   COWS 27 Sep 1861
BRYAN, Annie (late Milton) of St. Joseph St. Joseph Rev. E.S. Dulin

HICKMAN, Ezra R.   4 Feb in Raleigh NC   LEXC 27 Feb 1856
RALSTON, Rowena (Col. Samuel) "all of Jackson Co."

HICKMAN, Rev. Gary of Dover MO   6 Dec   LEXP 15 Dec 1852
CARPENTER, Mary (Deacon Nathan) of Foxcroft ME

HICKMAN, John L. of Boone Co.   10 Nov   COWS 12 Nov 1858
WALKER, Ella (Smith) of Cooper Co.

HICKMAN, Joseph G.   18 Apr in Florida, Monroe Co.   PALS 1 May 1863
CAMPBELL, Maggie K. (eldest dau/John I.)   Rev. John Leighton

HICKS, James E.   3 Apr   MORE 15 Apr 1855
KEEN, Elizabeth (James) "all of Audrain Co."   Elder T.M. Allen

HIGGINS, Henry   6 Jan in Chillicothe   GLWT 20 Jan 1853
PARKS, Sarah Ann (Samuel decd) late of Chariton Co.   T. Myers Esq.

HIGGINS, James C.   in Savannah by Elder Duke Young   MORE 5 Oct 1855
JOHN, Mary M. (eldest dau/Jesse)

HIGGINS, T.J. of Independence 29 Mar in Baltimore MD   WEBS 22 Apr 1859
MAGRAW, Jennie E. (James C.) of Baltimore   Rev. Burt

HILDEBRAND, John   in Montgomery Co. 30 Mar   MORE 6 May 1857
KELLERHALS, H.L.

HILDRETH, Samuel P. of St. Louis   10 Dec in Wheeling West VA   MORE 16 Dec 1856
LIST, Dorrie V. (Thomas)   Rev. Dawson

HILES, George of St. Louis   18 Jul in Philadelphia   MORE 26 Jul 1857
HOYLAND, Mrs. Mary Ann

HILL, Britton A.   14 Jan   MORE 16 Jan 1857
BEHRENS, Joanna (Dr. Henry) of St. Charles   Rev. Rudolph Large

HILL, James S.   19 Nov   Elder T.J. Marlow   MORE 25 Nov 1863
FLETCHER, Eliza I. (John F.)   "all of Callaway Co."

HILL, T.B.   MORE 5 Nov 1858
STEWART, Kate (2nd dau/John)   Rev. G.B. Weaver

HILL, Dr. W.C. of Sparta   12 Oct in St. Joseph   SJH 12 Oct 1865
HEATON, Lizzie G. (D.J.) of St. Joseph   Rev. G.T. Hougland

HILLS, Charles F.   7 Nov, Church of the Messiah   MORE 8 Nov 1864
SPARR, Sarah Louise (John N.)   Rev. Eliot

HINDS, Capt. John C. of St. Louis   in Peoria by Rev. Mayous   MORE 24 Nov 1851
GREENWOOD, Amanda of Hickman, KY

HINSON, S. of Glasgow   21 Jun   GLWT 28 Jun 1855
NEILLE, Kate (Joseph) of Arrow Rock

HITCH, G.H. of St. Charles Co. 16 Oct at New Hope, Lincoln Co.   MORE 25 Oct 1856
HAND, Mollie T. (late Absalom and Martha) formerly of Rappahannock Co. VA

HITCHCOCK, Abner of St. Louis at the home of the bride, in Plymouth,   MORE 5 Jan 1862
PATTERSON, Mrs. Helen E.   Wayne Co. MI by Rev. William B. Grow

HOARSMAN, John of Monroe Co.   last Thursday   HANT 31 Jan 1857
EUSTACE, Caraline (John) of Palmyra

HOBLITZELL, Joseph   1 Nov in Oregon (Holt Co.)   HOLS 3 Nov 1865
COLLINS, Lida A. (Stephen C.)   Rev. Edward Roszeli "all of this city"

HODGE, Robert M.   31 Mar   COWS 9 Apr 1858
HULEN, Nannie (John C.)   Rev. W.R. Wigginton

HODGMAN, John A.   in Troy NY   Rev. Vincent   MORE 10 Dec 1864
CROZIER, Jennie (Alex) "all of St. Louis"

HOGGE, John W.   10 Oct in Montgomery Co.   MORE 18 Oct 1855
JAMES, Elizabeth W.   Rev. W.W. Crockett

HOLEMAN, William H.   20 Apr   COWS 8 May 1857
GUTHRIE, Sarah (Samuel)   "all of Callaway Co."

HOLLAND, B.F.   14 Oct in Montgomery Co.   COWS 29 Oct 1858
TANNEYHILL, Rebecca (C.)   Rev. A. Taylor

HOLLISTER, John   17 Sep   Rev. Forman   SLMD 24 Sep 1861
HOLME, Annie (eldest dau/P.H.) of Hannibal

HOLLOWAY, Jesse of St. Louis   Logansport IN   MORE 19 Apr 1861
EWING, Lavinie (Col. G.W.) at the home of George B. Walker
                    (above item taken from a Fort Wayne newspaper)

HOLMAN, J. H. of St. Louis   25 Aug in Charleston MA   MORE 10 Sep 1864
ALDEN, Maggie   Rev. Everett

HOLME, Charles J.   10 Nov in Granby, Newton Co.   MORE 22 Nov 1859
FITZGERALD, Jeannie (John)   Hannibal pc

HOLME, Richard of St. Louis   30 May at Batavia OH   MORE 14 Jun 1860
FISHBACK, Lizzie (Judge O.T.)   Rev. Allen

HOLMES, Nehemiah   near Westport, Jackson Co.   MORE 21 Aug 1858
FLOWERIE, Mollie (Daniel)   Rev. Wallace

HOLT, Dr. S.W.   20 Aug   COWS 25 Aug 1865
HARRIS, Mary E. (late O.G.) "both of Boone Co."   Rev. W.L.T. Evans

HOLTZCLAW, H. of Paris MO in St. Louis at the home of William Fife, 8 Apr   MORE 10 Apr 1863
WHITE, Mrs. J.C. (Robert Fife) formerly of St. Louis, now of Paris
                          by Elder B.H. Smith

HOLTON, Charles A. of St. Louis 1 Jan in Chicago, Church of the Redeemer   MORE 15 Jan 1865
STRATFORD, Helen M. (eldest dau/Dr. H.R. of Waukegan, IL Rev. J.K. Tuttle

HOMER, Truman J. 20 Jun at the Rectory of St. Michael's Church   MORE 28 Jun 1860
HOGEN, Susan M. (eldest dau/Michael A.)   Rev. P. O'Brien

HOOD, James   15 Mar in Boonville   GLWT 25 Mar 1852
SMITH, Mary S. of Boonville   Rev. W.G. Bell

HOOD, John   1 Nov   MARD 21 Nov 1860
PURSEY, Miss __ (eldest dau/Jesse) "all of Saline Co." Rufus Bingham Esq.

```
HOOD, John                        27 Jun                              MORE 29 Jun 1865
RUTH, Lizzie  "all of this city"          Rev. Nelson
          "at the residence of her uncle Charles G. Ramsey"

HOOK, Zadock, Public Administrator   16 Sep                           COWS 16 Oct 1863
STEENBERGER, Mollie (Rev. Peter H.) all of Callaway Co.  Rev. John M. Robinson

HOOKER, William of Clay Co.          12 Oct                           SJH 13 Oct 1864
DAUGHERTY, Lou (A.A.) of the City Hotel, St. Joseph   Rev. T.W. Barrett

HOOPER, Philip of Chariton Co.       13 Mar                           COWS 23 Mar 1855
BAKER, Betty Ann (Joseph) of Callaway Co.       Elder T.P. Stephens

HOOPER, Thomas Jr. of St. Louis   First Presbyterian Church, Jerseyville IL   MORE 17 Oct 1864
JOHNSON, Anna M.                      Rev. Charles Foote

HOOPER, William P. of Parkville      12 Mar                           LIT 3 Apr 1857
ARNOLD, Sallie (Thomas) of Clay Co.       Rev. H. Hill

HOPKINS, E.H.                        4 Nov                            MORE 21 Nov 1858
(MANEFEE?), Mary S. (Alvin)               Rev. J.E. Waitman
               "all of Ralls Co."

HOPKINS, J.P. of St. Louis           20 Nov                          LEXC 3 Dec 1856
McPHERSON, Sally (2nd dau/E.B.) of Boonville   Rev. George P. Giddings

HOPKINS, Rev. Theodore A., Rector of St. George's Church, St. Louis 8 Aug   MORE 10 Aug 1855
DOOLITTLE, Alice L. of - at Rochester NY  at St. Paul's Church
          by the Rev. John H. Hopkins, Bishop of Vermont

HOPPER, John                         11 Jan                           COWS 20 Jan 1860
BELL, Sarah (James)                       Judge James W. Daily

HORNBEAK, W.C.                        14 Jun                          MORE 23 Jun 1860
OLIVER, Georgie E. (eldest dau/M.)          Elder Charles Carlton
               "both of Springfield MO"

HORNER, David                        27 Aug    Rev. John C. Keene     LIT 1 Sep 1865
MUSSER, Mrs. Martha "at the home of her mother, Mrs. Donaldson"

HORNER, Samuel                    in Marysville CA 28 Aug             MORE 29 Sep 1854
THOMPSON, Elizabeth       "both of Atchison Co."

HORNSBERGER, H.H. of Pettis Co., formerly of Rockingham Co. VA       WAVE 29 Oct 1859
GALBRAITH, Nannie (Hugh)     26 Oct in Saline Co. by Rev. William J. Brown

HORNSBY, D.C. of St. Louis Co.       22 Feb, 2nd Presbyterian Church  MORE 24 Feb 1859
PIM, Lizzie (only dau/Thomas F.) of South Missouri  Rev. J. Brooks
               Wilmington DE & Philadelphia pc

HORSLEY, Walter J. of Keytesville     23 Dec                          SLMD 8 Mar 1854
LASALTER, Ida Binda (Henry) of Huntsville

HORTON, Dr. Samuel M., Asst. Surgeon U.S. Army  6 Aug                MORE 8 Aug 1863
*DUNNIES, Sallie K. (youngest dau/Judge James)  Rev. S.A. Mutchmore

HOSKINS, Daniel                      21 Oct in Linnaeus               GLWT 4 Nov 1852
TISDALE, Mrs. Nancy (David Prewitt)       William Woodruff Esq.
               "all of Linn Co."

HOSTATER, Horis of Port Perry MO     23 Feb in Chester IL            MORE 26 Feb 1852
LYMAN, Ada     at the residence of W.W. Lyman

HOUGH, Warwick, Adj. General of MO  30 May  Rev. William Prottsman   COWS 21 Jun 1861
MASSEY, Nina (Col. B.F., Secretary of State)

HOUGH, William J., eldest son of the late Judge H.   15 Aug          CHAC 18 Aug 1865
WALTERS, Sallie (H.C.)                Rev. James E. Gardner
               "all of Wolf Island Twp." (Mississippi Co.)

HOUSE, H.W. of St. Louis             14 Oct  Rev. John A. Harrison   LEXP 20 Oct 1852
RELF, Gertrude (eldest dau/D.C.) of this county

HOWARD, H.C.                      in Hermitage, Hickory Co.          BOL 12 May 1860
GILL, Sarah Jane (Dozier) formerly of Bolivar

HOWARD, Harrison, publisher of the Legion, Bloomington MO  27 Jun   SLMD 10 Jul 1860
CALDWELL, Julia (Rev. S.B.F.)             Rev. O.R. Bouton

HOWARD, John H.                      8 Sep                            COWS 16 Sep 1859
WETZEL, Sallie (Judge John C.) of Dade Co.   Rev. W.J. Garrett

HOWE, John W.                     in Audrain Co.                     HANT 6 Feb 1858
WALLS, Sarah (W.H.) of Callaway Co.
```

*DUNNICA, not Dunnies

HUBBARD, John of Frytown   15 Jan   HAWU 23 Jan 1851
NASH, Mary (A.O.) of Hannibal   Rev. J.L. Bennett

HUBBARD, Richard B. of Rocheport 28 Oct   COWS 5 Nov 1858
MILLER, Mary (Alvin G.) of Howard Co.   Elder J.K. Rogers

HUBBARD, William L.   (9 Feb?)   COWS 17 Feb 1860
LYNES, Elizabeth (Perry)   Elder John G. White

HUBBELL, William P. of Missouri City 29 Aug in Washington Co. PA   LIT 9 Sep 1859
QUAIL, Mary C. (Robert) at her home   Rev. Thomas Hanna

HUBENSMITH, Fred A. of St. Louis 27 Sep   Rev. D.J. Beale   MORE 5 Oct 1864
SIDLE, Caroline (Henry) of E. Waterford, Juniata Co. PA

HUDGINS, John P. of St. Louis   19 Aug   LIT 26 Aug 1864
GANT, Anna J. (Capt. James)   Elder R.C. Morton

HUDSON, Henry of St. Louis   5 Jan in Davenport IA   MORE 10 Jan 1858
DONNEL, Mary Virginia of Davenport   Bishop Lee

HUDSON, Richard of Moniteau Co., formerly of Boone Co.   COWS 5 Feb 1858
SHAMOUS, Margaret Ellen (Kelly H.) of Cooper Co.   Rev. Robert Harris

HUDSON, Robert S.   14 Feb in Columbia   MORE 28 Feb 1854
SMITH, Martha (Hanson)   Rev. F. Wilhite

HUGGINS, Fielding   29 May at the home of Wm. Cooper   LIT 30 May 1856
HALL, Jane (late Anderson) "all of Clay Co."

HULETT, William P.   15 Jun in Rocheport   HANJ 1 Jul 1852
PHILLIPS, Zerelda (William H.) of Rocheport Rev. Fielding Wilhite

HULL, Edward Brodie 18 Jul at the home of his mother, Hillwood, Pike Co.   MORE 24 Jul 1861
CHAMBERS, Lizzie (late Col. A.B. of St. Louis)

HULL, Joseph A.   21 Nov in Philadelphia   MORE 4 Dec 1860
COZENS, Lue of Philadelphia   Rev. Cooper

HUME, Lafayette of Columbia   25 May   COWS 29 May 1857
HICKAM, Samira Ann (George) of Boone Co.   Elder L.B. Wilken

HUME, Reuben, merchant of Columbia   26 Jan   COSE 3 Feb 1853
ESTES, Catherine E. (Berkeley) of Boone Co.   Elder T.M. Allen

HUME, Reuben of Columbia   23 Aug   COWS 28 Aug 1857
WILSON, Henrietta (late Wm. E.) of Boone Co.   Pres. James Shannon

HUME, Reuben T. of Moniteau Co.   12 May   COWS 15 May 1857
CONLEY, Elizabeth (Francis) of Boone Co.   Elder P. Kemper

HUMPHREYS, David E.   31 Jan at the residence of Theodore Stanley   JINQ 11 Feb 1854
GOODE, Frances M. (late Thomas)

HUNN, Housan of Parkville   13 Jan   LIT 18 Feb 1853
DAVIS, Nancy E. (Martin) of Clay Co.   Rev. Woodward

HUNT, George   Rev. W.B. Watts   GLWT 30 Dec 1852
YATES, Sarah (Judge John M.) "all of Randolph Co."

HUNT, H.T.   15 Apr   SPRIM 17 Apr 1858
JONES, Jane (Rev. William) of Greene Co.   Rev. Carlton

HUNT, William B.   (9 Nov?)   COWS 16 Nov 1855
CONNELLY, Mary Ann (B.F.) of Boone Co.

HUNTER, Benjamin F. son of Col. Abraham   3 Apr   Rev. Alvin Rucker   CHAC 6 Apr 1860
BIRD, Mary (John) at the home of her father

HUNTER, John J. of Boone Co.   24 Nov in Audrain Co.   COSE 9 Dec 1852
POWELL, Julia A. (Robert)   Rev. W.R. Wigginton
                          Nicholas KY pc

HUNTER, John M.   7 Sep at St. John's Church   MORE 10 Sep 1858
ECK, Annie H. (late Joseph)   Rev. P. O'Brien

HURD, Caleb   25 Jan in Monroe Co.   HANT 28 Feb 1857
DeMOSS, Sophronia Ann (Rev. Thomas, pastor of the Hannibal Methodist Church)

HURST, George W. at the home of L. Baby, near St. Joseph, 29 Nov   MORE 4 Jan 1856
THOMPSON, Ann E. (eldest dau/F.)   Rev. G. T. Hoagland

HURT, James   S.A. Mutchmore, pastor Columbia Presbyterian Church   COWS 25 May 1860
McBRIDE, Mary (Hon. P.H.) "all of Boone Co."

HUTCHENS, Cyrus, late of Cumberland Co. KY   Elder S.J. Bush   COWS 12 Feb 1858
WADE, Fereby (William H.) of Boone Co.

HUTCHINSON, Cyrus of Chariton Co.   5 Sep   GLWT 7 Sep 1854
SNELL, Mrs. (Capt. R. Dicken) of Howard Co.   Elder A. Proctor

HUTCHINSON, E.R.   7 Jun at the residence of Dr. E.B. Smith   MORE 8 Jun 1865
MITCHELL, Mary S. (late Col. D.D.)   Rev. E.F. Berkeley
     "all of St. Louis"   Louisville pc

HUTCHINSON, I.W. of Cooper Co.   25 Oct by Rev. Brooks   MORE 27 Oct 1859
MACDONALD, M.C.D. (3rd dau/Isaiah) of Steubenville OH

IRVINE, Edwin H. of Buchanan Co.   1 Jun   SJWW 12 Jun 1859
FORBES, Nannie (Maj. Frank) of Platte Co.   Elder D.S. Burnett

HUTTS, George W.   25 Aug   FULT 2 Sep 1864
DAVIS, Margaret Ann (Joseph G.) "all of Callaway Co."   W.J. Gilman

JACKSON, Richard T. of St. Louis   3 Sep   Rev. Schuyler   MORE 6 Sep 1865
WHITE, Maria C. eldest dau/late Thomas of Liverpool ENG

JACKSON, Samuel   10 Apr   MORE 4 May 1855
WATSON, Josephine only dau/Andrew of Buchanan Co.   Judge Wyman

JACKSON, Thomas   12 Feb at 2nd Presbyterian Church, Hannibal   MORE 23 Feb 1860
CAMPBELL, Mary Ann (A.V.) late of NJ   Rev. A.P. Forman

JACKSON, William J.   7 Nov in Palmyra   MORE 13 Nov 1855
CLAGETT, Russie (William H.)   Rev. John Leighton

JACOB, Joseph   28 Nov   Rev. T.M. Cunningham   MORE 29 Nov 1854
LEE, Christina (Alexander)

JACOBS, John   12 Jan   COWS 20 Jan 1860
VANLANDINGHAM, Elenore (late Benjamin)   Elder R.R. Pace

JACOBS, William H. of Boone Co.   9 Nov   Rev. E. M. Marvin   COWS 11 Dec 1857
BAST, Julia C. (Dr. John) of Loutre Island

JACQUES, Capt. William   20 Jan   COWS 9 Feb 1855
McCOUN, Amelia (Maj. James) of Ray Co.   (SEE BELOW)

JACOBS, William of Richmond   RICE 9 Feb 1855
McCOUN, Amelia (Maj. James) of Ray Co.   Rev. J.B. Harbison

JAMES, John S. of Callaway Co.   14 Aug   COWS 24 Aug 1855
GIBBS, Russella (Robert F.) of Boone Co.
                    Frankfort & Georgetown KY pc

JAMES, Joseph   7 Sep   MORE 19 Sep 1854
ADAIR, Eliza (John) of Callaway Co.   Thomas P. Stephens

JAMES, William C. formerly of MO   2 Mar in Nevada   MORE 15 Apr 1854
BROADDUS, Mary Ann (eldest dau/Maj. J.)   Rev. J.R. Tansey

JAMISON, John W.   7 Sep   J.T.M. Johnston   COWS 10 Sep 1858
WHITE, Georgeanna (Allyn) "all of Boone Co."

JAMISON, William C. Jr. of St. Louis   30 Dec in Kaskaskia   MORE 7 Jan 1857
HAILMAN, Jane   Fr. pou---?

JAMISON, William E. of St. Louis   14 Jul in Madison WI   MORE 18 Jul 1865
NOE, Mary E. of Norfolk VA   Rev. W.L. Green
              NY, Baltimore & Norfolk pc

JEANS, Richard of Jackson Co.   20 May   Rev. George S. Woodward   LIT 13 Jun 1851
GASH, Lucinda (Joseph D.) of Clay Co.

JENKINS, Daniel D. of Boone Co.   20 Sep in Lincoln Co. KY   COSE 14 Oct 1852
SCOTT, Sue (Dr.)

JENKINS, James   25 Dec in Danville, Montgomery Co.   COWS 16 Jan 1857
OFFUT, Jemima

JENKINS, M.C. son of Albert of VA   in Christ Church   MORE 16 Jul 1858
BOWLIN, Jennie S. (only dau/James B.)   Rev. R.E. Terry

JENNING, Milford   14 Feb   Rev. Lane   WAVE 3 Mar 1860
FLOURNOY, Nannie C. (Gideon) "at her father's home in this county"

JENNINGS, Dr. P.S.   14 Jun, Bethlehem Church, Henry Co.   MORE 7 Jul 1857
VICKERS, Laura (Absalom)

JENNINGS, William H. of MO 25 Sep in Crab Orchard KY   MORE 4 Oct 1855
WELCH, Hadge Jane (Dr. Thomas)   Rev. John Gano

JEWELL, J.E. in Kansas City 7 Oct   Rev. J.H. Luther   WEBS 15 Oct 1860
BRANNAN, Mary V. (adopted dau/A.N. Lyons) formerly of Richmond VA

JOHNS, Dr. Montgomery of LaGrange in Baltimore 16 Sep   LANA 19 Sep 1857
DIFFENDORFER, Salome (youngest dau/Michael) Rev. Henry V.D. Johns

JOHNSON, Charles F. of St. Louis   4 Dec   MORE 10 Dec 1856
TYLER, Mary Lawrence (late Robert) of Louisville

JOHNSON, Charles P. of St. Louis   17 Jun in Washington DC   MORE 24 Jun 1861
PARKER, Estelle (only dau/Thomas)   Rev. Sunderland
        "at the home of the bride's father"

JOHNSON, Charles of St. Louis   13 April in Springfield   MORE 15 Apr 1859
SMIZER, Eliza H. (George)   Rev. W.D. Shumate

JOHNSON, Dr. C.M.   26 Feb in Troy, Lincoln Co.   MORE 13 Mar 1856
SMITH, Martha A. (Wright) of Warren Co.   W.M. Newland

JOHNSON, Greenberry of Boone Co.   29 Jan   FULT 7 Feb 1851
CARTER, Mary C. (Reed C.) of Callaway Co.   Rev. Noah Flood

JOHNSON, James   21 Nov in Callaway Co.   COWS 1 Dec 1865
STONE, Cecelia W. (Judge J.H.) at the home of Samuel Grant by Rev. Edward Cowen
        "all of St. Charles"

JOHNSON, James E.   21 Nov   PALS 23 Dec 1864
ROGERS, Judith (Stephen) "all of Marion Co."   Elder James S. Green

JOHNSON, John A. of Hannibal   5 Mar   MORE 7 Apr 1856
DeSPADA, Elizabeth (oldest dau/Charles, of Baltimore) Wm. G. Eliot

JOHNSON, Lieut. Marshall W.   13 Jan Rev. D.A. Wilson   COWS 30 Jan 1863
McCLURG, Mary Emma (oldest dau/Col. J.W.) of Linn Creek, Camden Co.

JOHNSON, William   Thursday last in Marion Co.   MORE 21 Feb 1856
HANSON, Margaret Ann (James)   Rev. James Phillips

JOHNSON, William B.   17 Jan   SJH 19 Jan 1865
COLHOUN, Mary K. (John, a banker in St. Joseph)   Rev. A.P. Forman

JOHNSON, William Henry   14 Feb near Washington MO   COWS 3 Mar 1865
HACKMAN, Mary E. (late F.W.) formerly of Columbia Rev. J.F. Benton
        "at the home of the bride's mother"

JOHNSON, William N.   1 Nov   BOBS 3 Nov 1860
TRIGG, Julia (Dr. William H.)   Rev. Painter

JONES, Andrew P.   8 Aug Rev. Kekelier   MORE 11 Aug 1863
RICE, Elizabeth (Vanrenstler and Elizabeth) "all of St. Louis Co."
        St. Joseph & CA pc

JONES, C.G. of Ray & Jones, Brunswick 26 May in Edwardsville IL   MORE 28 May 1851
MILLER, Sarah at the home of Hon. A. Miller   Rev. P. Young

JONES, George H.   8 May in Hannibal   LADB 21 May 1851
DRAPER, Maria (Judge Z.G.)   Rev. J.L. Bennett

JONES, George W. of Platte Co., formerly of Rappahannock Co. VA 28 Nov   MORE 8 Dec 1854
TILLERY, Martha Ann (Reuben) near Liberty by Rev. Price
        /of Clay Co.

JONES, James C. of Callaway Co.   21 Sep   MORE 12 Oct 1855
CLARK, Elizabeth Jane (W.N.) of Audrain Co.   Rev. S. Scott

JONES, James H. of St. Joseph   in Brownsville, N.T. 1 Jul   HOLT 9 Jul 1858
PROUTS, Anna of St. Joseph   Rev. Benjamin Baxter

JONES, John F.   8 Sep in Montgomery Co.   MORE 4 Oct 1859
HEELEY, Sarah E.   Rev. J. Livengood

JONES, P.H. of Howard Co.   5 Dec in Saline Co.   COWS 22 Dec 1865
STEPHENSON, Marietta (Augustus) of Saline Co.   Rev. John Montgomery

JONES, Thomas   2 Dec   MARD 10 Dec 1858
PETERSON, Susan Jane (Thomas) "all of Saline Co."   Rev. Talbott

JONES, William   4 Nov in St. Louis   MORE 7 Nov 1858
WOODWARD, Emily (late Rev. W.H.) "all of St. Louis" Rev. Francis J. Clerc

JONSON, G.W. of DeKalb TX   6 Aug   MORE 27 Aug 1856
KELLY, Mary Ann (John) of St. Louis   Rev. Fr Bryan

JOPES, Dr. William H., formerly of Springfield, 11 Sep in Greenfield   MORE 2 Oct 1855
BOWLES, Kate (Dr.)

JOUETT, William R.   30 Apr in St. George's Church   MORE 3 May 1861
SCHAUMBERG, Nannie (late Judge C.W.)

JUDGE, Dr. J. French of St. Louis   15 Jun in Cincinnati   MORE 24 Jun 1856
ROGERS, Mary Cornelia (eldest dau/late Rev. George & Ruth D.) Rev. I.D. Williamson

JUDY, George H. formerly of Frederick MD   4 Jan in Palmyra   SLMD 11 Jan 1854
KEHOE, Lizzie A. (2nd dau/late M. William of Washington D.C.) Rev. Murphy

KAHN, Aaron of St. Joseph   30 Aug in Baltimore   SJH 12 Sep 1863
SCHIPP, Henriette of Baltimore   Rev. Exold

KARNES, J.V.C.   3 Dec in Columbia   COWS 4 Dec 1863
CRUMBAUGH, Mollie (Henry, at his home) Rev. Montgomery

KARNES, John of Boone Co.   25 Jun   COWS 10 Jul 1863
POTTS, Sallie A. (Henry, of Nicholas Co. KY) Rev. John Holliday

KARNES, W.P.   4 Jun   COWS 21 Jun 1861
WIGGINTON, Mary C. (Joseph A.) "all of Boone Co." Rev. W.R. Wigginton

KARST, Emile of St. Louis 9 Jul at St. Vincent de Paul Church, New York MORE 18 Jul 1854
TOURNEY, Mina of Philadelphia

KARST, Eugene   29 Mar at St. Malachy's Church   MORE 3 Apr 1864
BOGY, Celeste (Col. Lewis V.) "all of St. Louis" Fr. Tobin

KEARNY, Charles of St. Joseph   25 Sep in Jersey City NJ   MORE 2 Oct 1855
STEWART, Annie   Rev. Charles K. Imbrie

KEENE, J.W.   11 Aug   COWS 14 Aug 1863
JOHNSTON, Sallie (Samuel) "all of Boone Co."   Elder J.M. Robinson

KEILL, G.R.   11 Nov in Boonville   BOBS 15 Nov 1856
CHRISMAN, A.E. (Col. Joseph) of Mount Hope, Saline Co. Rev. H.M. Painter

KEISER, Capt. John P. of St. Louis   27 Sep Rev. Brooks   MORE 29 Sep 1864
HOUGH, Laura (George W., at his home in Jefferson City)

KEITH, David of St. Louis   20 Nov in Clifton IL   MORE 26 Nov 1861
HOWE, Susan W. of Brookfield MA   Rev. Edwin Jaggar
                "at the home of the bride's brother"

KELLAR, Francis   6 Mar   SLMD 17 Apr 1854
MADDOX, Mary P. (Basil)   Rev. Mayhew

KELLY, James of St. Louis   25 Mar in New Orleans   SLMD 5 Apr 1854
FOSTER, Mary Ann F. (Benjamin) of New Orleans

KELSEY, Henry O. of St. Louis   26 Dec in Brooklyn NY   MORE 4 Jan 1865
DAVIS, Ellen M. of Brooklyn   Rev. David Moore, Jr.
                Leavenworth pc

KEMPER, James F. of Audrain Co.   13 Jul   MORE 24 Jul 1854
PARK, Ann Eliza (Capt. Levi)   Thomas P. Stephens

KEMPER, Tiliman T.S.   18 Nov   Rev. Benjamin Owens   COWS 26 Nov 1858
BRATTON, Sallie (William) "all of Boone Co."

KEMPER, Capt. William B.   November?   COWS 6 Jan 1865
SINGLETON, Alice G. (Capt. M.R.) of Andrew Co.

KENNARD, Dr. Thomas of St. Louis   12 Jun at Independence   MORE 17 Jun 1860
CATES, Edmonia H. (Owen G.)   Bishop Hawks

KENNEDY, Granville D.   28 May   CECB 1 Jun 1861
BLUE, Lizzie (Dr. John) "all of Brunswick"   Rev. W.A. Mayhew

KENNEDY, P.M. of St. Louis   MORE 15 Aug 1860
WHITING, Florida (Maj. D.P., US Army)

KERLIN, Henry T.   9 Nov   MORE 11 Nov 1856
CARBIS, Maggie, late of Lawrenceville PA Rev. Fr Henry

KERR, George C. of St. Louis   24 Jan   Rev. England   MORE 27 Jan 1865
ANTHONY, Fannie L. of Memphis TN   Memphis & NY pc

KESSLER, Julius, formerly of Dutch Flat, Placer Co. CA   10 May   MORE 17 Jun 1862
DOERBAU, Margaret   Julius Schneider, J.P.

KETCHAM, H.B. of St. Joseph   18 August at the Christian Church in SJH 20 Aug 1863
DENISON, Lucy Wetmore ygst dau late Chas./ Newport RI, Rev. R.H. Weller

KETCHUM, William W.   24 Oct in Sacramento by Rev. Kenny MORE 30 Nov 1854
KEEGAN, Elizabeth J.C. "both of St. Louis"

KIDWELL, William of Monroe Co.   12 Mar   HAM 16 Mar 1861
TAYLOR, Rebecca (Wesley) of Marion Co.   Rev. John Lindsay

KILE, George W. formerly of KY   5 Apr   JINQ 10 Apr 1858
DYE, Sallie E. (only dau/Thomas) of Platte Co.   Rev. C.C. Steel

KIMBROUGH, John W.   last Sunday in Weston   COSE 1 Sep 1853
BROUGHTON, Adelia (John) of Boone Co.   Rev. Thomas Abbott

KIMBROUGH, William H. of Randolph Co.   12 Feb by Elder W.L.T. Evans   COWS 27 Feb 1863
HARRIS, Bettie (Maj. W.H., of Boone Co., at his home)

KIMES, Mathias of Marion Co.   21 Sep   MORE 30 Sep 1854
HUDSON, Sarah Ann (Joshua)   William B. Phillips

KING, A.W.   21 Dec in Independence   MORE 22 Dec 1854
GANDEE, Virginia (Jesse) of Brunswick   Rev. Calhoun

KING, Christopher   6 Aug in Waverly   WAVE 13 Aug 1859
JENKINS, Mary (William)   Rev. J.R. Savage

KING, James A. of St. Louis   25 Jun in Louisville   MORE 29 Jun 1857
MONTGOMERY, Mary A. of Rockingham Co. VA   Rev. Semour

KING, John of Jefferson Co. 10 Jul at Temple Grove, Ray Co.   WAVE 20 Aug 1859
MOORE, Rebecca B. (late Col. William) of Ray Co. Rev. B.M. Hobson

KING, R.S. of St. Louis   25 Dec in Chambersburg PA   MORE 29 Dec 1860
SIMPSON, Lizzie A. of Chambersburg   Rev. Samuel Phillips

KING, Thomas B. of Liberty   26 Jul in Jefferson City   COWS 3 Aug 1860
CHILES, Emma A. (late Walter G.) of Glasgow

KING, Thomas B.   2 Jun   COWS 10 Jun 1864
BINGHAM, Clara F. (George C.) "all of Jefferson City" Rev. William Schofield

KING, William   in Platte Co.   LIT 9 Sep 1859
PENCE, Tetie (Edward)   Elder A. James

KINNEY, James of Harrisonville MO   16 Jun   RANC 24 Jun 1859
FINKS, Anna (Capt. J.F.) of Howard Co.   Rev. Noah Flood

KIRBY, F.B. of St. Louis   1 Sep in Syme, CT   MORE 14 Sep 1858
NOYES, Caroline I. (Daniel E.) of Syme   Rev. D.S. Brainerd

KIRKPATRICK, William R. of Boone Co. 18 Mar   COSE 25 Mar 1852
STRICKLIN, Zilphia Jane (Thomas) "   Elder T.M. Allen

KIRTLEY, Shelby   27 Nov   LEXC 3 Dec 1856
CHINN, Anna (Dr. Joseph B. of Lexington KY)   Elder Allen Wright

KNIGHT, C.F.   9 Feb   SJH 11 Feb 1864
KEYES, Annie M. (T.W.)   Rev. R.H. Weller

KNOTT, Lewis O. of St. Louis   5 Jun in New Orleans   MORE 16 Jun 1861
BENTZ, Mary H. of New Orleans   Rev. John A. Stevenson

KNOWER, Dr. Charles of the U.S. Army   22 Oct, Church of the Messiah   MORE 25 Oct 1863
LESLIE, Mary S. (Dr. A.M.)   Dr. Eliot

KUEMMEL, Frederick of St. Louis   18 May   SLMD 26 May 1858
WAGNER, Natalie (G.O.) of Glasgow   Judge F.W. Digges

KUMM, Louis   28 Nov in Sedalia, Rev. Greene   MORE 4 Dec 1865
BRENT, Rosalie V. (late Robert of Cooper Co., formerly of Fauquier Co. VA)

LaBARGE, Thomas J.   21 Mar   MORE 26 Mar 1865
PEERS, Julia (youngest dau/V.J.) "all of St. Louis"   Fr. Feehan

LACKLAND, H.C. of St. Charles   4 Dec   MORE 8 Dec 1856
HARDIN, Nannie (late Joseph) of Washington, MO   Rev. Cowan

LACKLAND, Norman of Audrain Co. 5 Jun at Christ Church Chapel   COWS 13 Jun 1862
LACKLAND, Augusta (late Matthew) of Richmond VA   Rev. M. Schuyler

LACY, Benjamin   23 Nov   Rev. Kendrick   MORE 26 Nov 1865
WHITAKER, Emma F. (B.D.)   "all of St. Louis"

LADUE, P.A. of St. Louis   in Quincy IL   MORE 25 Sep 1856
WOODWARD, Emma C. of Quincy   Rev. G.P. Giddings

LaFORCE, D.M. of St. Louis   25 Feb   STGAZ 26 Feb 1851
BENIGHT, Mary (late Thaddeus) of St. Joseph   Rev. T.S. Reeve

LAKE, Charles D. of St. Louis Co.   28 Dec at Webster Station   MORE 9 Jan 1862
FYLER, Louisa (late J.H.)   Rev. S. Hyde

LAKENAN, Robert   6 Mar in Hannibal   SLMD 22 Mar 1854
MOSS, Mary (Russell W.)

```
LAMAR, T.J.                          23 Oct                              LIT 9 Nov 1855
McDONALD, Mrs. M.E. (Thomas Arnold, of Liberty)     Rev. E.A. Carson

LAMB, Dr. Charles L.                 16 Feb in Marion Co.                HANT 18 Feb 1859
JACKSON, Luda J. (C.F.)

LAMB, P.H. of Greenville MO                                             MORE 24 Oct 1854
GUY, Lizzie (oldest dau/John)

LAMPTON, J.H.P., formerly of Monroe Co., 3 Apr in Diamond Spring CA     HANT 30 May 1853
POCKMAN, Lucy Ann formerly of Linn, MO          Rev C. Bonner

LAMPTON, J.P. of Liberty             15 Aug    Rev. Richard Valentine    COWS 27 Sep 1861
PASHAM, Annie R. (J.W. and Catherine J.) of Newcastle KY

LANE, John C.    4 Mar at the home of the bride's mother Rev. Chas. B. Parsons MORE 6 Mar '57
JONES, Matilda G.A. (sister of Rev. Charles J. of Boatmen's Church)
                NY, Philadelphia, & MD pc

LARUE, Dr. Robert T.                 26 Feb                              COWS 15 Mar 1861
CRUTCHER, Mattie (William M.) of Grand View, Boone Co.   Rev. James Marton

LAWNIN, Joseph D.                    25 Jul                              MORE 27 Jul 1861
WORTHINGTON, Ariadna (Mrs. Elizabeth)      W.D. Shumate

LAWS, Rev. S.S., President of Westminster College                       MORE 5 Feb 1860
DOUBLEDAY, Mrs. Anna M. (William Broadwell)       Rev. Jephtha Harrison

LAWSON, Leonidas M. of Platte Co.           13 Dec in Liberty           MORE 24 Dec 1860
THORNTON, Theodosia (Col. John)

LAY, John F.                  28 Jun in St. Louis Co.                   MORE 30 Jun 1865
MORGAN, Sophia A. (Stephen D.)         Rev. W.D. Shumate

LEACH, Richard of Kansas Territory in Oregon, Holt Co. 25 Oct          MORE 7 Nov 1855
MODIE, Sallie (John W. and Agnes)    Rev. W.R. Fulton

LEADER, George of Nodaway Co.        9 Jan                              STGAZ 22 Jan 1851
JOSLIN, Elvira (Josiah) of Andrew Co.           Rev. William Trapp

LEAHEY, John L.                      26 Nov                             MORE 29 Nov 1862
DOUGLAS, Jennie (James) "all of this county"      Rev. McClain

LEAR, John V.                   Thursday in Marion Co.                  PWH 14 Sep 1854
JACOBS, Mary (John) of Shelbyville

LEE, Woodruff H. of Palmyra          in Jacksonville IL                 LADB 24 Feb 1851
ALLSMAN, Sarah (Andrew) of Jacksonville

LEMONS, Stephen                      17 Feb                             LIT 25 Feb 1859
GRADY, Mary (William)                      Rev. James E. Hollis

LEONARD, Benjamin                    7 Feb                              COWS 17 Feb 1860
McCALESTER, Kate (Mrs. Harriette W. Brand)       Rev. Edward Berkley

LEONARD, James D., late of Pittsburgh      Tuesday                      MORE 28 Aug 1856
HALL, Julia L. (late Elisha)               Rev. S.J.P. Anderson

LEONARD, Dr. M.J.F.  14 Oct in Warren Co.    Rev. William Newland       LEXC 29 Oct 1856
HODGES, Mrs. R.A. (late Judge Griswold)
                     "at the home of Mrs. M. Griswold"

LEOPARD, A.                          4 Jun                              COWS 4 Jul 1862
CLATTERBUCK, Nancy (Cagely) "all of Callaway"   Rev. J.H. Tuttle

LEVEL, Thomas F. of Rockingham       28 Dec                            WAVE 15 Jan 1859
MUNDAY, Ella A. (John R.)                   Rev. B.F. Creel
             "of Standardsville VA"

LEVERING, A.R.                       4 Dec in Hannibal                  MORE 24 Dec 1860
PORTER, Ella (Gilchrist)

LEVERING, Aaron B. of St. Louis      6 Jan in Lexington MO             MORE 20 Jan 1858
STRATTON, Jeannie P. (Edward) of Lexington      Rev. Hobson

LEWIS, Augustus of St. Louis         21 Jan                            MORE 22 Jan 1851
MATHEWS, Elizabeth (Rev. William A.) of PA      Rev. Harsin

LEWIS, B.W.                          6 Oct.                            COSE 14 Oct 1852
TURNER, Eleanor (Talton) of Howard Co.

LEWIS, Charles H.                    5 Sep                             GLWT 7 Sep 1854
ROPER, Anna E. (William P.)                Elder A. Proctor

LEWIS or LEVIS, George M.  24 Feb, 1st Presbyterian                    MORE 26 Feb &
ROCHE, Emily J. (James) all of St. Louis   Rev. H.A. Nelson              2 Mar 1865
  Louisville & Alton pc
```

LEWIS, George T.   17 Feb   MORE 20 Feb 1863
PHILIBERT, Mary Elizabeth (Augustus)   Rev. Zeigler

LEWIS, Henry C.   19 Aug in Mexico, Audrain Co.   COWS 5 Sep 1862
WELLS, Mary E. (A.)   Rev. J.R. Taylor

LEWIS, J.W.   28 Oct   LEXC 29 Oct 1856
SILVER, Eliza (Silas, ex-mayor of Lexington)

LEWIS, Owen J. of St. Louis   19 Sep at Milford NH   MORE 29 Sep 1865
PROCTOR, Clara E. (Moses) formerly of West Cambridge MA   Rev. F.D. Ayer

LEWIS, William J. of St. Louis   6 Oct   COSE 14 Oct 1852
TURNER, Rebecca (Talton) of Howard Co.   Rev. C.D. Simpson

LINCOLN, George T.   Elder C.R. Morton   LIT 14 Jun 1859
PRYOR, Virginia M.   "all of Clay Co."

LINDELL, Will of St. Louis   31 May in DeSoto   MORE 1 Jun 1864
DAVIS, Eliza S. (J.J.) of DeSoto   Rev. Henrickson   Cincinnati pc

LINDSAY, L.D.   21 Jun   MARD 27 Jun 1860
BROWN, Miss __ (James) "all of Arrow Rock Twp."

LINDSEY, Herndon of Haynesville   1 Feb   LIT 25 Feb 1853
HUBBARD, Emma (Col. Moses) of Clay Co.   Rev. F. Graves

LINDSEY, O.W. of Kansas City 2 Nov at Grand Saline, Cherokee Nation   MORE 24 Nov 1859
BRIAN, Maria L. (Major John) of Grand Saline

LINGO, Levi   6 Jan at Chillicothe   MAG 21 Jan 1863
TOWNER, Timorah (Judge M.M.) "all of this city" Rev. W.T. Ellington

LINHOFF, Henry   22 May   MORE 27 May 1860
DeHODIAMONT, Josephine (Emanuel)   Fr. P. Brady

LINN, Dr. H.D.   18 Aug in St. Louis   JINQ 30 Aug 1851
PARSONS, Sarah (Gen. G.A.) "all of Jefferson City" Rev. Potts

LINVILLE, Capt. Richard B.   Rev. W.M. Leftwich   SJH 8 Jun 1865
RICHARDSON, Emma (Preston) of Andrew Co.

LIONBERGER, John R. of Boonville 20 Nov near Columbia   GLWT 27 Nov 1851
CLARKSON, Margaret (Dr. H.M.) of Boone Co.   Rev. N. Hall

LITTLE, John Watson   18 Nov   MORE 20 Nov 1860
RICHARDS, Priscilla (Benjamin C.) "all of St. Louis" Rev. J.R. Anderson

LITTLETON, Henry Dalton of St. Louis 3 Dec   MORE 16 Dec 1851
MOBLEY, Mary of Dubuque   Elder M. Mobley

LOAN, James of Weston   9 Feb in Weston   LIT 17 Feb 1854
TORRILL, Frances (youngest dau/John, of Clay Co.) Rev. William Caples

LOCKRIDGE, A.D.   7 Dec   GLWT 16 Dec 1852
SHEPARD, Martha Ann (Col. Jonah H.)   Elder T.M. Gaines

LOCKWOOD, J.M.   in Montgomery Co.   MORE 16 Jan 1861
RANDOLPH, Mollie

LOGAN, Francis   26 Sep near Wright City   MORE 29 Sep 1859
PRATT, Alice (Jonathan)   Rev. James E. Walch

LONG, Alvin M.   6 Oct   COWS 9 Oct 1857
SHAW, Eliza (late Wiley)   Green Carey

LONG, Edward   23 Oct   HANJ 6 Nov 1851
MAPPIN, Ann Eliza (late James) all of Monroe Co. Elder Henry Thomas

LONG, Gabe   24 Aug in St. Louis Co.   MORE 10 Sep 1865
SHUMATE, Ginnie A. dau/Rev. Walker D., who officiated

LONG, James of Boone Co.   15 Jul   COWS 17 Jul 1857
CREWS, Mrs. Susan E. (Creed Carter) of Callaway Co.   Rev. Green Carey

LONG, John D. formerly of Vermilion Co. KY at Linnaeus   MORE 22 Sep 1854
HARRISON, Sarah B. of Danville   Rev. Alton F. Martin

LORING, James Milton   26 Oct   MORE 27 Oct 1864
GLYCKHERR, Albertine (Mrs. Frida)   Rev. C. Smith

LOUCK, William   Felix Robidoux   SJH 31 Jan 1865
FALES, Sarah (Shepherd)   29 Jan

LOUDERMAN, Henry B. of St. Louis   5 Sep   MORE 6 Sep 1865
MARSHALL, Sallie R. of Lewes, DE.   Rev. Schuyler
 Baltimore, Philadelphia, NYC pc

LOUGHBOROUGH, J.M.   10 Nov in Carondelet   MORE 11 Nov 1857
WEBSTER, Mary (Dr. A.W.) of Carondelet   Rev. John F. Cowan

LOVEJOY, Benjamin M.   25 Nov in St. Louis Co.   MORE 2 Dec 1863
STOKES, Henrietta A. (W.H.)   Rev. S.H. Hyde
                  Cincinnati & Louisville pc

LOVELACE, Col. Walter L.   23 Jun in Danville   COWS 22 Jul 1864
BUSH, Nancy (W.D.) "all of Danville"   Rev. McIlhaney

LOWRY, James H.   (1 Mar? Rev. Han?)   COWS 9 Mar 1855
MAXWELL, Mary (John) "all of Boone Co."

LUCAS, Gen. Samuel D. of Independence 13 Jul in Independence   LIT 15 Jul 1851
SYMINGTON, Myra W. of Hanover IA   Rev. S.D. Symington

LUDLOW, Francis Maury of St. Louis   22 Nov in New York Rev. Hawks   MORE 5 Dec 1851
VAN NESS, Harriet (late William Maury) of Liverpool ENG

LUDWIG, Dr. Charles V.F.   23 Sep   Judge Schneider   MORE 25 Sep 1858
GANTIE, Emily (Theodore) "both of St. Louis Co."

LUNARD, Fred A. of St. Louis   12 Dec in Middleboro MA   MORE 14 Dec 1865
WEBSTER, Hattie A. of Middleboro   Rev. Abbott

LYNCH, F. Kirtley of Columbia   1 Oct   MORE 6 Oct 1863
WATSON, Davilla A. (James D.) of Ralls Co.   Elder L.B. Wilkes

LYNCH, Thomas   LIT 21 Nov 1856
HALL, A. (John B.) "all of Liberty"

LYNCH, Thomas   27 Nov at the Cathedral   MORE 30 Nov 1856
McDONALD, Mary Jane (Philip)   Rev. Fr Wheeler

LYONS, James of Edina   21 Feb   MORE 18 Mar 1859
HARRISON, Cynthia E. (Hiram) of Lewis Co.   Rev. James Lillard

McAMEY, Maj. Joseph H. of Monroe Co.   10 Oct   HANT 17 Oct 1854
McAFEE, Rebecca J. (Joseph)   Rev. Thomas Tatlow

McAFEE, John of Marion Co.   23 Aug   COWS 9 Sep 1859
BAILY, Anna (Mrs. Elizabeth) of Fulton   Rev. M.M. Fisher

McALPIN, J.H.   18 Feb   SPRIM 3 Apr 1858
DUVAL, M.E. (W.O.) of Lebanon   Rev. Archley

McARTHUR, James of St. Louis   22 Nov in Davenport IA   MORE 18 Dec 1855
MICHAEL, Esther Mary of Davenport   Rev. A.M. Prelamourges

McBAIN, Robert R.   26 Feb in Providence   COWS 6 Mar 1857
HARRIS, Marcus Ellen (John M.) of Boone Co.   Elder T.M. Allen

McBRIDE, Thomas   5 Mar in Monroe Co.   COWS 27 Mar 1857
DRAKE, M.S. (Samuel)

McCARTY, William   11 Dec   LIT 19 Dec 1851
RILEY, Alley (Maj. A.M.) "all of Clay Co."   Elder A.H.P. Payne

McCAUSLAND, William G. (of Waddell, McCausland & Co.) of-in Lexington   SLMD 31 Aug 1860
ARNOLD, Sue (Dr. E.G.)   Rev. Dunlop

McCLAIN, Peter of Jefferson City   JINQ 18 Feb 1854
SHEETS, Susan (Horace) of Callaway Co.

McCLELLAN, James N. 43rd Reg IL Vols. 29 Sep at Everett House   MORE 7 Oct 1863
HUGHES, Alvina (William H.) of St. Louis   Rev. J. Jermain Porter

McCLELLAN, Josiah G. of St. Louis   9 Sep in Hopkinsville KY   MORE 14 Sep 1856
SHARP, Mary E. (late Col. F.C.)   Rev. F.G. Strahan

McCLELLAND, Matthew V.L.   13 Dec at St. John's Church   MORE 18 Dec 1864
BAY, Sadie E. (late S. Mansfield)   Bishop Hawks

McCLELLAND, Dr. __ W. of Pleasant Green, Cooper Co. 18 Dec   COWS 20 Dec 1861
PHILLIPS, Mattie (Judge Hiram) of Boone Co.   Rev. Wm. R. Wigginton

McCLINTOCK, William   15 Nov   COWS 23 Nov 1855
KEANE, Rachel (James S.) "all of Audrain Co."

McCLURE, R.A. of St. Charles Co.   17 Nov   LEXP 7 Dec 1853
BROWN, S.E. (Rev. M.) of Fulton   Rev. Dodd

McCOLLOCK, Ben M.   in Perry Co. NY by Rev. E.T. Chambers   MORE 23 Sep 1864
HARSHAW, Josephine (late William) at the home of her uncle, Samuel Hatch
                  "all of St. Louis"

McCORD, B. Frank   near Lexington   7 May   Rev. J.H. Carter   COWS 30 May 1862
BROWN, Alice (late Hon. B.J.) of Richmond

McCREA, Peter of Callaway Co.   6 Jun   COWS 11 Jun 1858
CRUSE, Mary F. (Stanley) of Boone Co.   Elder T.M. Allen

McCREERY, Andrew B.   3 Jan at Grace Church, San Francisco CA   MORE 25 Feb 1865
SWARINGEN, Isabelle D. (late Richard S.) of St. Louis Rev. H. Goodwin

McCUTCHAN, Thomas K. late of New Mexico   15 Dec in Westport   SEE   KCJC 24 Dec 1858
BOGGS, Mattie R. (Dr. O.) of Westport   Rev. R.S. Symington   BELOW

McCUTCHEON, Thomas K. late of New Mexico   15 Dec in Independence   COWS 31 Dec 1858
BOGGS, Mattie R. (Dr. Joseph O.)   (of Independence?)

McDANIEL, William (Judy and John J.)   29 Jan Rev. D. Johnson   MORE 9 Feb 1860
HUCKSTEP, Sallie (J.N.) "all of Osage Co."

McCLUNG, Franklin   6 May   MORE 8 May 1854
MILLS, Eliza A. (youngest dau/Col. A.L.)   Rev. Rice

McCLURG, Calvin E. of St. Louis 14 Jun in Lexington KY   MORE 26 Jun 1855
MORGAN, Kitty G. (late Col. Calvin C.)   Rev. E.F. Beckley

McCORD, Charles W.   28 Feb   SLMD 2 Mar 1854
McSHERRY, Kate (P.T.) of St. Louis Co. Rev. S.S. Church

McCULLY, Valentine   25 Feb in Randolph Co.   MORE 7 Mar 1856
DRY, Elizabeth (John) of Monroe Co.   William Lamme Esq.

McDANALD, A.H. of St. Louis   7 Nov in Quincy IL   GLWT 17 Nov 1853
+   BUSHNELL, O.M. of Quincy   Rev. George P. Giddings

McDEARMON, William N.   29 May near St. Charles   MORE 31 May 1860
SIGERSON, Laura (William)   Rev. John F. Cowan

McDOWELL, James   17 Apr   COWS 18 Apr 1862
KEEN, Eliza (Matthew) "all of Boone Co."   Elder T.M. Allen

McDOWELL, Samuel (SEE McGOWEN?)   16 Jun in Lincoln Co.   MORE 3 Jul 1857
COOK, Elizabeth L. (Capt. William) of Pike Co.   Elder John Johnson

+ McDANNOLD, W.H. of St. Louis   20 May at Locust Grove   MORE 28 May 1857
COCHRAN, Mary D. (Rev. William, officiating minister)

McELWEE, Dr. J.J.   16 May in Fleming Co. KY   LAJ 23 May 1861
GOODMAN, Laura R. of Fleming Co.   Rev. J.T. Walker

McFAUL, John C. of St. Louis   1 May in Chicago   MORE 5 May 1864
SMITH, Sallie S. (Julius H.) of Chicago   Rev. Smith

McGEE, B.L.   14 Mar   LIT 1 Apr 1864
WILLIAMS, Annie (Stokely) of Ray Co.

McGEE, James H. of Kansas City   30 Jun near Liberty   LIT 8 Jul 1859
THOMPSON, R.M. (late Robert)   Rev. J. C. Thornton
                "at the home of the bride's mother"

McGOWEN, Samuel of Lincoln Co.   25 Jun   (see McDOWELL?)   HANT 30 Jun 1857
COOK, Elizabeth L. (oldest dau/Capt. William) of Pike Co.

McGRATH, Maj. John, U.S. Army 16 Nov at St. John's Church, Fr. Smith   MORE 19 Nov 1865
FINNEY, Mary (late Bernard) "all of St. Louis"   Memphis pc

McGUIRE, W.D. formerly of Boone Co.   21 Apr in Trenton   COWS 29 Apr 1859
FIELDS, Lizzy L.   Rev. S. Brady

McHOME, John of Brunswick   6 Feb   GLWT 21 Feb 1856
PERKINS, Mary (Rev. William)

McILVAIN, A.J. formerly of Liberty, Clay Co., in Nevada   MORE 15 Apr 1854
NORMAN, Jane (William)   Rev. J.R. Tansey

McILVANE, Col. J.H., State Senator from Washington Co. 23 Feb   COWS 9 Mar 1860
MARTIN, Emily D. (2nd dau/Daniel Dunklin) 23 Feb at Cliffton, Jefferson Co.

McKENNA, James K. of St. Louis   5 Jun at Memphis   MORE 26 Jun 1865
ROBERTSON, Ariadne H.M. of Memphis   Rev. James W. Edilen

McKENZIE, Fountain S. of Jefferson Mo. 1 Mar in San Francisco   MORE 22 Apr 1856
MILLER, Mrs. Mary A. of St. Louis

McKINNEY, John C. of Boone Co.   1 Feb   GLWT 24 Feb 1853
TUTT, Mrs. Elizabeth (Porter Jackman) of Howard Co.   Rev. N. Flood   COSE 10 "

McKITTRICK, Hugh   24 Jan   Rev. Dr. Eliot   MORE 26 Jan 1859
CUTTER, Mary W. (eldest dau/Norman)   "all of St. Louis"

McKOWEN, William M.   14 May   MORE 16 May 1861
TURNER, Blanche (only dau/Spencer decd)   Rev. Staples

McLANAHAN, J.W.   12 Jun   MORE 14 Jun 1862
GREENE, Edith E. (W.W.)   Rev. S.B. McPheeters

McLAUGHLIN, Henry   11 Aug in Lafayette Co.   LEXP 17 Aug 1853
WHITSETT, Martha (William)   Rev. C.A. Davis

McLAUGHLIN, Thomas   8 Nov   MORE 16 Nov 1861
DAVIS, Dolthera P. (J.H.)   Rev. Parks

McLEAN, F.L. of St. Joseph   14 Nov   Rev. A.P. Foreman   SJH 15 Nov 1865
ARMSTRONG, Susie J. (eldest dau/late Andrew of Baltimore)
                         Louisville & Baltimore pc

McLEAN, Finis M.   6 Oct   HANT 16 Oct 1856
STEWART, Virginia (Judge C.B.) "all of Randolph Co."   Rev. Pritchett

McLEOD, Joseph T.   28 Jun in Independence   COWS 9 Jul 1858
SCRUGGS, Anna E. (Capt. N.H.)

McMAHAN, Robert J. at Locust Grove 1 Nov   BOBS 5 Nov 1859
WING, Sarah (Freeman)   Rev. H.M. Painter

McMAHAN, William H. of Cooper Co.   20 Oct Rev. J. Clark   BOBS 5 Nov 1859
HORNBECK, Luclie L. of Bullett Co. KY "at the home of her uncle,
                                    William F. Tindall"

McMICHAEL, John of St. Louis   5 May near Liberty Elder Alex Proctor   LIT 6 May 1864
LINCOLN, Julia (Julia Ann) "at the residence of her mother"

McMILLEN, James A.   19 Mar   Elder John M. Johnson LAJ 16 Apr 1864
CASH, Susan E. (eldest dau/Thomas Sr.) "all of Pike Co."

McMILLIN, John T.   16? Feb Elder M.M. Mollisett   LAJ 25 Feb 1865
MARTIN, Nannie (eldest dau/William G.) of Pike Co.   (Modisett?)

McMURRY, T.P. of Palmyra   29 Jul in Louisville KY   CANE 18 Aug 1853
WRIGHT, Lizzie (late John) (of Hannibal? CANE says she was of Louisville.)   HANJ 15 "

McMURTREY, Richard G. of St. Louis   16 Jul in Hopkinton IA   MORE 24 Jul 1857
FOWLER, Mary Jane formerly of St. Louis   Rev. M. Hammond

McNAIR, Charles A. of Glasgow   9 May   MORE 20 May 1855
DONAHO, Louisa (Stephen) of Howard Co.   Rev. William M. Rusk

McNAIR, James L. of Marshfield   10 Jan in Buffalo   MORE 27 Jan 1860
JOHNSON, Delilah P. (Col. J.W.) of Polk Co.   Rev. L.T. Satterfield

McNEIL, Daniel M.   8 Apr in Shelby Co.   HANT 17 Apr 1858
SHEETS, Annie M. (Henry T.) "all of Shelby Co."

McNEILL, William S.   10 Nov in Daviess Co.   SJWW 19 Nov 1859
PRYOR, Mary (Westly) "both of Daviess Co."   Rev. J.D. Vincil

McNUTT, George M. of Jefferson Co.   14 Mar   Rev. Farmer   MORE 28 Mar 1855
SWINK, Sarah A. (oldest dau/William) of Ste. Genevieve Knoxville TN pc

McPHAIL, William A. of Linn Creek   12 Sep in Polk Co.   BOL 17 Sep 1859
CAMPBELL, R.P. (E.M.)   Elder J.H. Callaway

McPHEETERS, S.A. of St. Louis   1 Jul, Calvary Church, Memphis MORE 12 Jul 1865
WILLIAMS, Jannie C. of Memphis   Rev. White

McPHEETERS, Rev. Samuel of St. Louis 27 May   MORE 14 Jun 1851
SHANKS, Eliza C. (Col.) of Fincastle VA   Rev. W.S. White

McPHERSON, Henry of Boonville   29 Oct   COWS 6 Nov 1857
CHANDLER, Maria Louisa (Leroy) of Cooper Co.   Rev. Giddings

MacQUEEN, William N. of St. Louis   18 Nov   MORE 22 Nov 1863
McKELLOPS, Grace (William) of Corunna MI   Rev. E.E. Gregory

McREYNOLDS, David of Saline Co.   in Lafayette Co. 11 Sep   WAVE 29 Sep 1860
JOHNSON, Rebecca (Washington)   Rev. J.J. Warder

McVEIGH, J.H.   COWS 24 Aug 1855
McBRIDE, Mary E.   "all of Paris MO"   7 Aug

MACK, Charles B. of St. Louis   5 Sep in Cape Girardeau   MORE 10 Sep 1865
GARAGHTY, Eliza D. (youngest dau/Eugene) of Cape Girardeay Fr. O'Reagen

MACKAY, Alfred of St. Louis   10 Feb   MORE 22 Feb 1857
JUDSON, Maggie (only dau/late James, of New York) Rev. William Adams

43

MACKENNIS, Dr. Thomas   23 Dec   MORE 25 Dec 1858
COGSWELL, Isabella (oldest dau/W.A. and Caroline)   Rev. Peter Walsh

MADDOX, Jacob L.   28 Jun   MORE 12 Jul 1854
MORRIS, Lou (late Judge George W.)   in Callaway Co.

MADDUX, Henly J.   24 Jan   PWH 3 Feb 1855
McDANIEL, Mary Harriet (Mrs. C.)   Rev. J.T. Williams

MAGINN, John Alexander   3 Jul   MORE 6 Jul 1854
LENNON, Margaret (Patrick) "all of St. Louis"

MAGRUDER, Dr. D.L., US Army   15 Oct   MORE 17 Oct 1863
LARKIN, Mary C. (Thomas) of St. Louis   Rev. Montgomery Schuyler

MAGUIRE, Constantine of St. Louis   15 Sep in Springfield KY   MORE 18 Sep 1859
PULIN or POLIN, Mary A. (Dr. J.)   Fr. O'Brien

MAGUIRE, Francis   17 Oct, St. Lawrence O'Toole Church MORE 22 Oct 1865
WALSH, Mary J. only dau late/Thomas   Rev. James Henry
                  NY and Lancaster PA pc

MAJOR, C.W. of Henry Co.   26 May   COWS 13 Jun 1862
WALLACE, Sarah A. (John) of Callaway Co.   Rev. J.H. Tuttle

MALONE, Theodore B., only son of G.B. 16 Jan   R.S. Dean   HAM 1 Feb 1861
EVERETTE, Beatrice G. only dau/J.M. "all of Ralls Co."

MANEUL, Thomas   30 Dec   COWS 12 Jan 1855
ABERNATHY, Zerelda B. (__.R.) of Paris, Monroe Co.

MANN, R.S.   5 Jan   CAWN 15 Jan 1859
ANDERSON, Susan "both of Cass Co."   Rev. R.M. Whaley

MANNING, Lee B.   5 Oct in Chillicothe   MORE 24 Oct 1854
CRAWFORD, Catherine (Samuel)   Rev. W.B.A. Carter

MANNY, J.D. of St. Louis   in New Haven (CT?) St. Paul's   MORE 30 Nov 1851
SMITH, Jane E.D. (John Durris)

MANTER, Charles T. of New Orleans   8 Jan   Rev. Love   SLMD 12 Jan 1861
EVENS, Mary (John) at Hopewell Furnace, Washington Co.

MARKS, W.A. of Lewis Co.   16 Mar   CANE 31 Mar 1853
KEISTER, Caroline C. (Mrs. E. Heywood) of Clark Co.   Rev. J.B. Callaway

MARMADUKE, Darwin W. of St. Louis 13 Sep in Arrow Rock Twp., Saline Co. MARD 26 Sep 1860
SAPPINGTON, Jennie (late E.D.) "at the home of the bride's mother"

MARMADUKE, M.M. Jr.   16 Feb in Saline Co.   COWS 5 Mar 1858
BRUCE, Mollie (A.F.)   Elder J. McGarver

MARMADUKE, Vincent of Saline Co.   JINQ 23 Jul 1853
EAKIN, Julia (John) of Nashville TN (no date or minister shown)

MARSH, C. Waldo of St. Louis   St. James Church, Roxbury MA   MORE 11 Jan 1861
KING, Anna H. (eldest dau/John) of Roxbury

MARSHALL, Winfield J. of Lewis Co.   6 Dec   HANT 15 Dec 1853
PEAK, Mary A.M. (James L.) of Palmyra   Rev. Hopson

MARTIN, Abner   COWS 20 May 1859
TUTTLE, Arena M. (G.S.)   of Boone Co.   Elder J.M. Robinson

MARTIN, Andrew J. of Independence   6 Sep   GLWT 8 Sep 1853
FRISTOE, Elizabeth M. (Rev. Thomas)   Rev. Addison M. Lewis

MARTIN, Charles of Canton   21 Oct in Winchester MO   CANE 1 Nov 1855
GLASCOCK, Maria Louisa (B.R.) of Clark Co.   Elder Musgrave

MARTIN, James of Saline Co.   18 May   Rev. John Dejarnatt   COWS 10 Jun 1859
SMITH, Bettie (youngest dau/Gen. George) of Georgetown MO

MARTIN, Lincoln R.   7 Feb   COWS 16 Feb 1855
LANHAM, Nancy (Richard) "all of Boone Co." Rev. D. Doyle

MARTIN, Dr. M.   12 Jul at the home of E.C. Sloan   MORE 15 Jul 1864
TRACY, Mrs. Ella M. (George Martin) "all of St. Louis" Rev. Montgomery Schuyler

MARTIN, M.G.   5 Jan   COWS 8 Jan 1858
HUNTER, Bettie (Enoch) of Boone Co.   Elder J.M. Robinson

MARTIN, Nicholas of Callaway Co.   8 Feb   MORE 23 Feb 1854
SEIF, Eliza J. (Philip) of Boone Co.   Elder Wren

MARTIN, Zachariah F.   16 Aug in Monroe Co.   HANT 25 Aug 1855
QUIREY, Ann Eliza (Judge Samuel M.)

MASON, A.G., Editor of the Paris Mercury   4 May in Randolph Co.   MORE 21 May 1854
RUBY, Lavenia M. (Thomas F.)   Rev. J.W. Morrow

MASON, Thomas of St. Louis   6 Oct in Chicago   MORE 9 Oct 1859
CHAPMAN, Mrs. Mercy B. of Natchez   Rev. N.I. Rice

MATHEWS, Maj. George W.   13 Mar in LaGrange   Rev. James Holt   PALS 24 Mar 1865
FULLER, Mrs. Mary S. (Rev. James M. and Martha Lillard) at her sister's home

MATHEWS, Preston   16 Mar   HAM 3 Apr 1862
VALIANT, Rosalaire (John) "all of Palmyra"   Rev. William B. Conger

MATTHEWS, Prof. George H.   25 Nov   Rev. X.X. Buckner   COWS 26 Nov 1858
WOODSON, Olevia A. (Judge Warren) "all of Columbia"

MATTHEWS, John J.   10 Dec   MORE 14 Dec 1865
LONG, Maggie L. (H.)   Rev. J.V. Schofield

MATTHEWS, John W.   20 Nov in Wellington   LEXC 28 Nov or
CORSE, Mattie (William)   Rev. T.P. Akers   5 Dec 1855

MATTHEWS, Leonard   2 Oct   Rev. James S. Brooker   SLMD 8 Oct 1861
NISBET, Mary Spottswood (only dau/William) "all of St. Louis"

MATTHEWS, Oliver D.   24 Apr in St. Louis   MORE 26 Apr 1865
BROWN, Harriet (eldest dau/Robert E.(?)) of Carondelet Rev. Berkley

MATSON, A.W. of Utica   25 Jan   RICE 27 Jan 1854
PIXLEE, Caroline J. (William) of Clay Co.   Rev. William H. Price

MAUGHAS, Dr. M.M.   Rev. E.M. Marvin of St. Louis   COWS 26 Nov 1858
OFFATT, E.C.L. (Eli) of Callaway Co.

MAUPIN, Chauncey C. of Boone Co.   18 May   COWS 16 Jun 1865
BOSS, Lizzie (late Peter) of Henry Co.   Rev. Kellie

MAUPIN, Garland D.   11 Mar   GLWT 25 Mar 1852
WOODS, Sarah J. (Larkin K.)   Elder William Proctor

MAUPIN, Joel A.   28 Jan   HANT 31 Jan 1857
FIELD, Rebecca (Benjamin) "all of Marion Co."

MAUPIN, Thomas H. of Monroe Co.   29 Jan   HANT 31 Jan 1857
MAUPIN, Mary Frances (Joel) of Marion Co.

MAURO, Charles G. of St. Louis   3 Apr in Washington DC   MORE 11 Apr 1856
DAVIS, Charlotte (George M.) of Washington   Rev. Boyle

MAXWELL, William B. of Cass Co.   24 May   HANT 2 Jun 1853
SMITH, Mary E. (Elkanah) of Callaway Co.)   Rev. M.M. Modisett (Baptist)

MAYHEW, Allen of St. Louis   Delhi Twp., Hamilton Co. OH, 6 Dec   MORE 9 Dec 1860
DARBY, Margaret (H. decd) at the home of her mother Rev. Horace Bushness

MAYNARD, James C. of Randolph Co.   10 Mar in Cooper Co.   RANC 19 Mar 1857
HENDERSON, Mary J. (Rev. J.T.A.) of Cooper Co.

MEAD, W.E., son of Edward of St. Louis   3 Sep Rev. J.C. Thornton   MORE 10 Sep 1856
HOY, Therese M. "all of Utica"

MEEK, John   19 Aug   Rev. Loup   MORE 20 Aug 1857
KILGOUR, Margaret, formerly of Fifeshire SCOT. "Both of St. Louis."

MEIER, Theodore G., son of Adolphus of St. Louis 7 Sep, Jefferson Co. KY MORE 12 Sep 1863
BASHAM, Hattie E. (late Charles) of Louisville KY   Rev. Whittier
                "at the residence of Theodore Schwartz"

MENEFEE, Robert M.   22 Apr in Chillicothe   COWS 30 May 1862
SHIRLEY, Scottie (Maj. James A.) "all of Chillicothe" Rev. William M. Rush

MERRY, D.S. of Chariton Co.   18 May in Mt. Pleasant, Saline Co.   GLWT 3 Jun 1852
HARRIS, Sarah Jane (Capt. Nathan) of Mt. Pleasant   Rev. Bell

METCALF, John   12 Jun   Rev. John Leighton   MORE 18 Jun 1855
HANLEY, Harriet (Francis)   "all of Marion Co."

MEYER, S. of St. Louis   6 Dec   Rev. Illoway   MORE 10 Dec 1855
LATZ, Nathalie (youngest dau/Louis)

MICHEL, Joshua C. of St. Louis   25 Nov at Little Prairie MO   MORE 29 Nov 1862
WISHON, Josie E. (Benjamin)

MICKY, David of St. Louis   1 May at Rock Hill Church   Rev. S.H. Hyde   MORE 14 May 1864
BROOKS, Mary Miller (eldest dau/Joseph and Catherine) living "3 miles
                from Manchester on Clayton Road"

45

MILAN, James A.   7 Oct in Prairieville, Pike Co.   GLWT 21 Oct 1852
BARNETT, Mary E. (Rev. William B.) of Prairieville Rev. J.C. Berryman

MILES, Richard, late of KY   14 Jan in Fulton   MORE 4 Feb 1856
SHERIFF, Rosanna (E.)   Rev. Fentem

MILLAN, George E.   26 Feb   SJH 1 Mar 1865
WEST, Sallie (Capt. Charles) of Buchanan Co.   Rev. R.H. Weller

MILLER, D.D.   4 Jul   LIT 21 Jul 1854
STONE, Martha R. (George)   Rev. E.S. Dulin

MILLER, D.S.   6 Jul   LIT 14 Jul 1854
ARTHUR, Cordelia (Michael)   Rev. E.S. Dulin

MILLER, Edgar   28 Nov   MORE 30 Nov 1865
GAMBLE, Mary Coalter (only dau late Ham. R.) Rev. James H. Brooks

MILLER, James   2 May   MORE 16 May 1855
BAKER, Martha S. (Robert E.)   Rev. D. Coulter

MILLER, John A. of St. Francois Co.   1 Sep   MORE 16 Sep 1853
TURLEY, M.C. (Aaron P.)   Milton Poston Esq.

MILLER, John S.J.   27 Apr at Christ Church   MORE 28 Apr 1859
WILLIAMS, Rachel (late Willis L.)   Rev. Schuyler

MILLER, Lewis of High Hill   15 Jul   COWS 23 Jul 1858
TRIGG, Sallie (late Joseph) of Columbia   Rev. R.L. McAfee

MILLER, S.K., Representative State House of Reps. from Buchanan Co.   JINQ 24 May 1851
BASYE, Margaret (A.) of Jefferson City   Rev. R.H. Weller 22 May

MILLER, Thomas S. of Hannibal   4 Sep   HANJ 11 Sep 1851
WARDLAW, Annie F. (Judge) of St. Louis Co.   Rev. J.A. Lyon

MILLER, Thomas S.   6 Nov at Council Grove   HANT 10 Nov 1855
BOWER, Sue M. (G.M.) of Monroe Co.

+ MILLER, Rev. W.G. of the MO Conference 6 Jul Rev. R.C. Hatton   COWS 4 Aug 1865
HAMILTON, N.P. (oldest dau/Col. J.R. of Wilson Co. KY)

MILLER, Walter T.H. of St. Louis 10 Dec, St. Luke's Church, Baltimore   MORE 29 Dec 1863
TAYLOR, Helen M. (late John) of Baltimore   Rev. Charles Ranken

MILLER, William B. of Saline Co. at East Bend, Clark Co., 20 Mar   MORE 29 Mar 1856
WAYLAND, Ann R. (only dau/Dr.)

+ MILLER, Rev. W.G. of the Mo Conference 6 Jul in Wilson Co. TN Rev. R.C. Hatton MORE 27 Jul'65
HAMILTON, N.P. (oldest dau/Col. J.R.) at father's residence

MILLINGTON, Jerome clerk of the Robert Campbell 16 Sep near Bridgeton   MORE 18 & 21
STOKES, Mrs. Mally (Mrs. Catherine Martin) "both of St. Louis Co." Rev. Morris Sep 1863
     /later Mollie Amelia   "at her mother's residence"

MILTON, Dr. George R. of Danville   20 Nov   MORE 2 Dec 1856
McILHANEY, Bettie (Mortimer) of Montgomery Co.   Rev. William Taylor

MING, James of Callaway Co.   (8 July?) in Bethany VA   MORE 4 Aug 1856
PASLOW, Mrs. Anna B.   Elder A. Campbell

MINOR, Ephraim of St. Joseph   3 Dec in Chicago   SJH 12 Dec 1863
STORK, Amanda of Mankate MN   Rev. W. Patterson

MITCHELL, A.S. of St. Louis   29 Sep in Louisville   MORE 6 Oct 1851
TALBOT, Mary Brent (A.G.)
          (GLWT 16 Oct gives location as Frankfort, date as 25 Sep, and
                         minister as Elder R.C. Ricketts)

MITCHELL, Alexander M. of MO   11 May in Chicago   MORE 27 May 1857
HIBBARD, Mrs. Mary A. of Chicago   Rev. H. Curtis

MITCHELL, John W. of Mexico, Audrain Co.   18 May H.P. Steenberger   COWS 21 May 1858
SNELL, Eliza (John) of Callaway Co.

MITCHELL, Newman T.   6 Oct   COWS 24 Oct 1856
JACKMAN, Hannah (Porter)   Rev. N. Flood

MITCHELL, Newman T.   3 Dec   COWS 11 Dec 1857
SLACK, Kittie (Maj. John) "all of Boone Co."   Rev. Fielding Wilhite

MITCHELL, William D. of St. Louis   16 Apr in Florence IL   MORE 23 Apr 1863
FENBY, Jennie at the home of her mother

MODISET, Rev. William of Louisiana MO 19 Jul Rev. J.T. Williams   MORE 6 Aug 1855
CARSON, Mary A. (Col. William) of Marion Co.

MOFFATT, Edgar R.   25 Jul   MORE 27 Jul 1865
WOODRUFF, Helen S. (oldest dau/Horace W., at his home) Rev. Dr. Schuyler

MOFFETT, William A. of St. Louis   20 Sep in Greene Co. KY   HANJ 2 Oct 1851
CLEMENS, Pamela A. of Hannibal

MONTGOMERY, Capt. Richardson at Conranville, Cape Girardeau Co. 13 Dec   MORE 9 Jan 1865
CONRAN, Julia (James C.) formerly of St. Louis, now on Conranville
                Fr. O'Regan   New York pc

MOONEY, James T.   25 May   COWS 29 May 1857
LAUGHLIN, Nancy (Levi)

MOORE, Dr. Benjamin J.   13 Mar at the home of Charles Archer   CHAC 16 Mar 1860
BADGER, Althea (only dau/late Felix)   Rev. Josiah McCary

MOORE, J.C. of St. Louis   4 Sep in Howard Co.   COWS 19 Sep 1862
WHITE, Laura (Col. John R.) of Howard Co.   Rev. Christy Gentry

MOORE, James   20 Jul in Knox Co.   MORE 27 Jul 1854
KING, Bettie (ex-Gov. Austin)   Rev. Bush

MOORE, James P.   1 Jun in Dade Co.   COWS 10 Jun 1859
BISHOP, Missouri (Col. Thomas J.)   Rev. Beckley

MOORE, John of San Jose CA, formerly of Fulton, in Callaway Co. 16 Sep   COSE 7 Oct 1852
CHAPPELL, Mary Susan (John)

MOORE, John R. of St. Louis   24 Oct in Dayton OH   MORE 1 Nov 1865
DARROW, Millie (W.L.) of Dayton

MOORE, S.M. of Hannibal   1 Nov in Philadelphia   HANT 10 Nov 1853
GORGAS, Caroline M. of Philadelphia   Rev. C.J.H. Carter

MOORE, Dr. W.   10 Oct   Rev. I.B. Allen   MORE 3 Nov 1854
DAVIDSON, Eliza Jane (2nd dau/Rev. S.C.) "all of Macon Co."

MOORE, William N.   4 Oct   Rev. D. Coulter   COWS 26 Oct 1855
EWING, Margaret (Capt. P.) "all of Callaway Co."

MOREHEAD, S.T. of Howard Co.   15 Oct in Huntsville   MORE 18 Oct 1863
HEAD, Texie A. (Mrs. H.P. Boulware) Rev. W.R. Rothwell

MORRIS, Henry   21 Jul in Hannibal   HANT 24 Jul 1858
WALLER, Margaret (F.) "all of Hannibal

MORRIS, James N. of St. Louis   22 Jun in Cleveland OH   MORE 26 Jun 1859
BURNHAM, Louise (eldest dau/Thomas) of Cleveland
       Ceremony performed by her uncle, Rev. S. Hanfield, of Syracuse NY.

MORRIS, Joseph D.   4 Nov   Rev. N.I. Fish   COWS 19 Nov 1858
CAUTHORN, Martha L. (Carter) "all of Audrain Co."

MORRIS, Moses   20 Jan   Rev. Edward ____   MORE 27 Jan 1853
HART, Rachel (Aaron) formerly of Edmundton, Middlesex, ENG.

MORRIS, T.A.   25 Oct   MORE 27 Oct 1864
GREENE, Cora Willey (Oliver)   Rev. Post

MORRIS, William   26 Jun in New Madrid   MORE 16 Jul 1854
ROUTH, Ann (John)   R.G. Baber Esq.

MORRIS, William H.   7 Nov   Rev. William Douglas   LEXP 7 Dec 1853
McMURTRY, Nancy (James) "all of Callaway Co."

MORRISON, Rev. A.A., 4th St. Methodist Church in Louisville KY   CANE 17 Mar 1853
SCANLAN, Susan of Marion Co. KY   Rev. A.H. Redford

MORRISON, Robert P. of San Francisco   18 Oct   MORE 22 Oct 1854
STETTINIUS, Julia (Joseph)   Rev. Dames

MORROW, Jacob B.   23 Feb   Rev. W.A. Tarwater   CANP 2 Mar 1865
BROWN, Mary E. (John) "all of Lewis Co."

MORROW, Rev. James W. of Monroe Co.   19 Oct   GLWT 17 Nov 1853
TWYMAN, Elizabeth G. (Paschal) of Howard Co.   Rev. Samuel C. Davis

MORROW, William   17 Jul   Rev. B.B. Black   MORE 23 Jul 1855
GREGORY, Mrs. Martha "all of Montgomery Co."

MORTIMER, Edward   9 Oct   MORE 11 Oct 1859
BRISON, Mary Ellen (late Benjamin)   Rev. Eads

MORTON, Clark J. of St. Louis   10 Jan in Jacksonville IL   SLMD 17 Jan 1854
ISRAEL, Mattie M. of Jacksonville   Rev. Dodge

MORTON, Henry of Missouri   7 Sep in Germantown PA   MORE 11 Sep 1857
SOWERS, Mary A. (only dau/late Col. Jonathan) Rev. William Suddard

MORTON, James   (of?)Exeter, Devonshire 17 Apr   MORE 20 Apr 1856
KIRGAN, Mary Ann Crowell (Thomas) formerly of Harper's Ferry   Rev. Eliot

MOSEBY, John H.   6 Feb   LIT 16 Feb 1855
HALL, Sarah (John D.) "both of Clay Co."   Elder M.E. Lard

MOSELEY, John P.   14 Sep   COWS 15 Oct 1858
CRAIG, Pollie Ann (William) of Callaway Co.   J.M. Robertson

MOSES, Julius L. of St. Louis   7 Dec in New York City   MORE 10 Dec 1859
JACKSON, Rebecca (eldest dau/John D.)   Rev. J.J. Lyons

MOSS, Reason A.   1 Dec   PALS 11 Dec 1863
BOONE, Susan (Daniel, at his home)   Rev. E.H. Hudson

MOSSE, John H. of Jefferson Co. 1 Jan in Springfield IL Rev. J.F. Brooks   MORE 4 Jan 1861
BARROWS, Mary P. of Springfield, at her mother's home

MUDDOCK, William L., late of Philadelphia   29 Feb   Rev. Hawks   MORE 3 Mar 1852
DUNCAN, Caroline J. (late T.O.)

MUIR, W.D.   14 Jan at Waverly Place   BOBS 22 Jan 1851
JONES, Sarah A. (Caleb) "all of Boonville" Rev. Wm. W. Jones

MULFORD, Joseph S. of St. Louis   3 May at Waybridge VT   MORE 8 May 1854
BROWNELL, Harriet L. of Waybridge   Rev. Merrill

MULLER, Christopher   18 Nov   MORE 2 Dec 1856
CHINN, Mary   all of Danville, Montgomery Co.

MULLINS, Augustin of St. Louis   6 Jun in Memphis   MORE 9 Jun 1857
BRESH, Mrs. L.M. of Carroll Parish, LA   Rev. Grundy

MUNDY, Ezra of St. Louis   31 Jul in Rahway NJ   MORE 3 Aug 1851
MUNDY, Rebecca (late Henry)   at the 1st Presbyterian Church

MURDOCK, Charles T. of Platte Co.   6 Sep   in Bourbon Co. KY   MORE 6 Oct 1855
CHINN, Malinda M.

MURPHY, E.G. of Linn Creek   4 Oct   JEX 13 Oct 1855
YOUNG, Mary C. (Col. William C.) of Cole Co.

MURPHY, M.J.   22 Jan   Rev. Fehan   MORE 26 Jan 1863
ARNOT, Annie L. (youngest dau/Jesse) at father's home; all of St. Louis

MURPHY, Michael J.   20 May   MORE 22 May 1857
CLINTON, Esther (John)   Rev. Fr. Wheeler

MURRY, Alfred D.   in Columbia 16 Feb   MORE 28 Feb 1854
THALSON, Elizabeth (Fountain)   Elder D. Cary

MUSIC, E. Combs of Co. G, 8th MSM   19 Jan   MORE 29 Jan 1865
DUNN, Sarah E. (Preston) of Randolph Co.   Rev. Rothwell

MYERS, A.S. of St. Louis   21 Jan   MORE 26 Jan 1857
GERSHON, Maria (eldest dau/George) of London   Rev. H. Kutner

NAILOR, John P.   30 Sep   COWS 15 Oct 1858
GRAVES, Nancy Jane (Mrs. Edward)   Rev. Green Carey

NALL, C.H.   10 May   LIT 11 May 1860
WYMORE, Lottie D. (William H.)   Rev. A.B. Jones

NANSON, John T.   24 Apr   Rev. W.T. Lucky   GLWT 1 May 1851
PATRICK, Elizabeth (Garrison)   "all of Howard Co."

NANSON, Joseph S.   24 Aug   Rev. C.D. Simpson   GLWT 25 Aug 1853
BILLINGSLEY, M. Belle (Col. E.)

NAPTON, William B. Jr.   9 Oct   Rev. Comten   COWS 10 Oct 1862
SHELBY, Mary Pindell (R.P.) "all of Saline Co."

NASH, William P. of St. Louis   6 Apr   COWS 15 Apr 1864
BONIFACE, Hattie F. (George) of Huntsville   Rev. W.R. Rothwell

NEAL, J.R.   14 Apr   Rev. Benjamin Terrill   RANC 29 Apr 1859
OLIVER, Mittie J. (Dr. P.T.)   "all of Randolph Co."

NEILL, Henry of Lexington   3 Nov   GLWT 10 Nov 1853
ELLIOTT, Sarah (Col. N.G.) of Howard Co.   Rev. C.A. Davis

NELSON, Thomas H.   Fr. Ryan, date not shown   MORE 1 Jul 1864
WARREN, Elizabeth A. (Peter) "all of St. Louis"

```
NELSON, William of Brunswick          13 Jun                          COWS 29 Jun 1855
LOURY, Mary Benton (Dr. John G.) of Howard Co.

NELSON, Capt. William S.              21 Nov    Rev. W.G. Eliot        MORE 24 Nov 1855
FRANCIS, Diana B. (Dr. Thomas S.) of Hamilton Co. OH

NEUENDEUTEL, Ernst of Erlangen Bavaria  31 May   Justice Herkenrath    MORE 2 Jun 1856
SCHWEINECK, Sophia of Erfurt, Prussia

NEVENS, William T.                    7 Jan                            COWS 15 Jan 1858
HERMON, Elizabeth Frances (Shadrach)            Elder B. Wren

NEWMAN, S.S.                          12 Jun                           COWS 28 Jun 1861
BARTLEY, Mary A. (George) "all of Callaway Co."  Elder T.J. Marlow

NEWSOM, Major Ben J,                  5 Jan in Westport                WAVE 14 Jan 1860
EWING, Annie (F.Y.)                             Rev. Robert Sloan

NEWSOM, Daniel                        26 Apr    in Callaway Co.        MORE 7 May 1855
DURHAM, Mary A. (Daniel)                        Elder A. Rice

NICHOLS, Amos B.                      1 Sep                            COWS 9 Sep 1859
BENNETT, Eliza Jane (Page)                      Elder B. Wren

NICHOLS, Elias Newton                 13 Oct                           COWS 21 Oct 1859
HOLTOM, Eliza Jane (George) "all of Boone Co."  Rev. James Watson

NICHOLSON, Peter of St. Louis      at the Railway Arms, Glasgow, SCOT  MORE 25 Aug 1857
ROBERTS, Mary (3rd dau/James) of Glasgow        Rev. Harper

NICKLAS, Daniel                       2 Feb                            MORE 3 Feb 1861
SCHULTE, Gertrude (only dau/John)               Rev. Fr. C. Dobbner

NISBET, Arch K.                                 Rev. T. Hill           MORE 4 Mar 1859
WOOD, Josephine (Horatio)     "all of St. Louis"

NOEL, Hyram of Monroe Co.             17 Feb                           COSE 4 Mar 1852
MARTIN, Martha E. (late Samuel) of Randolph Co.  Elder Henry Thomas

NOEL, William H.                      1 Jan                            HANT 9 Feb 1856
NOEL, Sarah Frances (Moses) "all of Monroe Co."  Elder James Barry

NOLEN, George A. of St. Louis         16 Jan in Philadelphia           MORE 1 Feb 1862
THROCKMORTON, Annie (Thaddeus)                  Rev. Benjamin Watson

NORISS, James G.                                                       LIT 31 Oct 1856
KELLER, Mary Eliza (James M.)         23 Oct

NORRIS, Edmond K. of St. Louis        1 Jul near Lexington KY          MORE 7 Jul 1858
MARTIN, Anna E. (late Lewis Y.)                 Rev. Pinkerton
                    Cincinnati & Baltimore pc

NORRIS, James                         21 Dec in St. Louis              MORE 23 Dec 1857
WISE, Margaret (Thomas J.)                      Rev. Proctor

NORTH, Henry C. of St. Louis          1 Dec                            MORE 2 Dec 1857
INGE, Fannie (Hon. C.B.) of Franklin Co.        Rev. John Cowan

NORTHCUTT, George W. of Newton Co.    20 Aug                           COWS 28 Aug 1857
McGUIRE, Ann E. (Levi) of Boone Co.             Elder T.P. Stephens

NORTHCUTT, Lemuel                     24 Apr in Boone Co.              FULT 9 May 1851
PEMBERTON, Talitha (Lewis)                      Elder Levi McGuire

NORTHCUT, William H.                  22 Apr                           COWS 29 May 1857
MORROW, Mary J. (Samuel)                        I. Winfrey

NOWLIN, Samuel S. of Lincoln Co.      19     in Montgomery Co.         MORE 6 Oct 1860
GRAVES, Lucy C.

NUGEN, Thomas H. of St. Louis         in New Orleans 22 Nov.           MORE 17 Dec 1859
JORDAN, Mrs. M.L. of Louisville                 Rev. Ostan

NUMELLY, Daniel                       6 Sep in Montgomery Co.          MORE 19 Sep 1855
SEE, Catherine

OBEAR, J.H.                           8 Jul                            MORE 11 Jul 1856
BRYAN, Maria (Dr. John Gano Bryan)              Rev. T.M. Post

OBER, R.H. of St. Louis               4 Aug                            GLWT 6 Aug 1857
DAVIS, Joella (Col. Jo.) of Howard Co.

OBER, William A.                      24 May    Rev. F.A. Morris       MORE 28 May 1863
NEWMAN, Mary S. (Dr. S.T.)     "all of St. Louis"

OBERMAYER, Morris of Jefferson City   28 Jun in Cincinnati            JINQ 8 Jul 1854
FRIDAY, Fanny of Nashville TN
```

O'CONNOR, P. of St. Louis   11 Jan in Jefferson City   MORE 14 Jan 1859
BOLTON, Josie (Dr. William) of Jefferson City   Rev. S.D. Longhead

OFFUT, Clagget of Audrain Co.   9 Dec   Rev. J.F. Cowan   SJH 13 Jan 1864
BUCKNER, Pinkie (youngest dau/Col. Robert R.) of Callaway Co.   COWS 25 Dec 1863
       (COWS spells his name "Cleggett")

O'FLYNG, Rev. I.M.   7 Jul   Rev. William Hypes   SLMD 10 Jul 1860
TAYLOR, Rachel A. (late Mark P., of Cincinnati)

OREAR, Allen   15 Jul   MORE 23 Jul 1855
SLAVEN, Susan O. (late William) "all of Boone Co."

OREAR, E.J. of Saline Co.   13 Oct in Lexington KY   COWS 31 Oct 1856
OREAR, Julia (Thomas C.)

OLIVER, Capt. Thomas Howard, 7th MO Inf 30 Jun   Rev. Hyde   MORE 2 Jul 1864
REDMAN, Helen J. (Capt. M.T. and Mary W.)

OSBORNE, J.D. of St. Louis   in Louisville   MORE 17 Oct 1851
GRAVES, Harriet   Rev. Wm. L. Breckenridge

O'TOOLE, John L. of St. Joseph   7 Aug in Cape Girardeau   MORE 22 Aug 1854
WOODS, Mary Pauline (John)   Homer Parr

OTTER, Col. William H. of Bolivar   3 Feb in Richmond VA   BOL 26 Feb 1859
CRUMP, Mary S. of Richmond   Grace St. Baptist Church. Rev. Jeter

OTTERMAN, Henry   23 Sep   MORE 26 Sep 1858
MARTELL, Melina (Joseph)   Rev. Paige

OVERALL, Dr. Samuel of St. Charles   8 Oct in Danville   JINQ 18 Oct 1851
ROBINSON, Mary A. of Jefferson City   Rev. Francis Morris
       "at the residence of J.H. Robinson"

OVERSTREET, E.B. of Danville   MORE 16 Jan 1861
WOOLEY, Lizzie of High Hill   Montgomery County

OVERSTREET, John, late of Virginia   21 Dec   MORE 26 Dec 1859
SHARK, Amanda, at the residence of her father   Elder T.T. Johnson
               "all of Montgomery Co."

OWEN, Austin A.   2nd Baptist Church, St. Louis   MORE 14 Apr 1856
COUZINS, Adeline (Capt. J.E.D.)   Rev. Reed

PAGE, John Y.   11 Jan at Christ Church   MORE 14 Jan 1859
WASH, Elizabeth (late Judge)   Rev. Schuyler

PAGE, Dr. James C., formerly of Columbia   19 Jul in St. Louis   COSE 5 Aug 1852
GAMBLE, Mary E. (Archibald)

PAGE, St. Clair   18 Apr in Roanoke   COWS 30 Apr 1858
TWYMAN, Nannie (Paschal) of Howard Co.   Elder T.N. Gaines

PAINTER, George   27 Sep in Morgan Co.   MORE 14 Oct 1860
RAINS, Mary Ann (Henry)   Thomas Bradbury

PAINTER, Harrison J.   13 Apr, in Carondelet   MORE 15 Apr 1864
FINKBURGH, Ella T. (Rev.) at her father's home
       "by Rev. A.C. Osburn, pastor 4th Baptist Church"

PALMER, DeMarcus   18 Nov in Boone Co.   COWS 23 Nov 1855
TUCKER, Elmira (late Edward)

PALMER, George S.   24 Aug   RANC 17 Sep 1857
TERRILL, Louisa (A.J.) "all of Macon Co."   Rev. S.B.F. Caldwell

PALMER, James B.   28 Apr   COWS 6 May 1859
PALMER, Tabitha (Hendron)   Elder Peter Kemper

PAPIN, Dr. T.J. of St. Louis   10 Jan in Keokuk   MORE 19 Jan 1865
YARNALL, Lida (J.J.) of Wheeling VA   Fr. Donnelly
       "at the residence of James R. Cox, the bride's uncle"

PARISH, George T.   8 Mar   GLWT 9 Mar 1854
MORGAN, Sarah, late of Prince Edward Co. VA   Rev. Wm. Thompson

PARK, William W. of Jefferson City   in Jefferson City 25 Jul   MORE 9 Aug 1855
SHANKS, Helen P. (2nd dau/Collon of Aberdeen, SCOT)   Rev. Boil

PARKER, Alfred A. of St. Louis   30 Mar in Orange MA   MORE 4 Apr 1857
WHIPPLE, Fannie A. (J.R.)   Rev. David Peck

PARKER, Col. Charles W. of Troy   Near Troy 24 Oct   MORE 28 Oct 1865
HUTT, Valeria B. (Thomas G.)   Rev. J. Spencer

PARKER, Horace M.   15 Mar at Sulphur Springs   MORE 18 Mar 1860
KENDALL, Olly (Mrs. Peggy, decd)   Judge Johnston

PARKER, I.C., City Attorney in St. Joseph 13 Dec   Rev. John Henesy   MORE 16 Dec 1861
O'TOOLE, Mary E. (James D.)

PARKER, Joseph age 17   Samuel M. Woods Esq   MORE 8 Apr 1859
THOMPSON, Caroline ae 14 (stepdaughter of William Brantley)

PARKER, William B.   29 Nov   MORE 30 Nov 1859
ALLEN, Mary D. (L.L.)   Rev. Berkeley

PARKS, Simpson of Platte Co.   1 Jul Elder Henry Hix   LIT 4 Jul 1862
PETERS, Martha A. (late John) of Clay Co.

PARKS, Waide of Moniteau Co.   12 Sep in Versailles   MORE 27 Sep 1860
PRICE, Mrs. M.E. (Samuel H. Woods) of Morgan Co.

PARKS, William H.   13 Nov   Rev. A. Greenlee   HAM 28 Nov 1861
WALKER, Susan (William)   "all of Philadelphia, Marion Co."

PARROT, James of Cape Girardeau at Benton, Scott Co.   LEXP 1 Dec 1852
HUNTER, Mary M. (late Joseph) of Benton   Rev. Dr. Y. Rice

PARTRIDGE, George of St. Louis   6 Jan in Boston   MORE 12 Jan 1858
COTTER, Mrs. Clarence E. of Boston

PATRICK, Garrison   25 Sep in Fayette   COSE 7 Oct 1852
CAREY, Mary Jane (Joseph)   Elder William C. Boon

PATTERSON, Daniel of St. Louis Co.   15 Nov   COWS 25 Nov 1859
HARRISON, Virginia (Judge James) of Audrain Co.   Rev. Baldwin

PATTERSON, John F.   16 Dec   COWS 24 Dec 1858
SHORT, Minerva (only dau/late John P.)   Rev. Green Cary

PATTERSON, Lemuel W.   19 Mar at the home of Dr. John B. Johnson   MORE 21 Mar 1863
NYE, Harriet J. of New Bedford MA   Rev. E.F. Berkeley

PATTERSON, Robert D. of St. Louis   17 Feb at Duncan Place, Erie Co. PA   MORE 3 Mar 1857
PHILLIPS, Velona A. (niece and ward of Hon. Archie Duncan, Erie Co.)
              by Rev. D.D. Gregory

PATTON, James W.   4 Feb   COWS 14 Mar 1862
DUDLEY, Eliza (Elder J.W.) of Audrain Co.   Elder Theodoric Boulware

PAULIS, Modeste of Venviers   31 May   MORE 2 Jun 1856
FOURDIGNIERS, Josephine of Antwerp   Justice Herkenrath

PAYNE, A.G.   Elder J.T.M. Johnston   COWS 3 Dec 1858
HARRINGTON, Sophia (William) "both of Boone Co."

PAYNE, Ben Woolley M.D.   Thursday last   G.M.T. Smith   CANE 7 Apr 1853
PAYNE, Sarah (oldest dau/George C.)   "all of Scotland Co., late of Kentucky"

PAYNE, Madison of Marion Co.   in Smith's Flat, CA   MORE 12 Jul 1856
COATS, Catherine, formerly of Wisconsin   J.C. Garber Esq.

PAYNE, William   7 Nov in Palmyra   MORE 13 Nov 1855
CLAGETT, Mary (William H.)   Rev. John Leighton

PAYNTER, Reese of Carrollton   in Carroll Co.   GLWT 27 Oct 1853
THOMAS, Isabella (Judge N.B.)   Rev. J.M. Goodson

PEABODY, Dr. Adams   17 Mar   COSE 24 Mar 1852
ROBINSON, Dorithy F. (John M.) "both of Boone Co."   Rev. M.L.A.Vie

PEARCE, H.L. of B.C. Pearce & Son, St. Louis in Columbus OH 19 Oct   MORE 22 Oct 1865
KELTON, Anna (eldest dau/F.C. of Columbus)   Rev. Richards of Trinity Church

PEARSON, Joseph   21 Oct   COWS 19 Nov 1858
DANIELS, Ann (A.B.) "all of Audrain Co."   Rev. Wm. R. Wiginton

PECK, J.W. of St. Louis   17 Apr at the home of John Ramsey   MORE 19 Apr 1860
RAMSEY, Mary J. (Andrew and Mary of Philadelphia) Rev. S.J.P. Anderson

PECK, John W. of St. Louis   22 Jun in Ashland Co. OH Rev. William Hughs   MORE 28 Jun 1864
RAMSEY, Annie E. (Andrew and Mary) at her father's home in Ashland Co.

PEERS, V.C. of Farmington   23 Sep near Somerville TN   MORE 30 Oct 1855
DUPUY, Sarah L.   Rev. T.C. Smith

PEEVY, Dr. Thomas of Montgomery Co.   22 Mar (in Paris - Missouri?)   SLMD 1 Apr 1854
MAUPIN, S.J. of Albemarle Co. VA

PENN, Rev. James of the Mo Conference, Methodist Church near Canton 6 Jul   CANP 16 Jul 1862
BAYNE, Sally (Thomas) at their home near Canton Rev. Vandeventer

PENNY, William F.   20 Oct in Randolph Co. at the home of Capt. J.F. Finks   COWS 22 Oct '58
MORRIS, Mary J. (late Judge John)   Rev. William Pinkard

PEPPER, G.P., merchant of Spring Hill
STEWART, Elizabeth J. (John) of Spring Hill   Rev. B.S. Ashby   GLWT 3 Jun 1852

PERDEE, John A.   Rev. W.M. Pitts   LEXP 31 Aug 1853
SHAFER, Nancy (Henry)   "all of Johnson Co."

PERRY, Richard Jr.   3 May   MORE 6 May 1863
PERRY, Fannie (late Dr. L.F.)   Rev. Edward Berkley
                        Pike Co. IL pc

PETEFISH, Samuel   12 Apr   MORE 14 Apr 1855
DOVENER, Charlotte (William V.) "all of St. Louis"   Rev. Hill

PHILLIBER, Richard   12 Nov at Putah Creek, Yelo Co. CA   MORE 30 Nov 1854
MONTGOMERY, Elizabeth late of Shelby Co. MO

PHILIPS, B.D.   1 Sep   HANT 10 Sep 1853
THOMAS, Nancy S. (Rev. Henson) of Monroe Co.   Rev. H.H. Tilford

PHILLIPS, Franklin W. of Boone Co. 2 Feb   MORE 28 Feb 1854
ALLEN, Mary Ann (late Col. Walker) of Callaway Elder Thomas Allen

PHILLIPS, J.F.   11 Apr in Georgetown   COWS 29 May 1857
BATTERTON, F. (W.W.) of Danville KY

PHILLIPS, Thomas   30 May Rev. Y.A. Anderson   MORE 19 Jun 1855
GIBSON, Elizabeth E. (John)   "all of Greene Co."

PHILLIPS, Dr. William C.   28 Apr in Boone Co.   COSE 5 May 1852
HALL, Penelope P. (Rev. Dr. N.H.)   Dr. N.H. Hall   GLWT 19 "

PHIPPS, George   Tuesday   GLWT 10 Dec 1857
THIXTON, James Ann (L.)   Rev. N.G. Berryman

PICKEN, John A.   10 Jan   HANT 15 Jan 1855
STEVENS, Annie (Rev. Benjamin)   Rev. D.T. Morton

PICKENS, John L.   24 Nov Rev. A.D. Landrum   COSE 9 Dec 1852
BAXTER, Elizabeth A. (Jacob)   "all of Pike Co."

PIGOTT, John T.   17 Apr in Lexington MO   COWS 22 Apr 1859
TRIGG, Jose H. (Dr. William H.) of Boone Co.

PIKE, David J.   25 Feb in New York City   MORE 1 Mar 1857
JACKSON, Eve R. (2nd dau/John J.)   Rev. J.J. Lyons

PIPER, James M. of St. Louis   8 Jun in Jefferson City   COWS 20 Jun 1862
THOMAS, Mollie B. (late Rev. R.S.) formerly of Columbia   Rev. James E. Welch
                "at the residence of G.C. Bingham"

PITTMAN, Edward T. of St. Louis   13 Nov in Fayette Co. KY   MORE 15 Nov 1860
HARRISON, Annie (Dr. George B.) of Fayette Co.   Rev. Elisha Pinkerton

PITTS, John S.   25 Mar Elder J.M. Robinson   COWS 6 Apr 1860
WINFREY, Sallie (Israel) "all of Boone Co."

PIXLEE, William F.   21 Sep Rev. William H. Price   LIT 1 Oct 1852
PRICE, Sarah J. (Winfrey E.)   "all of Clay Co."

PLANT, George P.   27 Jan, Christ Church Chapel   MORE 29 Jan 1863
DOUTHITT, Martha Gleim (youngest dau/late Robert H. of Pittsburgh) Rev. Schuyler

PLASS, William G.   14 Mar   (also see Broch)   SLMD 19 Mar 1861
BLUMENTHAL, Dora (apparently Augustus A.)   Rev. G.W. Wall

POINDEXTER, R.   13 Mar near Milton   RANC 20 Mar 1855
HALEY, Mattie J. (Benjamin) "all of Randolph Co."

POOL, John, merchant in Mexico MO   27 Sep Elder T.M. Allen   MORE 24 Oct 1854
KELLY, Lucy J. (late James) of Boone Co.

POOL, M.P.   2 Feb in Audrain Co.   COWS 26 Feb 1858
WILLIAMS, Mary (James H.)   Rev. Brooks

POOR, Dr. Thomas C.   24 Sep   CHAC 28 Sep 1860
SMITH, Annie (Samuel)   Josiah McCary

PORTER, James J. of St. Louis   23 May in Hannibal   MORE 27 May 1854
HONEYMAN, Lavenia P. (Robert D. and Amanda)   Rev. D.T. Shearman

PORTER, R.S.   in Lexington   MORE 20 Sep 1854
HALE, Judith P. (Street)   Rev. Boyle

POSEGATE, F.M. of St. Joseph 6 Sep at New Lexington OH HOLT 17 Sep 1858
JOHNSON, S.A. Rev. Gratz

POWELL, Dr. A.M. at the home of Dr. A.M. Davidson near Cambridge, 21 Jun WAVE 7 Jul 1860
DAVIDSON, Ann M. "all of Saline Co." Rev. O. Buckley

POWELL, John C. 14 Jul MORE 15 Jul 1857
WEBSTER, Emma (late James) "all of St. Louis" Dr. Schuyler

POWELL, John P. 13 Mar RANC 20 Mar 1855
JOHNSTON, Virginia (Col. R.M.) "all of Macon Co."

POWELL, R.R. 18 Jun in St. Louis Co. MORE 21 Jun 1862
HUNT, Ann (C.L.) Fr. Van Huest

POWELL, William M. 13 Jul COWS 30 Jul 1858
PRICE, Annie E. (W.) "all of Chariton Co." Rev. S.M. Barbee

POWER, James Columbus in Danville, Montgomery Co. Rev. James Love FULT 16 May 1851
CHANEY, Mary Ann (James) formerly of Jefferson Co., now of Callaway Co.

PRATHER, Isaac N. Jr. 3 Jan MORE 20 Jan 1858
ELLIS, Rosanna (T.L.) "both of Nodaway Co." Elder Trapp

PRATT, Benjamin C.T., formerly of Binghampton NY 6 Nov at Flint Hill MORE 23 Nov 1856
ENGLISH, Helen T. (Dr. B.) Rev. D.S. Sherman

PRATTE, Bernard A. of St. Louis 5 Jun at Chatsworth near Louisville MORE 11 Jun 1856
EDWARDS, Eliza J. of Chatsworth Rev. Beckett

PREVATT, Isadore last Monday HANT 29 Mar 1856
MILSTED, Emily G. (Inment) "all of Palmyra"

PRICE, Alonzo D. of Springfield MO 12 Sep in Warsaw IL MORE 16 Sep 1864
WHALEY, S. Augusta of Warsaw Rev. Rankins

PRICE, Edwin V. of Chariton Co. 1 May BRUNS 12 May 1855
BRADFORD, Kittie E. (Austin) of Boone Co. Elder T.M. Allen

PRICE, James S.? of St. Louis 4 Feb in Saline Co. MORE 13 Feb 1864
STUART, Maggie E. (Robert) of Saline Co. Rev. J.W. Clark

PRICE, R.B. Cashier of the Columbia Exchange Bank 1 May COWS 18 May 1860
HOCKADAY, Eva (Judge I.O.) of Fulton Rev. Mayhew

PRICE, Sterling J. of the University of MO at Ste. Genevieve 23 Sep MORE 25 Sep 1858
BRYAN, Mary (Thomas) of Ste. Genevieve Dr. J.C. Farmer

PRICE, Thomas of Brunswick 2 Nov in Prince Edward Co. VA BRUNS 18 Nov 1854
ALMOND, Bettie Rev. A.J. Blackwell

PRICE, Thomas D. of Hannibal 10 Dec Rev. W.R. Rothwell MORE 19 Dec 1863
KEEBAUGH, Addie (S.D.) of Huntsville (Cows gives his initials as S.M.) COWS 15 Jan 1864

PRICE, Gen. Thomas L. of Jefferson MO 25 Apr at Luray VA MORE 8 May 1854
LONG, C.V. of Virginia Rev. Beston

PRICE, William 23 Nov at Howell's Prairie, St. Charles Co. MORE 11 Dec 1864
SCANLAN, Maggie (late Thomas)

PRICE, William Clem of Brunswick 22 Feb in Prince Edward VA COWS 25 Mar 1859
ALMAND, Lou W. "at the residence of Henry A. Allen" Rev. Benjamin Smith

PRICE, William R. of St. Louis last Thursday HANT 11 Mar 1858
McVEIGH, Ada W. (Hiram) of Hannibal

PRIMM, Hubert 14 Feb in Carondelet MORE 19 Feb 1860
LYNCH, Mary E. (only dau/William A.) Rev. McFaul

PRITCHARD, James of St. Louis at the residence of Dr. N.C. Saloner on Deer MORE 14 Apr 1865
LAWS, Gertrude F. Creek, MS, 2 Mar Rev. Stephenson Archer
    /dau/late Elijah of Philadelphia

PROCTOR, Alexander of St. Louis 29 Aug in St. Francois Co. MORE 13 Sep 1859
PREWITT, Mrs. Carrie M. (William Shaw) of St. Francois, at his home

PROWELL, James of Cedar Co. 25 Aug in Cedar Co. MORE 7 Sep 1856
DAWSON, Barsheba (John W.) of Monroe Co. Rev. O. Smith

PULLINS, William S. 9 Dec in Chillicothe Rev. Ellington LIT 20 Dec 1861
BARNES, Alice (adopted dau/Lucien Eastin, ed. of the Chillicothe Chronicle)

PURNELL, George W. of St. Louis 10 Oct, Rev. G. Anderson, 2nd Bapt. Ch. MORE 11 Oct 1859
BUCKINGHAM, Lizzie M. of New Haven CT

QUARLES, Benjamin L. 24 Mar by Rev. J.B. Mitchell HANT 29 Mar 1853
SWINDELL, Emily M. (James B.) "all of Monroe Co."

QUARLES, J.A. of Boonville   11 Oct in Eldon, Pettis Co.   WAVE 5 Nov 1859
FIELD, Carrie W. (W.H.)

QUINETT, F.A.   13 Jul in Kirkwood   MORE 14 Jul 1858
LEFFINGWELL, Sophie (niece of H.W.)   Rev. John F. Cowan

QUISENBERRY, Inskeep   22 May in Boone Co.   HANT 12 Jun 1856
OREAR, Elizabeth (Jesse)   Rev. Gentry

RAGLAND, Francis T.H.   1 Dec at Union Valley Church   PALS 6 Dec 1864
GRIFFITH, Sallie (Enoch H.)   Rev. Pearton

RAMSEY, John H.   9 Jun   MORE 10 Jun 1864
CLARK, Mary E. sister of Capt. John H.   Rev. Dr. Post

RANKIN, Newton 7 Sep at the residence of William H. Jones, Cheltenham   MORE 14 Sep 1865
SPIES, Mrs. Catherine, widow of John "all of St. Louis" Rev. C.S. Osborn
        Cincinnati and Louisville pc

RANNELS, C. of St. Louis Co.   12 Jul in Fayette Co. KY   MORE 2 Aug 1854
STAMPS, Cordelia A.   Dr. Dudley Nathan

RAWLINGS, C.P.   19 Sep   COWS 21 Sep 1855
ADAMS, Pauline (Robert) "all of Howard Co."   Rev. M.U. Payne

RAWLINGS, Samuel of Paris, Monroe Co.   14 Jul   HANT 23 Jul 1853
CROW, Lizzie (Dr. Samuel) of the Paris vicinity

REABURN, J.J. editor of the Alexandria Delta   27 Nov   LAJ 6 Dec 1860
MUSGROVE, Fannie (A.)   "all of Clark Co."

REED, Thomas B. of Huntsville   28 Nov   MORE 19 Dec 1855
DENNY, Rachel Eliza (James) of Howard Co.

REED, Tilden of St. Louis   19 Oct in Webbertown (CA?)   MORE 10 Nov 1851
FREAKS, Ellen of Michigan   Squire William Stone

REEL, John of St. Louis   28 Apr in Pittsburgh   MORE 3 May 1859
EDRINGTON, Virginia S. (late Dr. E.G.)   Rev. McMahan

REESE, Addison of Canton   2 Sep in Keokuk   Rev. W. Dennet   PALS 11 Sep 1863
BODTON, Mrs. Sarah of Indianapolis "at the residence of her sister."

REESE, Dr. W.A.   18 Feb   Rev. J.H. Baker   MORE 4 Mar 1862
PEMBERTON, Lucy R. (M.G.)   "all of Ralls Co."

REGAN, James F.   16 May   Rev. F.A. Morris   MORE 17 May 1864
JULIAN, Ophelia F. (J.M.)   "all of St. Louis"

REID, Henry M.   19 Mar   HAM 22 Mar 1861
WELLS, Rachel M. (L.M.) of Ashley, Pike Co.   Rev. E.B. Smith

REID, Walker D.   Judge Wyman   MORE 4 May 1855
CUNETT, Miranda (Maj. W.C.) of Buchanan Co.

RENFROW, William   28 Mar in Rocheport   COWS 5 Apr 1861
FREEMAN, Malvy Ann (late Harrison) "both of Moniteau Co." Wm. H. Phillips Esq.

RENOE, James   22 Sep   COSE 7 Oct 1852
BOYD, Eveline (Thomas) of Callaway Co.   Rev. W.W. Robertson

REYNOLDS, Dr. Francis M.   4 Nov in Louisiana, Pike Co.   MORE 12 Nov 1856
BUCHANAN, Nancy (J.S.)   Rev. Vandeventer

REYNOLDS, J.C. of St. Louis   14 Jan in New Orleans   MORE 27 Jan 1851
MUDGE, Annie (Col. S.H.)   Rev. Neville

REYNOLDS, William T.   24 Nov by Pres. Thompson (of Wm. Jewell College) LIT 2 Dec 1859
MELONE, Fannie (Cullen decd)

RICE, Edward P.   11 Nov, 1st Congregational Church   MORE 16 Nov 1862
EDGAR, Fannoe B. (T.B. or T.N.?)   Boston pc   Rev. Post

RICHARDS, Caernarven L.   8 Sep in New York   MORE 13 Sep 1859
TAYLOR, Mary C.   "both of St. Louis"

RICHARDS, J.P. of Quincy 15 Jan   S.S. Meacham   HAM 27 Jan 1861
THOMPSON, Lou F. of Burton IL at the home of her father

RICHARDS, John R.   10 May in Boone Co.   COWS 20 May 1859
CARUTHERS, Margaret (John)   Rev. B.F. Johnson

RICHARDS, T.T.   17 Jan   Rev. S.J.P. Anderson   MORE 18 Jan 1865
FILLEY, Ellen (oldest dau/O.D.) Troy NY, Boston, & Hartford CT pc

RICHARDSON, Nathaniel   30 Sep in Newark, Knox Co. by Elder E. Ballenger   PALS 1 Oct 1856
BRAGG, Mary (Giles, at his home)

RICHMOND, Rollin of St. Louis 30 Mar in Johnstown WI   MORE 4 Apr 1865
RICE, Mrs. E.G. of Johnstown   Rev. S.K. Warner

RICORDS, J.B.   14 Jan   MORE 16 Jan 1852
COTIER, Ellen of New York   J. Boyle

RILEY, William of St. Louis   3 Jul   MORE 7 Jul 1861
HORINE, Sue M. (late Capt. Thomas) of Jefferson Co.   Rev. P.J. Ryan

RITCHEY, Dr. Stephen   Elder A.B. Jones   LIT 16 Sep 1859
STONE, Nannie (George)

RIVES, Dr. F.L.   .   at Centennial Church   MORE 14 Feb 1857
SHELTON, Gillie (John G.)   Rev. Marvin

ROBBINS, C.B. of St. Louis   14 Sep   MORE 15 Sep 1859
DAVIS, Lottie (C.E.K.) "   Rev. G. Anderson

ROBBINS, H.S.   12 Oct in St. Louis Co.   MORE 17 Oct 1864
TUNSTALL, Mary (Thomas)   Rev. J.W. Lewis

ROBBINS, Dr. L.H. of St. Louis   25 Jun   Rev. C.H. Foot   MORE 28 Jun 1863
WYCKOFF, Mary A. (David G.) of Jerseyville IL Chicago Times & NY pc

ROBERTS, Aquilla   11 Feb   COWS 19 Feb 1858
ROBERTS, Martha A. (Jesse)   Elder Stephen Bush

ROBERTS, Francis M.   Elder Chrisman   COWS 27 Mar 1857
HEULEN, Mrs. Mary (Calvin Armstrong)

ROBERTS, Henry H.   2 Oct   RANC 16 Oct 1856
COATES, Sarah C. (Capt. Thomas P.) "all of Randolph Co.

ROBERTS, John   9 Oct   RANC 16 Oct 1856
TERRILL, Sarah (William) "all of Randolph Co."

ROBERTS, Dr. John W.   16 Nov   Elder T.M. Allen   COWS 24 Nov 1865
SKINNER, Ann Eliza (Maj. John) "all of Boone Co."

ROBERTS, William M.   24 Oct in Boone Co.   COWS 2 Nov 1855
FORBIS, Elizabeth (Robert)

ROBIDOUX, Edmond F. of St. Joseph   1 Jun   STGAZ 4 Jun 1851
RIDDLE, Martha C. (Benjamin) of Andrew Co.   ___ Bond, JP

ROBINSON, Andrew   12 Apr, vicinity of Lexington   WAVE 23 Apr 1859
YOUNG, Matilda (J.C.)

ROBINSON, George R. of St. Louis 20 Sep, Trinity Church, Shepherdstown VA MORE 27 Sep 1855
ANDREWS, Annie   Rev. W.C. Andrews

ROBINSON, James E. of Marion Co.   22 Nov   HANT 24 Nov 1855
GLASCOCK, Maria Louisa (French) of Ralls Co.

ROBINSON, James M.   25 Mar in Rocheport   COWS 9 Apr 1858
STREET, Mary (Corbin J.)   Rev. Fielding Wilhite

ROBINSON, James W. of Greene Co.   20 Sep   MORE 2 Oct 1855
PAYNE, Martha Jane (Larkin)   F.C. Howard Esq.

ROBINSON, John S. of Boone Co.   Rev. Green Cary   COWS 23 Feb 1855
HARRIS, Ann Eliza (William H.) of Randolph Co.

ROBINSON, John S. of Boone Co.   31 Oct   COWS 19 Nov 1858
PALLER, Permelia (Samuel) of Howard Co.   Rev. Green Cary

ROBINSON, John William of Jackson Co. 28 Jun in Callaway Co.   MORE 12 Jul 1854
BEDFORD, Sallie (late Stephen)

ROBINDS, William A. of St. Louis   29 Jun in Collinsville IL   MORE 16 Jul 1865
NELSON, M.A. of Collinsville   /pc:Memphis MO Albany IN /Rev. Halsey

RODDY, James H.   6 Nov   COWS 9 Nov 1855
BALLENGER, Sarah E. (James E.) "all of Boone Co."

RODDY, Robert   26 Oct in Boone Co.   COSE 10 Nov 1853
TUTTLE, Sarah C. (Judge) of Nashville   Elder W. Cunningham

ROEDLER, C.H. (or O.H.)   8 Jun Rev. F. Melchor   MORE 21 Jun 1865
WEISENECKER, Minnie (youngest dau/P.) all of St. Louis
                     Philadelphia & NY pc

ROEVER, Frederick of St. Louis   21 Jun at Euskirchen GER   MORE 31 Aug 1856
HAENISCH, Natalie of Euskirchen

ROFF, Nat. of St. Louis 7 Dec at Mt. Vernon near Mays Lick KY   MORE 10 Dec 1854
MITCHELL, Lizzie H.   Rev. Gardner

ROGERS, Charles L.   25 Mar in Weston   MORE 30 Mar 1856
BURNES, Victoria (Col. Lewis) of Weston

ROGERS, Henry C.   6 Dec near Tipton Rev. J.B.H. Wooldridge
NEWKIRK, Sallie E. (Drake)   "all of Moniteau Co."   CAWN 15 Dec 1860

ROGERS, Hugh   22 Dec   MORE 25 Dec 1863
MONTGOMERY, Lottie (Dr. Edward) "all of St. Louis" Rev. S.J.P. Anderson
                New Orleans & Middleton MS pc

ROGERS, James V. of Marion Co.   Elder T.M. Allen   COWS 26 Oct 1855
GUITAR, Lizzie (late John) of Columbia

ROGERS, John   15 Nov   Rev. H.M. Painter   COWS 23 Nov 1860
WHITAKER, Jane (Hiram) "all of Andrew Co."

ROGERS, Elder J.R. of St. Joseph   in Hannibal 17 Aug   MORE 24 Aug 1855
ROBARDS, Jennie E. (Capt. A.S.) of Hannibal Elder D.T. Morton

ROGERS, Thomas S. of Clinton MO   1 Dec   Rev. J. Boyle   LEXP 8 Dec 1852
FLETCHER, Lucinda S. (Maj. John) of Lafayette Co./Montgomery Journal pc/

ROHRER, William   29 Jan   Joseph R. Cooper   MORE 10 Feb 1865
STEPHENS, E.A. (Andrew J. and Martha) "all of Clay Co."

ROLAND, Samuel   6 Aug in Ralls Co.   LAJ 22 Aug 1863
SHULZE, Susan Mary (2nd dau/William A.) of Ralls   Elder John M. Johnson

RONEY, Henry   7 Apr in Weston   MORE 13 Apr 1859
WOODS, Lou (youngest dau/Jerry)   Rev. John Stone

ROOTES, George F. of St. Louis   11 Aug in Panola Co. MS   MORE 17 Aug 1859
VANCE, Mrs. C.C. of Panola Co., at her home   Rev. James Bates

ROSE, Johnson   in Macon Co.   GLWT 29 Jun 1854
AUSTIN, Sally Ann (Judge)

ROSS, Dr. James W. of Newark, Knox Co.   25 Jan   HANT 6 Feb 1855
BONNER, Sarah Catherine (A.)   Dr. White

ROSS, Dr. J.W. of Pettis Co. in Salt Pond Twp., Lafayette Co. 17 Jan WAVE 28 Jan 1860
FRANCISCO, Sophia (George) at her father's home   Rev. J.W. Clark

ROSS, Thomas P., formerly of Liberty   20 Jul in Marion Co.   MORE 25 Jul 1854
MORTON, Fulvia (Samuel)   Rev. James Williams

ROTHWELL, Dr. W.A., late of Kentucky 3 Apr   MORE 15 Apr 1856
ROTHWELL, Sallie C. (Dr. J.) of Callaway Co.   Elder T.P. Stephens

ROTHWELL, W. Renfro   25 Jun in Howard Co.   COWS 27 Jun 1856
HUGHES, Lou M. (Allen)

ROWLAND, D.P.   17 Nov at Mound View, near St. Louis MORE 18 Nov 1863
SHACKELFORD, Mattie H. (William H.) "all of St. Louis" Rev. S.J.P. Anderson
            Lexington & Louisville pc

ROWLAND, Eli G. of Bates Co.   11 Feb   COWS 19 Feb 1858
GRAVES, Lucy Ellen (Edward) of Boone Co.   Rev. B.S. Woods

ROWLAND, Joshua M.   27 Feb   COWS 29 Mar 1861
KING, Nancy E. (late James)   Rev. Green Carey

ROWLAND, William J. of Boone Co.   2 Feb   SLMD 14 Feb 1854
THOMPSON, Amelia (late Elmore) of Howard Co.

ROYLE, John C.   23 Apr, Presbyterian Church, Lexington COWS 8 May 1857
KIRTLEY, Eliza (Sinclair) formerly of Columbia

ROZIER, Edward of Ste. Genevieve   5 Oct at Richwoods (Washington Co.) MORE 9 Oct 1854
STEWES, Lavinia (William)   Rev. J.J. Caffrey

RUBEY, Charles W. of Nevada, Vernon Co. Thursday near Paris, Audrain Co. MORE 20 Jun 1859
NESBIT, Mary J. (John T.)   Rev. Fenton

RUCKER, James   10 Jun   Rev. W.R. Rothwell   MAG 18 Jun 1863
SMITH, Kate (Joel)   "all of Randolph Co."

RUCKER, Richard S.   in Ralls Co. Elder E. Ballinger   PALS 17 Mar 1858
BOULWARE, Elizabeth J. (eldest dau/John) at her father's home

RUMMANS, Andrew J.   9 Feb   COWS 17 Feb 1860
TOALSON, Mary Ann (James)   Elder Peter Kemper

RUSH, Tandy Q.   4 Jan   SLMD 26 Jan 1858
ROBERTS, Elvira (David R.)   "all of Boone Co."

RUSSELL, A.J.   12 Feb   MORE 28 Feb 1856
STRODE, Nannie M. (Jacob)   "both of Boone Co."   Rev. A. Plina

RUSSELL, Jefferson   11 Aug in Washington Co.   MORE 13 Sep 1854
BYRD, Mary Bruce (Thomas decd)   Rev. Genty

RUSSELL, John W.   23 Nov in Fulton   COWS 3 Dec 1858
WIGGS, Mary Jefferson (A.D.)   Rev. W.W. Robertson

RUSSELL, William F. formerly of St. Mary's Co. MD   2 Oct   MORE 3 Oct 1856
HULL, Eliza (D.R.) of St. Louis   Rev. Parsons

RUSSELL, William H.   4 Nov   LIT 12 Dec 1856
STARKE, Ann E. (William) "all of Clay Co."

ST. CLAIR, E.C.   30 Jul in Huntsville   MORE 22 Aug 1854
BRADLEY, Fannie (Judge)

SALISBURY, Lord. W.   18 Nov   Rev. William Taylor   MORE 2 Dec 1856
CUSTER, Mollie J. (Joseph) "all of Danville"

SALMON, R.G.   (1 Mar?)   COWS 18 Mar 1859
GRANT, Matilda (Daniel)   Elder J.M. Robinson

SAMUEL, Charles W. of Jefferson City 18 Jan   JINQ 30 Jan 1858
FERGUSON, Anna E. (Swan) of Callaway Co.   Elder A. Rice

SAMUELS, Mark "High Priest of the United Hebrew Congregation" last evening   MORE 26 Feb 1852
BLOCK, Mary, of Germany   Rev. Edward Myers

SANDERSON, Robert M. formerly of Lynchburg VA   20 Jul   GLWT 5 Oct 1854
KING, Lizzie C. of Barren Co. KY

SAPP, Berryman   7 Aug   Elder B. Wright   COWS 15 Aug 1856
WILCOXSON, Tabitha (Samuel) "all of Boone Co."

SAPP, John C. of Benton Co.   24 Nov   COWS 10 Dec 1858
COLVIN, Nancy (Elijah) of Boone Co.   Elder B. Wren

SAPP, Samuel of Boone Co.   1 Nov   COWS 9 Nov 1855
WATSON, Mary Jane (John K.) of Callaway Co.

SAPPIERE, Z.M. of Cape Girardeau   3 Jan in Jackson MO   MORE 8 Jan 1865
WELLING, Mary J. (Charles)   Rev. A. Munson

SAPPINGTON, D.D.   Elder J.M. Robinson   COWS 18 Mar 1859
EDWARDS, Harriet (John Sr., decd)

SAPPINGTON, Richard   (16 Feb?)   COWS 11 Mar 1859
BALLENGER, Martha (James)   Elder Wm. Cunningham

SAUNDERS, Horace of Springfield   1 Feb in Bridgeton NJ   SPRIM 19 Feb 1859
BUCK, Hannah (late Dr. Ephraim)   Rev. Joseph Saunders

SAUNDERS, T.P.   7 Dec   MORE 8 Dec 1854
JONES, Mary S. (Jonathan)   Rev. William Homes

SAWYER, Charles B.   31 Jul in Boston   MORE 16 Aug 1851
TURNER, Elizabeth E. (Jacob)   Rev. Gannett

SCHAEFERMEYER, Christian, merchant in Lexington 18 Jun   LEXP 30 Jun 1860
TAFT, Eliza A. of Lebanon IL

SCHOFFLER, C.   Bishop Hawks, no date shown   MORE 12 May 1853
HEINEGEN, Mrs. Sarah of Brunswick

SCHOONOVER, J.   19 Jan   JINQ 30 Jan 1858
WILSON, Elizabeth H.C. (A. & Mary)   Rev. Leftwich

SCHOULTON, Henry, formerly of St. Louis 7 Oct in Lincoln Co.   MORE 17 Oct 1858
MOORE, Delilah (William)   A.G. Mitchell

SCHRATER, George   14 Dec in Hannibal   HANT 19 Dec 1854
HAINES, Carrie A. (Sidney P.)   Rev. Phillips

SCOBEE, Stephen   10 Feb in Monroe Co.   MORE 7 Mar 1861
WHITE, Lucy C. (R.G.)   Elder D.V. Inloe

SCOTT, E.T., MD of Fulton   21 Oct   Rev. W.W. Roberson   MORE 27 Oct 1858
OFFUTT, Lou M. (Eli) of Callaway Co., at her father's home

SCOTT, John, merchant of St. Louis   2 Oct in Nashville   MORE 28 Oct 1860
ERWIN, Caroline C. (late John P.)   Rev. J.T. Edgar

SCOTT, John D. of Ste. Genevieve   25 Jun in St. Louis Rev. Bullard   MORE 26 Jun 1855
McKNIGHT, Louise E. (Thomas) of DuBuque IA

SCOTT, William J.   21 Feb   COWS 24 Feb 1860
HUNTER, Lucy (Enoch)   John M. Robinson

SCROGGINS, Dr. F.M.   Thursday by Rev. F.A. Savage   MORE 30 Jul 1854
SWITZER, Martha (Davis) "all of Chariton Co."

SCUDDER, Charles of St. Louis   23 Jun   PWH 1 Jul 1858
ROGERS, Virginia (Clifton R.) of Marion Co.   Rev. W.H. Hopson

SCUDDER, John   1 Jun   Rev. J. Boyle   GLWT 10 Jun 1852
WHITE, Mary Ann (James H.)   "all of St. Louis"

SCUDDER, William H. of St. Louis   17 Jan in Newport KY   SLMD 27 Jan 1854
HINDS, Kate   Rev. Kavanaugh

SEARCY, J.N.   4 Mar in Boone Co.   COWS 12 Mar 1858
COCHRAN, Amanda (William)   P. Kemper

SEARCY, Jasper J.   25 Dec in Boone Co.   MORE 8 Jan 1856
BARRETT, Sarah (Richard)   Elder Peter Kemper

SEARS, James M.   14 Feb near Huntsville   MORE 22 Feb 1865
MATHIS, Dona (Thomas)   Elder M.J. Sears

SEAVER, George L.   29 Nov   MORE 30 Nov 1859
CALVERT, Mary Belle (Jesse)   Rev. Barnhurst

SEAY, Ed A.   at the Virginia Hotel, St. Louis   MORE 24 Aug 1860
POMEROY, Gracia (only dau/W.G. of Steelville MO) Rev. P. Renick

SEAY, William of St. Louis   12 Nov in Iberville Parish LA   MORE 1 Dec 1857
EDWARDS, Eliza (late William F.) of Louisiana   Rev. Selleck

SEE, John F.   21 Sep   Rev. John G. Swinney   MORE 2 Oct 1858
GRIFFIN (GRIFFITH?), Lucinda H. (William G. and Ann) "all of Macon Co."

SEELY, S.P.   6 Jan at the home of the late Capt. Alex Gilham   KCJC 10 Jan 1860
GILHAM, Lizzie (Samuel)   Rev. R.S. Symington

SELBY, James of Callaway Co.   1 Aug   COWS 10 Aug 1860
VANDIVER, Missouri J. (Capt.) of Boone Co.   Rev. W.G. Miller

SELBY, William of St. Louis   24 Oct   Rev. M. Schuyler   MORE 26 Oct 1865
WALLINGFORD, Sue E. (D.P.) formerly of Weston MO   Wheeling VA pc

SELL, Walter E.   10 Apr at Central Presbyterian Church   MORE 11 Apr 1855
WEST, Martha E. (Thomas H.)   Rev. Anderson

SELTNER, John H. of Co. E 9th MSM   19 Jan   Rev. W.R. Rothwell   MORE 29 Jan 1865
DERINGE, Elizabeth (Abraham) of Randolph Co.

SETTLE, John D.   26 May   Elder N. Flood   GLWT 23 Jun 1853
DUDGEON, Martha (Alexander) "all of Howard Co."

SEXTON, D.M.   13 Dec at St. John's Church   MORE 18 Dec 1864
DONNELLY, Margaret (only surviving dau/Charles)   Fr. Ring

SEXTON, George S. of St. Louis   30 Jul   COWS 7 Aug 1857
SHIRLEY, Mary (James S.) of Fayette   Elder William C. (Been?)

SHACKELFORD, J.T. of St. Louis in Clark Co. KY at the home of J.C. Woodward   MORE 1 Feb 1862
BATES, Mary C. of Clark Co. KY

SHACKELFORD, Thomas of Glasgow   Tuesday   GLWT 19 Jun 1851
HARRISON, Sarah (John) of the Glasgow vicinity   Rev. W.T. Lucky

SHAFFER, F.D. of St. Louis   2 Feb near Bridgeton, St. Louis Co.   MORE 5 Feb 1864
MARTIN, Jennie A.E. (late Col. Daniel)   Rev. J. Hickman
   "at the home of William Palmer"   Chicago & New York pc

SHANNON, John H.   MORE 21 Apr 1854
McENTIRE, Margaret (Capt. John) "all of St. Louis" Rev. Banner

SHANNON, Elder Richard D. of Columbia   11 Jun Elder E.S. Dulin   COWS 19 Jun 1863
LARD, Lizzie (eldest dau/Elder Moses E.) of Buchanan Co.

SHAPLEIGH, Frank   6 Jun   Bishop Hawks   MORE 8 Jun 1865
DOGGETT, Mary L. (John D.) "all of St. Louis"

SHARP, B.W. of St. Louis   6 Oct   Rev. John Saxe   MORE 18 Oct 1856
CHAMBERLIN, Mrs. Ann Eliza of Vienna, Ontario Co., NY

SHARP, Benjamin J. of Callaway Co.   12 Oct in Pike Co.   COSE 28 Oct 1852
ROBERTS, Mary (J.)   Rev. William Barnett

SHARP, George W.   23 Nov   RANC 2 Dec 1859
MARMADUKE, Jennie C. (Wm. D.) "all of Bloomington" Rev. S.B.F. Caldwell

SHARP, Jacob L.   14 Jan   Rev. Richard Bond   MORE 19 Jan 1852
REDMAN, Mrs. Evalina (widow of Rev. W.W.) "all of Danville"

SHARP, Rev. James of Macon Co.   15 Sep   HANT 28 Sep 1853
HANNA, Louisa (Robert) of Randolph Co.   Rev. M.C. Patton

SHARP, Leander J.   21 Oct   Rev. Hobson   BOBS 8 Nov 1856
CHADWICK, Mary (H.S.) "all of Lexington"

SHAW, Howard   27 Oct at St. John's Church   MORE 30 Oct 1864
TRACY, Eliza R. (only dau/late Edward)   Rev. Hawks

SHAW, Capt. John S. of St. Louis   24 Jul in Lexington KY   MORE 27 Jul 1860
ELBERT, Mary (John L.) of Lexington   Rev. Buckner

SHAW, Thomas M.   25 Mar in Scott Co.   COSE 29 Apr 1852
WAUGH, Mary (Dr. A.)

SHEELEY, John W.   14 Jan   Elder James F. Smith   MORE 4 Feb 1856
LYTES, Albina (Washington) of Callaway Co.

SHELTON, John G. Jr. of St. Louis   23 Jun in Cincinnati   MORE 4 Jul 1864
DE LA VEGA, Donna Lula of Havana Cuba   Rev. Antonio La Barge
     "at the home of the bride's uncle, Don Jose Gomez"

SHEPHERD, George   Sunday in St. Louis   MORE 9 May 1855
HARVEY, Estella Anna (David)   Rev. Gillasgoe

SHEPPARD, Charles of Springfield   15 Nov in Walden VT   SPRIM 4 Dec 1856
DOW, Lucy A. of Walden   Rev. J.P. Stone

SHERMAN, Henry   20 Apr   COWS 23 Apr 1858
SMITH, Julia (William J.)   Rev. N.H. Hall

SHIELDS, Thomas W. of St. Louis   13 Nov   MORE 25 Nov 1856
TRIGG, Lizzie (W.R.) of Lafayette Co.   Rev. Dunlap

SHIFFER, R. of Columbia   3 Oct   COSE 7 Oct 1852
HARRIS, Rebecca A. (Capt. John) of Boone Co.   Elder T.M. Allen

SHINKLE, F.L. of St. Louis   19 Jan in Oldham Co. KY   MORE 30 Jan 1864
CRIDER, S.C. (Capt. E.P.) of Oldham Co.

SHOLL, Cyrus R.   14 Jun Rev. D.S. Warden   MORE 21 Jun 1855
PARR, Eliza J. (oldest dau/John) "all of Jackson Co."

SHORT, L.D.   23 Jun   MARD 1 Jul 1859
BARLEY, Mary Margaret (Samuel) of Blackwater   Elder Hancock

SHORTRIDGE, A.L. of Hannibal   5 Dec   HANT 11 Dec 1855
PRIEST, Maddie M. (Henry) of Ralls Co.

SHORTRIDGE, B.F.   28 Mar in Bloomington MO   SLMD 17 Apr 1854
HOCKERSMITH, Emma of Franklin Co. KY   Rev. F. Hodges

SHORTRIDGE, Jonathan   19 Jan in Jackson Co.   SLMD 3 Feb 1854
CHILDS, Isabel (Hon. James)   Elder F.R. Palmer

SHRYOCK, William P. of St. Louis   27 Oct in Bourbon Co. KY   MORE 31 Oct 1863
GARTH, Alice E. (late Thomas) of Bourbon Co.   Rev. J.W. Venable

SHUTTER, Charles of St. Louis   11 Jan in Peoria IL   SLMD 21 Jan 1854
SOLOMON, Susan Emily (Joel) of Peoria   Rev. Ferris

SIMPKINS, William H.   17 Jan, 1st Unitarian Church   MORE 22 Jan 1865
MOORE, Mary Ann (late Davis) "all of St. Louis"   Rev. Cox

SIMPSON, Rev. C.D. of Glasgow   13 May in Piermont NY   BRUNS 17 May 1856
HOUGHTON, R.J. "at the home of Mrs. H.C. Seymour"

SIMPSON, George W. 6 Jun at the home of C.W. Townsley Rev. S.J.P. Anderson MORE 7 Jun 1865
MICHAEL, Mary Louise (youngest dau/late D.C.) "all of St. Louis"

SIMPSON, Robert H.   27 Sep in Paris MO   HANT 6 Oct 1855
McGEE, Mary A. (Robert H.)

SINCLAIR, Robert W. of Audrain Co. 21 Oct   Rev. P. Donan   COWS 12 Nov 1858
NELSON, Mrs. Eliza Ann (James Clark)   .of Monroe Co.

SINCLAIR, William H.   13 Feb   COWS 26 Feb 1858
ROCHFORD, Bedelia (John)   Rev. Alderson

SINGLETON, Jackson of St. Louis/30 Aug in Albuquerque NM at the home of MORE 28 Sep 1855
SKINNER, Elizabeth P.   /Maj. J.H. Carlton   Rev. H.W. Read

SIPPLE, W.C.   13 Dec in Sidney IA   LIT 28 Dec 1860
WOOD, Kate (Judge) of Liberty   Rev. Guflee

SISK, Simeon   in High Hill 8 Dec   Elder T.T. Johnson   MORE 26 Dec 1859
MOREHED, Ann Amanda at her father's home   "all of Montgomery Co."

SISK, William Y. of High Hill   12 Nov in Middletown   MORE 24 Nov 1857
SMITH, Mary M. of Montgomery Co.   Col. Seneca Hammock, Notary Public

SIVIRHER, Noah   last Wednesday   HANT 23 Feb 1859
CARSON, Sarah A. (Simon)

SKELLY, John P., formerly of VT   30 Dec in Mora   Fr. Salpoint   MORE 5 Feb 1864
ST. VRAIN, Mary Louise, niece of Col. Coran St. Vrain of Taos, at the
        home of Vicente St. Vrain in Mora

SKINNER, Truman of St. Louis   12 Nov, Church of the Ascension, Baltimore   MORE 17 Nov 1863
CONSTABLE, Isabelle (late William S.) of Kent Co. MD   Rev. Callaway

SLACK, Henry of St. Joseph   24 May   COSE 26 May 1853
ALLEN, Anna (Elder T.M.) of Boone Co.   Elder A. Proctor

SLOAN, M. Harrison (or H) near Emerson MO   19 Sep   Rev. John Leighton   HAM 3 Oct 1861
HICKS, Kate (Peter) at her father's home   "all of Marion Co."

SLOSS, James C.   22 Apr   Rev. William H. Park   MORE 24 Apr 1851
TUPPER, Mary Frances (only dau/L.B.)   "late of Baltimore"

SMART, Reuben   25 Jan   Rev. P. McKim   MORE 29 Jan 1865
HAMBLETON, Robyna (eldest dau/Samuel)   "all of St. Louis"

SMELSER, Henry   18 Feb   Rev. George Rice   HANT 22 Feb 1853
WOLF, Mary Ann (Henry C.) of Lick Creek, Ralls Co.

SMITH, Byrd of Kentucky   22 Feb   LIT 27 Feb 1857
MILLER, Nancy (William) of Clay Co.   Elder W.C. Barrett

SMITH, Dr. C.E. of Saline Co.   13 May   Rev. W.D. Shumate   GLWT 20 May 1852
PENN, Virginia (Dr. George) of St. Louis Co.

SMITH, Elon G.   18 Dec at Trinity Church   MORE 21 Dec 1856
DERBY, Cornelia (Charles)

SMITH, Francis J. of Jefferson Co.   at Windsor Harbor 15 May   Rev. Proctor   MORE 20 May 1860
O'FALLEN, Ellen (youngest dau/late Maj. B.) of Indian River
        "at the residence of D.M. Cooper"

SMITH, George W. of Audrain Co.   9 Feb   Elder A. Rice   MORE 28 Feb 1854
BASKETT, Elizabeth (Judge James) of Callaway Co.

SMITH, Gilman, formerly of Vermont   26 Apr in St. Louis   GLWT 1 May 1851
GRIFFITH, Mrs. Margaret formerly of Fayette   Rev. J.B. Jeter

SMITH, J. Bailey of St. Louis   1 Nov   Rev. James Craik   MORE 5 Nov 1858
WATKINS, Mary J. (Sim) of Louisville

SMITH, James M.   21 Jan   Rev. M. Kirby Miller   HAM 3 Feb 1861
CALDWELL, M.E. (R.H.)   "all of Ralls Co."

SMITH, Johnson   24 Apr   Rev. R.C. Mansfield   MORE 17 Jun 1855
NORTON, Sarah Ann (D.) late of Audrain Co.

SMITH, Joseph B.   20 May   Rev. Prottsman   GLWT 3 Jun 1852
LAND, Harriet H. (Robert)   "all of Saline Co."

SMITH, Robert   8 Oct in Boone Co.   COWS 10 Oct 1857
LAMPTON, Martha Jane (William)   Rev. Via

SMITH, Thomas M. of Columbia   8 Oct in Washington D.C.   MORE 17 Oct 1851
KIRBY, Sallie (Maj. E.F.)   Rev. F.H. Evans

SMITH, Thomas M. of Rocheport   6 Oct   COWS 22 Nov 1861
DAVIS, Sue C. (Z.T.) of Warrensburg   Rev. Warden

SMITH, Thomas M.   7 Apr   Rev. H. Cox   MORE 11 Apr 1865
BURK, Mollie M. (Capt. John H.)   "all of St. Louis"

SMITH, William A.   22 Jun   JINQ 1 Jul 1854
WOOD, Eliza H. (L.L.) of California, Moniteau Co.

SMITH, William H.   14 Aug in Callaway Co.   COWS 22 Aug 1862
CURD, Die (Gen. John) of Callaway Co.   Rev. Marlin

SMITHLAND, Franklin of Savannah MO   30 Nov   SAND 20 Dec 1856
HILTIBIDAL, Harriet E. (Jacob) late of Andrew Co.

SNELL, Charles A.   29 Nov   MORE 3 Dec 1855
VOELKER, Maria (Emanuel)   Louis Dubreuil JP

SNODDY, Robert M.   30 Apr   Rev. James M. Green   GLWT 7 May 1857
WOODS, Clemency (L.K.) "all of Howard Co."

SOHCALING, George L. of Lafayette Co. 10 Feb in Nelson Co. KY   SLMD 16 Feb 1858
STYLES, Caroline (Lewis, at his home)

SOMBART, Julius   7 Feb   BOBS 9 Feb 1856
BRENNEISEN, Louisa (Reinhard)   Henry S. Brant, Esq.

SORIA, Henry, formerly of New Orleans   27 Oct at Christ Church   MORE 30 Oct 1858
JOHNSON, Henrietta (late Edward) of St. Louis Rev. Montgomery Schuyler

SOUTHWORTH, Dr. J.W. Jr. of Glasgow   10 Oct in Georgetown KY   MORE 20 Oct 1865
MORRISON, Helen (Judge J.G.) of Georgetown Rev. T.J. Stevenson

SPARKS, S. of Newcastle ENG   28 Sep   MORE 6 Oct 1859
GALLAHER, Julia O. of Dublin   Rev. E.F. Berkley

SPEAR, William   26 Apr   Rev. C.D. Simpson   GLWT 29 Apr 1852
EARICKSON, Susan E. (Perregrine) "all of Howard Co."

SPELBRINK, Louis   28 Nov   MORE 30 Nov 1865
LAUMAN, Emilia (Fred) "all of St. Louis"   Rev. A.W. Boder

SPENCE, Joseph   14 Oct in Clinton Co.   MORE 30 Oct 1855
TALBOTT, A. Kate (Benjamin) formerly of Bourbon Co. KY Rev. E.A. Martin

SPENCER, Charles W.   24 Nov in Brunswick   COWS 3 Dec 1858
JOHNSON, Bettie B. (Dr. A.C.) of Chariton Co.   Rev. Beebee

SPENCER, Samuel M.   22 Nov in Payson   HANT 1 Dec 1853
ELLIOTT, Jane (oldest dau/Joseph)   Z.K. Hawley

+ SPIER, Dr. __ (a dentist, first name, not shown)   MORE 17 Nov 1865
GOLDSOLL, Nattie (Meir) (A Hebrew wedding, in the local news column.)

SPOTSWOOD, E.R.   9 Mar in Glasgow   GLWT 23 Mar 1854
MONTMOLLIN, Sallie P. of Lexington KY   Rev. John D. Matthews

SPOTSWOOD, John W. of Audrain Co.   11 Nov   COWS 20 Nov 1857
SCOTT, Margaret Isabella (James M.)   W.W. Robertson

+ SPENCER, Sherman   15 Nov   Rev. James A. Paige   MORE 20 Nov 1858
DONALDSON, Lizzie H. (eldest dau/Andrew) Cincinnati, Newport KY pc

SPRINKLE, D.A., formerly of Hannibal 8 Jan in Monroe Co.   MORE 5 Feb 1856
BARCLAY, Fannie (Maj. John) of Boone Co.   Rev. A. Monroe

SPROUL, Dr. Samuel   28 Oct in Greenfield   SPRIM 6 Nov 1856
SEVERSON, Margaret (Josiah) "all of Dade Co." Br. W.I. Garrett

STANTON, Lieut. John L.   19 Apr in Savannah MO   MORE 28 Apr 1864
HOLT, Elvira (Ben)   Rev. Sheldon

STARKEY, William (Hickory Co.?)   Sunday last in this vicinity   BOL 14 Feb 1857
HART, Elizabeth (Judge Moses P.)

STASEY, Thomas B. of Marion Co.   6 Oct in Monroe Co.   HAM 13 Oct 1859
SPARKS, Margaret A. (Osborn) at her father's home

STEBBINS, Charles J. of St. Louis   7 Sep in St. Louis   MORE 8 Sep 1858
SQUIRE, Sarah J. (Samuel) of Madison Co. IL   Rev. J.G. White

STEBBINS, Oscar F.   11 Jun   MORE 12 Jun 1863
WARNE, Sallie (M.W.)   Rev. H.A. Nelson

STEEDMAN, Dr. J.G.W.   at St. George's Church, Monday   MORE 1 Nov 1865
HARRISON, Dora (James)   Rev. Schuyler
             Montgomery AL & Columbia SC pc

STEELE, John J.   6 Sep   Pres. T. Skelton   RANC 16 Sep 1859
LANDER, Mollie (Israel) "all of Mexico MO"

STEELE, Zebulon T.   27 Jul in Calumet Twp. (Livingston Co.?)   MORE 1 Aug 1856
GIBSON, Mary D. (Dr. J.D.) of Utica, Livingston Co.   Elder Erret

STEEN, Frederick, son of Col., 22 Feb in Owensville   COWS 11 Mar 1859
BEMPSON, Martha (stepdau/Col. Steen)   Rev Ben Leath

STEEN, Robert   22 Apr in Ralls Co.   HANT 16 May 1856
MENEFEE, Mary Tabitha (Arthur)   Rev. Vanemen

STEMMONS, J.M.   9 Jul in Greenfield   SPRIM 16 Jul 1857
ALLISON, R.S. (Judge M.H.)   Rev. S.S. Headlee

61

STEPHENS, Absalom   in Boone Co.   COWS 14 Sep 1855
BURCH, Harriet (Joseph)   Rev. T.P. Stephens

STEPHENS, Edward W. of St. Louis   28 May, 4th District New Orleans   MORE 7 Jun 1857
KEEN, Harriet Isabella (H.D.)   Rev. Thomas Markham

STEPHENS, J.B.L. of Gilroy MO   1 Jun
SMALLWOOD, Agnes S. (late Russell) of Moniteau Co. Rev. Thomas Grear   BOBS 10 Jun 1854

STEPHENS, Dr. T.L.   3 Mar   Elder T.P. Stephens   COWS 11 Mar 1859
BRIGHT, Sarah (Judge Michael)   "all of Callaway Co."

STEPHENSON, James late of Montgomery Co. KY 27 Nov   COWS 30 Nov 1855
BRUTON, Sarah J. (James) of Boone Co.   Elder T.M. Allen

STEPHENSON, James M.   13 Mar   GLWT 24 Mar 1853
HALLEY, Arzela E. (Francis) of Chariton Co.   Rev. James W. Morrow

STEPHENSON, J.S.   8 May   COWS 13 May 1859
STEPHENSON, Mary (late Samuel)   Elder Larue

STERLING, E.J. of St. Louis   3 Sep in Williamsburg NY   MORE 7 Sep 1851
BARR, Sallie E. (Jonathan)

STEVENS, Thomas of Montgomery Co.   8 Oct in Hudson OH   MORE 24 Oct 1855
SALISBURY, M.M.

STEWART, John   23 Dec in Callaway Co.   MORE 24 Jan 1855
STEWART, Elizabeth (James)   Elder Rice

STEWART, Robert, formerly of Philadelphia, now of Osceola in Philadelphia   OVAS 10 Jan 1861
BUNTING, Elizabeth   Rev. John Patton 25 Dec

STEWART, T.W.   2 Feb near Sturgeon   COWS 10 Feb 1860
PALMER, Mary (Joel)   Rev. M.L. Eads

STICHTER, F.G. of Louisiana, Pike Co. 19 Dec in Chester Co. PA   LAJ 2 Jan 1862
WILSON, Emma (William) of Chester Co., at her father's home Rev. T.J. Umsted

STICKLES, Dr. __ of St. Louis   29 Nov in Mechanicsville NY   MORE 30 Dec 1857
FARNAM, Mrs. Renetta Wilcox of St. Louis   Rev. Fulton

STIGALL, B.M.   13 Mar in Independence   MORE 3 Apr 1860
TRUSLOW, Amanda (Rev. J.F.)   Rev. Cavanaugh

STILLWELL, Enoch of St. Louis   17 Jun   MORE 21 Jun 1851
HUTCHINSON, Margaret of Danville KY   Rev. Boyle

STILLWELL, William H.   in Frankford Elder John M. Johnson   HAM 1 Nov 1859
DEVIN, Emily Jane (William) "all of Pike Co."

STINDS, Conrad R. of St. Louis   31 Aug in Walberstadt Prussia   MORE 4 Oct 1854
WEST, Augusta A.

STITH, James Wilmer   27 Aug at the home of L.H. Terry, south St. Louis   MORE 28 Aug 1857
TAYLOR, Fannie L. (Dr. S.T.) of Virginia   Rev. S.J.P. Anderson

STITH, Judge M.S. of Texas   22 Jan in Christ Church   MORE 23 Jan 1859
MILLS, Matilda (late Col. A.L.) of St. Louis   Rev. M. Schuyler

STIVERS, Dr. James H. of Boone Co. 27 May   COWS 5 Jun 1863
BROWN, Mary (Thomas) of Audrain Co.   Rev. Green Carey

STOCKWELL, James Miller   12 Aug   LIT 20 Aug 1852
NORRIS, Ann E. (John) "all of Clay Co."   Rev. D. Patton

STONE, Isaac H. of St. Louis   20 Dec in Cedar Rapids IA   MORE 8 Jan 1858
LITTLE, Marion B. (eldest dau/James) of Linn Co. IA   Rev. Morrow

STONE, James S. "one of the proprietors of the American" Thursday last   RANC 4 Mar 1859
BRADLEY, Lucretia A. (Terry) "all of Randolph Co." Rev. Noah Flood

STONE, Jo. W.   28 Sep in Columbia   COWS 10 Oct 1858
DOZIER, Elvira (Capt. James) of St. Charles Co.   Rev. Anderson

STONE, N.R.   26 Dec in Kansas Territory   LIT 26 Jan 1855
DOTY, Miss   "both of Clay Co."   Rev. Barker

STONE, Richard A. of Marion Co. 2 Mar at the home of Rev. Lewis Duncan HANJ 11 Mar 1852
DUNCAN, Sarah C.   in Lincoln Co.   Rev. James F. Smith

STONE, Samuel M. of St. Louis   22 Oct   HANT 24 Oct 1857
SMITH, Lizzie C. (J.P.) of Hannibal

STOUTENBURG, T.W. of New Haven MO in Lacon IL 10 Dec Rev. B.B. Parsons MORE 13 Dec 1861
BENTON, Hattie P. of St. Louis   "at the home of her sister"

STRAWBE, Francis M.   4 Aug in Montgomery Co.   MORE 12 Aug 1864
MULHERIN, Mary E. (Capt. John M.)   John M. James, J.P.

STREET, J.C. of Rocheport   7 Feb   COWS 17 Feb 1860
HART, Elizabeth (Thomas) of Boone Co.   Elder John G. White

STRIKER, Isaac O. of Marshall   31 Aug in Cincinnati   MARD 10 Sep 1858
STERN, Henrietta   Rev. Kean

STRINGER, T. of St. Louis   7 Feb in Newburgh NY   SLMD 20 Feb 1854
EAGER, Sarah J. McBride (Samuel W.)

STRODE, Lieut. J.G.   15 Dec in Mexico, Audrain Co.   COWS 25 Dec 1863
WHITE, Mattie (Rev. William) of Mexico   Rev. N.L. Fish

STROTHER, James P.   last Tuesday in Marshall   MARD 24 Oct 1860
LEWIS, Mildred E. (2nd dau/Mrs. Rebecca)   Rev. J.W. Clark

STROUD, Robinson F. of Benton Co. 13 Jul in Van Buren AR   MORE 31 Jul 1854
FINE, Sophronia of Washington Co.   John Reed Esq.

STUART, Moses   2 Aug   MORE 3 Aug 1859
JOHNSTONE, Jane Ann of Monahan Co. IRE   Rev. Terry

STURGEON, Isaac   16 Dec   COWS 24 Dec 1858
ALLEN, Nannie (Mrs. Beverly) of St. Louis

STURGES, John A. of St. Louis   13 Aug in Galesburg IL   MORE 18 Aug 1857
ZIMMERMAN, Augusta of Galesburg   Rev. Blanchard

SULLINS, Amos G.   30 Dec   COWS 6 Jan 1860
SHOCK, Rebecca (David)   T.M. Allen

SULLIVAN, James of Saline Co.   1 Jan   Rev. William Brown   BRUNS 5 Jan 1856
WHITESIDES, Mary (ygst dau/late John) of Chariton Co.

SUMMERS, H.C.   1 Feb at the home of Col. J.C. Orr   COWS 3 Feb 1860
THORNTON, Mattie (Joseph decd)   Elder W.A. Wigginton

SUMMERS, Mason T., merchant of Parkville   7 Oct   Rev. Calomel   GLWT 21 Oct 1852
BEEDING, America (C.P.) of Parkville

SUTER, J.J. of Marion Co.   25 Nov   HANT 20 Dec 1856
SMITH, Lucy A. (Judge F.) of Clark Co.

SUTTON, George W. by Judge Michael Bright at his home in Callaway Co. COSE 26 May 1853
PETTUS, Martha (Stephen D.)   "both of Boone Co."

SWITZLER, William B.   25 Feb in (of?) Woodville, Macon Co. COWS 12 Mar 1858
MARTIN, Agnes A. (Col. J.S.) of Monroe Co.   Rev. J.P. Finley

SWON, Edwin at Portland, Callaway Co. 5 Dec by Rev. H.A. Bourland   SLMD 17 Dec 1861
DARNES, Ella (only dau/late Simon of Fairfax VA) at her grandmother's home

TACK, Cary Jr.   26 Dec at the home of Joseph Bledsoe by J.H. Fulkerson COWS 11 Jan 1861
BLEDSOE, Sarah Frances (Loven) "all of Boone Co."

TANNER, Joseph   9 May   Rev. McPheeters   MORE 11 May 1860
BLOCK, Delia M. (Emmanuel) "all of St. Louis"   Nashville pc

TARR, B.F. of Brunswick   1 Jun   Rev. H. Hall   GLWT 10 Jun 1852
PHILLIPS, Harriet (John G.) of Boone Co.

TATE, John, late of Clark Co. KY   27 Dec   MORE 8 Jan 1856
ROBERTS, Frances A. (Lewis)   Elder S.J. Bush

TATE, Dr. N.C.   23 Feb   SLMD 8 Feb 1854
WILSON, Mary E. (Rev. J.M.)   "all of Fulton"

TATLOW, Rev. Thomas H. of New-Ark, Knox Co. 22 Dec   HANT 30 Dec 1854
LAFON, Susan (Dr. Joseph) of Palmyra   Rev. John Leighton

TAYLOR, James of Platte Co.   22 Jan   LIT 30 Jan 1857
WALKER, Virginia (John) of Clay Co.   Rev. John G. Fackler

TAYLOR, Rev. John R. of the MO Annual Conference (5 or 9 Aug?)   MORE 21 Aug 1865
PORTER, Andromache (Richard, at his home) of Monroe Co. Rev. L. Rush

TAYLOR, M.G.   18 Mar   Rev. Samuel Johnson   RICON 26 Mar 1863
BRASHER, Mollie (A.D.) "all of Ray Co."

TAYLOR, W.T.   5 Apr at Huntsville   MAG 15 Apr 1863
BROOKING, Julia (James R.) of Huntsville   Rev. Sutton

TAYLOR, John R.   5 May   Rev. D. Coulter   WAVE 14 May 1859
KEITH, Bell (Dr. James M.)   "all of Lafayette Co."

TAYLOR, John M.   24 Apr   Bishop Hawks   MORE 27 Apr 1854
SHEAFFE, Margarette H. (late Jacob) formerly of Pottsville PA and
+   Portsmouth NH

TERRILL, George   Tuesday   PWH 1 Nov 1855
HAYDEN, Delila (Col. E.C.)   Rev. Ayres

+ TAYLOR, Philip C.   7 Mar   St. John's Church   MORE 9 Mar 1859
STOUT, Leontine (youngest dau/Moses)   Fr. Bannon

TERRY, Rev. E.A., Rector of St. John's, Boonville at Christ Church, St. Louis MORE 12 Jul 1854
THOMAS, Flora (2nd dau/Lucy) of Woodburn IL

TEBBS, Dr. William B. of Camden   Rev. J.A. Prather   LIT 24 Dec 1852
RINGO, M. Louisa (A.H.) of Richmond

THACKSTON, William   Tuesday last   GLWT 18 Sep 1856
BOGGS, Ann E. (R.W.)   Rev. N. Flood

THATCHER, John of Callaway Co.   14 Jan in Audrain Co.   HANT 6 Feb 1858
SMITH, Permelia (J.T.) of Audrain Co.

THATCHER, J. Milton   29 Jun in Clay Co.   MORE 12 Jul 1854
SULLIVAN, Frances C. (oldest dau/Capt. James)   Rev. Moses Lard

THAW, Charlie of St. Louis   17 Nov in Boonville   MORE 22 Nov 1859
SMITH, Lissie (Judge C.H.)   Rev. H.M. Painter

THEOBALD, Griff P. of St. Louis   at the Female Academy, Nashville 17 Jul   MORE 1 Aug 1854
LOVE, Harriet of Columbus MS

THOMAS, George W.   Rev. Sullivan   MORE 14 Dec 1856
RYAN, Kate Fitzgerald (Thomas)

THOMAS, Dr. J.L.   1 May   Rev. N.T. McNeily   MORE 29 Jun 1860
CUSTER, Lou M.   "both of Montgomery Co."

THOMAS, James P. of Callaway Co.   16 Feb   COWS 14 Mar 1862
McDANIEL, Sallie (William) of Benton Co.   Rev. William Gray

THOMAS, John B.C.   27 Oct in Quincy   PALS 30 Oct 1863
WILCOX, Lizzie A. (D.P.) "all of Palmyra"   Rev. Gallaher

THOMAS, John W.   25 Aug "all of Callaway Co."   COWS 9 Sep 1859
THOMAS, Julia Ann (Presley E.)   Elder A. Rice

THOMAS, William of Callaway Co.   25 Feb   COWS 5 Mar 1858
GRIFFIN, Elizabeth (Jesse) of Boone Co.   Elder B. Wren

THOMPSON, Charles   18 Sep in Cole Co.   MORE 25 Sep 1855
GORDON, Mary (John T.)   Rev. M.D. Noland

THOMPSON, Charles L. of St. Louis 8 Feb in Danville KY by Rev. Yantiss   MORE 12 Feb 1860
SHACKELFORD, Bettie (W.H.) of Danville "at the home of William Duke"

THOMPSON, John of Liberty   14 Feb at New Franklin   MORE 23 Feb 1860
JACKSON, Mary C. (G?) (Dr. W.D.) late of Charleston VA

THOMPSON, John C.   9 Dec   CAWN 11 Dec 1859
ADAMS, Susan J. (Judge D.D.)   Rev. J.M. Hardy

THOMPSON, Macklot of St. Louis   26 Jun in New Bedford MA   MORE 6 Jul 1861
NYE, Amelia H. (late A.B.) of New Bedford   Rev. Tusten

THORNTON, Charles H. of Independence   13 Mar in St. Joseph Rev. Fackler   COWS 14 Mar 1862
HOWARD, Annie (Col. Joseph) of St. Joseph, formerly of Columbia

THORNTON, Rev. J.C.   29 Nov in Clay Co.   LIT 7 Dec 1855
BIRD, Catherine (G.)

THORNTON, John G.   28 Jan in Clinton, Henry Co.   COWS 12 Feb 1858
CHILTON, Mary Ella (Dr. Edward) of Cooper Co.   Rev. Robert Harris

THORNTON, James T. of Cass Co.   2 Oct in Winchester KY   MORE 30 Oct 1855
SIMPSON, Mary H. (Judge James)

THORP, Alonzo, MD of California, Moniteau Co. St. John's Church   MORE 17 Nov 1855
TAYLOR, Sarah (Thomas) of St. Louis   Rev. Clerc

THORPE, James   21 Apr   Rev. W.C. Randolph   MARD 29 Apr 1859
KING, Martha Ann (Thomas) "all of Miami (Saline Co.)"

THURSTON, John W.   in Boone Co.   COWS 12 Mar 1858
ELLIOTT, Fanny (Epps)   Rev. Green Cary

TICKNOR, Edward   5 Mar   Rev. H.A. Nelson   MORE 7 Apr 1859
BOSWELL, Josephine (Charles)   "all of St. Louis"

TILDEN, John B. of St. Louis   16 Nov, Greenton Valley, Lafayette Co.   COWS 26 Nov 1858
SLAUGHTER, Mollie (Martin)

TILFORD, Capt. J.G., 3rd MS Cav   9 Feb   Fr. Ryan   MORE 12 Feb and
DEAN, Cornelia V. (youngest dau/Harriet and John) (later notice omitted   later 1864
        John) "at the home of her mother" New York & Louisville pc

TILLAY, John T.   4 Oct, St. George's Church   MORE 6 Oct 1859
OWEN, Annie (oldest dau/O.J.) formerly of Remsen NY   Rev. Berkley

TILTON, Peter of Newton Co.   4 Jan in Jacksonville IL   BOL 15 Jan 1859
ROBERTSON, Mattie A. of Jacksonville   Rev. Morrison

TIPTON, William B. of Montgomery Co.   19 Nov   Elder W.S. Browne   COWS 4 Dec 1857
OLDHAM, Mary E. of Madison Co. KY

TISDALE, A.J. of Lafayette Co.   14 Dec   Rev. Samuel J. Cornells   GAL 21 Dec 1865
HUNTER, Martha E. (Samuel) of Gallatin

TOALSON, G.W.   5 Jan   COWS 20 Jan 1860
COWDEN, Mag E. (Addison)   Green Cary

TODD, Washington   3 Oct   Rev. William G. Eliot   MORE 5 Oct 1865
DAVIS, Mary L. (late Samuel) "all of St. Louis"

TOMPKINS, A.R. of Randolph Co.   10 Oct   Rev. J.M. Butts   MORE 30 Oct 1855
SNELL, Eliza J. (Greenup) of Callaway Co.

TOMPKINS, Benjamin of Boonville   11 Nov in St. Louis Bishop Hawks   GLWT 18 Nov 1852
CLARK, Sue (youngest dau/late Gov. James of KY)

TONES, H.S. of Santa Clara CA   22 Mar at Bowling Green, Pike Co.   SLMD 3 Apr 1854
BLAIN, Mary Frances (oldest dau/William J.)

TOOLEY, Clifton of Chariton Co.   8 May   GLWT 15 May 1851
CASON, Susan (George) of Howard Co.   Rev. Thomas Fristoe

TOWNER, George L. of Bloomington   8 Jun   GLWT 19 Jun 1851
ROBIOU, Frances V. (L.) of St. Aubert   Rev. Deventer

TOWNSEND, John Hendrick   4 Jan   Rev. Alvin Rucker   MORE 11 Jan 1855
SEBASTION, Mary Catherine (Moses) "all of St. Francois Co."

TOWNSLEY, Charles W.   5 Mar at the home of James Comfort   MORE 6 Mar 1863
MICHAEL, Julia (late D.C.)   Rev. T.M. Post

TOWSON, James F.   19 Jul in Hannibal Rev. Sherman   MORE 23 Jul 1854
COOPER, Lizzie (D.H.) "all of St. Louis"

TRABUE, S.R.   Rev. F. Graves   LIT 26 Feb 1858
CAVE, Susan (Uriel) of Clay Co.

TRASK, William R. of St. Louis   28 Jul near Caledonia Rev. Spencer   MORE 4 Aug 1861
PEYTON, Ella S. (Capt George W., at his home)

TRAVIS, William   23 Mar near Liberty   Rev. J.M. Holt   CANP 30 Mar 1865
SMITH, Mary A. (Rice, at his home)   /Church, Clark Co.

TREDWAY, John G. of Keytesville   8 May   GLWT 15 May 1851
SEARS, Elizabeth (Joseph) of Howard Co.   Rev. W.T. Lucky

TREVATHAN, F.M. of Mississippi Co.   22 Mar in Columbus KY Rev. Henry Porter CHAC 23 Mar 1860
GREEN, C.E. at the home of her father

TREVOR, James   24 Jul on Fish Lake   CHAC 29 Jul 1859
WADLEY, G.E. (J.E.?) (Eden)   Judge William G. Corley

TRICKEY, E.E. of St. Louis   22 Oct   COWS 6 Nov 1857
PARSONS, Julia M. (Gen. G.A.) of Jefferson City   Rev. Longbeed(?)

TRIPLETT, C.M. of Palmyra   in Palmyra 12 May   MORE 27 May 1859
BANKS, Lizzie (William M.)   Rev. William Newland

TROEB, Philip of St. Louis   27 Jul   MORE 8 Aug 1854
KESSLER, Barbara (Jacob)   M. Thackaberry

TRUITT, William of Callaway Co.   8 Feb   COWS 11 Feb 1859
PEMBERTON, Ann Eliza (Harvey) of Boone Co.   T.M. Allen

TRUMBLE, James H. of Weston, formerly of Frederick MD 19 Oct   LEXP 20 Oct 1852
HAYS, Rebecca (youngest dau/Abraham) "of this county" Rev. John A. Harrison

TUCKER, Frank H. of St. Louis   25 Oct   Rev. Joel Campbell   MORE 2 Nov 1854
HAINES, Annie (Hon. Daniel) of Hamburg NJ

TUCKER, John   15 Nov in Boone Co.   COWS 23 Nov 1855
WHITE, Lizzie (late David)

TUCKER, Johnson M. of St. Louis   24 Jun in Cincinnati   MORE 7 Jul 1858
FRIES, Carrie V. (eldest dau/Dr. George) of Cincinnati   Rev. J.L.G. McKown

TUCKER, Joseph of near Boonville   26 Nov in Cincinnati   COWS 17 Dec 1858
SMITH, Kate (Lee) of near Jacksonville, Boyle Co. KY

TUREMAN, James H.   26 Jun in Callaway Co.   MORE 12 Jul 1854
EVERHART, Margaret (Joseph)

TURNER, George W.   19 Oct   COWS 29 Oct 1858
MARTAIN, Elizabeth (William) of Audrain Co.   Elder John O. White

TURNER, Samuel D.   5 Nov   L.G. Berry Esq.   COWS 13 Nov 1863
TUCKER, Frances (W.W.) "both of Boone Co."

TURNER, Thomas T. of St. Louis   10 Oct at Baltimore   MORE 18 & 22
BROWN, Harriet S. of Nashville (dau/Mrs. General Ewell) Archbish. Spalding   Oct 1865

TURNER, W.J.   25 Apr   MORE 30 Apr 1865
COCHRAN, Medor (James)   Rev. Dr. Boyle

TURNER, William   6 Jan   Rev. Beebee   GLWT 20 Jan 1853
BUTLER, Martha V. (Hon. N.)   "all of Chariton Co."

TURNER, William of Glasgow   23 Feb in Fayette   MORE 5 Mar 1865
SEBREE, Lucy (J.P.) of Fayette   Rev. J.A. Quarles

TURNER, William N. of Macon City   2 May   Pres. J.K. Rogers   COWS 6 May 1859
HOPPER, Mollie of Bourbon Co. KY

TUTT, D.G.   14 Mar   Rev. W.G. Bell   GLWT 25 Mar 1852
SMITH, Jessie C.)Judge C.H.) "all of Boonville"

TUTT, Thomas E. of St. Louis   in Richland, Boone Co., 4 Dec   MORE 10 Dec 1855
BENNETT, Sallie Rollins (Dr. James H.) of Columbia   Rev. Terry

TUTTLE, Samuel M. of Boone Co.   27 Nov   HANT 13 Dec 1856
BASS, Sallie (G.W.) of Howard Co.

TUTTLE, Thomas G.   19 Jun   Elder Thompson   MORE 2 Jul 1855
LOWRY, Gilly (James S.)   "all of Boone Co."

TWOMBLEY, Benjamin H.   Sunday last in Jackson   MORE 2 Nov 1855
BUNYIN, Mrs. Augusta B., late of Auburn NY   Rev. D.Z. Smith

UBSDELL, John A. Jr.   17 Nov in New York   MORE 24 Jan 1865
EADS, Genevieve (eldest dau/James B.) of St. Louis   Rev. Wm. F. Morgan

ULMAN, W.F. of St. Louis   17 Feb, Church of the Unity, Boston   MORE 24 Feb 1863
ADAMS, Lizzie (Isaac)   Rev. E.H. Sears

ULRICI, Rudolph of St. Louis   17 May in Winchester VA   MORE 27 May 1854
HAM, Georgetta Jacqueline   Rev. A.H.H. Bond

UNDERWOOD, Benjamin   18 Feb   Rev. George Rice   HANT 22 Feb 1853
WOLFE, Louisiana (Henry C.) of Lick Creek, Ralls Co.

UNDERWOOD, Drury of Virginia City, Idaho Territory 22 Dec   MORE 25 Dec 1863
LINK, Lou J. (C.) of St. Louis Co.   Rev. J. Hickman

UPTON, William L., formerly of the Louisiana Herald Warrensburg   MORE 16 Sep 1858
WILLIAMS, Kate (Rev. A.P.)   Rev. G.W. Johnson, Methodist Church

URBAN, Dom. formerly of Mulhausen France 19 Jun Justice Heckenrath   MORE 22 Jun 1856
KLAUSER, Carolene formerly of New York "both now of St. Louis"

UTTERBACK, I.T. of St. Louis   11 Nov   Episcopal Church   COWS 26 Nov 1858
PERRY, Hannah (R.D.) of Boonville   Rev. Giddings

UTTERBACK, J.T. of St. Louis   8 Nov in Howard Co.   MORE 17 Nov 1865
TURNER, Abbie (youngest dau/late Tarlton)   Rev. Schuyler

URZ, James   last Saturday, Salt Pond Twp., Saline Co. WAVE 17 Nov 1860
ERWIN, Ann M. (William B.)   Rev. G.M. Compton

VAN COURT, J.B. of St. Louis   17 Jan in New York   Rev. Sprigg   MORE 4 Feb 1853
MITTNACHT, Amelia (George H.) of Baltimore

VANDERFORD, Charles F. of St. Louis   16 Dec   Rev. R.B.C. Howell   MORE 25 Dec 1858
ANDERSON, Florence (H.I.) of Nashville

VANDERFORD, James D. of St. Louis   29 Oct in Boonville Rev. S.J. Anderson   MORE 31 Oct 1863
SMITH, Anna M. (Judge Charles H.) of Boonville Philadelphia & Nashville pc

VANLANDINGHAM, John   12 Aug   Rev. R.R. Price   COWS 20 Aug 1858
RICE, Mary (Wesley)   "all of Boone Co."

66

VANLANDINGHAM, William   13 Dec in Boone Co.   MORE 8 Jan 1856
BATTERTON, Lizze (John)   Rev. J.B. Watson

VAN NOSTRAND, J.   3 Nov   Congregational Church   MORE 5 Nov 1863
POST, Frances H. (Rev. T.M., who officiated)

VASSE, Dr. W.W.   4 Nov   Rev. D.H. Roots   MORE 9 Nov 1863
LOWRY, Mary (eldest dau/Thomas G.) "all of Randolph Co."

VAUGHAN, George H. of Osceola   11 Dec in Amherst Co. VA   OVAS 3 Jan 1861
BROWN, Mollie H., at her mother's home   Rev. John E. Edwards

VAUGHN, S.C.   15 Sep in Springfield   COWS 15 Oct 1858
DADE, Julia (Judge John)   Rev. Charles Carlton

VEITCH, Isaac M. of St. Louis   11 Sep at Newburgh NJ   MORE 17 Sep 1854
DU BOIS, Sarah of New York City   Rev. R.R. Veitch of Baltimore

VEMER, Paul   12 Dec near Rockbridge Mills   MORE 19 Dec 1854
MARTIN, Sarah G. (Amos) "all of Boone Co."

VIA, William W.   19 Jul   Rev. James Watson   COWS 24 Jul 1857
FORSHEY, Nannie (John)   "all of Boone Co."

VILIE, Alexander, late of Keokuk   24 Nov in Hannibal   HANT 27 Nov 1858
BUCHANAN, E. Fannie (youngest dau/Robert)

VIVION, Irvin C. of Boone Co.   24 Jan   Rev. F.A. Savage   COWS 3 Feb 1865
WALLACE, Mollie A. (Robert) of Callaway Co.

VON PHUL, Henry Jr. of St. Louis   12 Jan in Baton Rouge   MORE 4 Feb 1859
DAIGRE, Mary E. (Gilbert) of E. Baton Rouge   Rev. Hubert

VOORHEES, Capt. T.K. of St. Louis   28 Jul in Cincinnati   MORE 2 Aug 1857
GIBBONS, Mollie E. of Cincinnati   Rev. Yourtree

VOORHIES, Cornelius   21 Oct, North Presbyterian Church   MORE 24 Oct 1858
HULL, Lou B. (Joseph S.)   Rev. Parks

VOORHIES, George of St. Louis   12 Oct in Brownsville PA   MORE 23 Oct 1865
FINLEY, Mary of Brownsville   Rev. G. Dunlap

VUCHER, Auguste of St. Louis   12 Aug, New York, St. Vincent de Paul MORE 16 Aug 1860
LUTZ, Marie of Phalsburg FRA   Fr. Gamberville

WADE, G.W. of St. Louis   29 Jan in Washington Co. PA   MORE 3 Feb 1857
BROWN, Annie E. of Washington Co.   Rev. Alex McCar---

WADE, Robert of Callaway Co.   Elder E.E. Chrisman   COWS 4 Dec 1857
MOURNING, Emily Jane (Daniel) of Boone Co.

WALDEN, Lewis F., a printer   2 Nov   HANT 3 Nov 1853
COFFMAN, Kate (Jacob)   Rev. James W. Phillips

WALKER, Anthony of Cooper Co.   13 Sep   COWS 16 Sep 1859
BRANHAM, Laura (late Richard C.)   Elder J.T.M. Johnston

WALKER, Capt Benjamin   17 Feb   MORE 20 Feb 1859
McGUNNEGLE, Lizzie S. (George G.)   Rev. Montgomery Schuyler

WALKER, Edward G.   24 Jan   MORE 1 Feb 1860
HOPE, Mattie (J.R.) of Jackson, Cape Girardeau Co.

WALKER, John   13 Apr   Rev. T.N. Gaines   GLWT 15 Apr 1852
ROBINSON, Eliza (Gerrard) "all of Howard Co."

WALKER, John C. of Palmyra   7 Jun   HANT 13 Jun 1857
FARRICE, Mary Jane (William D.) of Marion Co.

WALKER, Leonidas D. of St. Louis   16 Feb in Charleston SC   MORE 28 Feb 1851
TURNBULL, Elizabeth C. (Andrew)   Rev. Paul Keith

WALKER, Willis C.   9 Aug in St. Louis   MORE 10 Aug 1860
WATSON, Russilla (late James S.)   Rev. James A. Page

WALL, J.F.   6 Sep   Rev. Benjamin Goodwin   COWS 30 Sep 1859
WOOLFORK, Bettie (C.F.) formerly of Boone Co.

WALLACE, Clarence of St. Louis   3 Nov   Justice John M. Young   MORE 6 Nov 1864
SHULL, Sarah of Philadelphia

WALLACE, H.C. of Lexington   4 Jun in Weston   Rev. E.S. Dulin   COWS 19 Jun 1863
SHARP, Lizzie (late Abraham) of Christian Co. KY

WALLACE, William of Cooper Co.   29 Aug   COWS 7 Sep 1855
SWITZLER, Frances Jane (Simeon) of Howard Co.   Rev. John C. Henning

WALLACE, William Cyrus of Sacramento City CA   Thursday last   LEXP 7 Dec 1853
EWING, Mary B. (Col. Thompson) "of this county"   Rev. C.A. Davis

WALLACH, Richard   3 Apr   MORE 11 Apr 1856
BROWN, Rosa (Marshall)   Rev. Cummings

WALLER, John E.   18 Feb   Rev. Green Cary   COWS 26 Mar 1858
TOALSON, Polly (Fountain) "all of Boone Co."

WANN, John   5 Jan in Christ Church   MORE 6 Jan 1860
STETTINIUS, Bertha (youngest dau/Joseph)   Rev. Schuyler

WALTON, Robert D.   23 Aug in St. George's Church   COWS 9 Sep 1859
COPHIER, Adelia Helen (George) of Lincoln Co.   Rev. D.T. Sherman

WARD, Thomas   3 Sep in Howard Co.   COWS 18 Sep 1857
TALBOT, Alice (Dr. John A.)

WARD, William J.   23 Apr   Rev. C. Jeter   MORE 29 Apr 1851
DONELLY, Alice, formerly of Louisville

WARE, E.H.   14 Aug in Warsaw   BOL 21 Aug 1858
HENRY, A.B. (eldest dau/Capt. R.C.)   Rev. J.V. Barks

WARFIELD, Ben, of Fayette   17 Dec in Louisville   MORE 22 Dec 1857
COCHRAN, Eliza (late John O.)   Rev. Whittle

WARNE, Charles G.   22 Feb   Rev. William Hendrickson   MORE 25 Feb 1860
BUREN, Sallie E. (P.H.) "all of Jefferson Co."

WARREN, Daniel   yesterday at St. Patrick's Church, Fr Ziegler   MORE 29 Aug 1865
MURPHY, Mary (D.B.)   "all of St. Louis"

WARREN, Dr. J.S. of Lafayette Co.   in Dover by Elder John W. McGarvey   COWS 10 Jun 1859
WARREN, Anne E. (J.) formerly of St. Louis, now of New Orleans
             "at the home of her uncle G.B. Warren in Dover"

WARRENSTAFF, Col. John   11 Oct in Richmond   WAVE 29 Oct 1859
AKERS, Mary L. (John)

WASH, Philip T.   22 Dec   LANA 24 Dec 1859
TAYLOR, Elizabeth N. (Samuel K.)   Rev. G.K. Taylor

WASH, Thomas   21 Nov   MORE 24 Nov 1854
BETTS, Isabella (Robert)   Rev. A. Dasham

WATERS, Israel, eldest son/late Capt. G.W.   at Peach Orchard Grove in   MORE 27 Oct 1855
JOHNSTON, Sarah (Benjamin)Rev. J.N. Gilbreath / Jefferson Co.

WATERS, Louis K.   Windsor Harbor, Jefferson Co.   MORE 16 Apr 1857
JOHNSTON, Moriah (Benjamin)   Rev. Galbreath(Gilbreath?)

WATSON, John Christy   29 May in St. Charles   SLMD 7 Jun 1858
PATTERSON, Jennie M. (S.D.) of St. Charles   Rev. Calhoun

WATSON, John (R.D.) of St. Louis   31 Dec in Sacramento   MORE 3 Mar 1852
BROWN, Isidora Ritter (Dr. B.B.)

WATSON, John W. of Columbia   20 Oct   COWS 30 Oct 1863
STAPLES, Fannie (James M.) of Brunswick   Rev. Starr

WAUGH, William A.   2 Feb near Bowling Green, Pike Co.   LAJ 19 Feb 1863
HODGES, Mary (2nd dau/Dr. George) "all of Pike Co." Elder J.M. Johnson

WAY, J. Clark of St. Louis   27 Jun in Ironton Rev. James Oakley MORE 29 Jun 1865
DUNYER, Fannie (Joseph, at his home)   Philadelphia pc

WEBSTER, Francis O. St. Louis   8 Dec at Trinity Church   MORE 9 Dec 1864
WASHINGTON, Mrs. Caroline M. of Newbern NC   Rev. E.C. Hutchinson

WEED, Frederick of St. Louis   4 May in Springfield OH   MORE 13 May 1856
HARRISON, Amanda J.   Rev. J. Sutherland

WEIR, William C. of St. Louis   3 Nov in Nashville   MORE 9 Nov 1864
HILL, Sallie M.   Rev. B.C. Howell

WELCH, John K. of Savannah MO   8 Apr in Louisville Rev. James Hill MORE 15 Apr 1851
FISHER, Mrs. Elizabeth D. of Jeffersonville IA

WELLER, Rev. R.H., Diocese of MO   24 Jul, Christ Church, Collinsville IL   JINQ 2 Aug 1851
LOOK, Emma Amanda (Horace)   Rev. Darrow

WELLER, W.W.   15 Dec   MARD 24 Dec 1858
JOHNSON, Philena (Berryman and Theresa) of Saline Co.

WELLS, George W. of Westport   8 Apr in Cincinnati   MORE 16 Apr 1857
MILLER, Lizzie of Cincinnati   Rev. W.M. Marsh

WELLS, Henry C.   5 Mar   MORE 12 Mar 1856
DYER, Emily H. (late Thomas) of Callaway Co.   Rev. W.W. Robertson

WELLS, John G.   18 Jan, Trinity Church   MORE 25 Jan 1865
GARRISON, Anna (eldest dau/Oliver) "all of St. Louis" Rev. E.C. Hutcheson

WELLS, Thomas of Troy   11 Mar   COSE 25 Mar 1852
SHELTON, Martha (Judge) of Lincoln Co.   Elder T.J. Wright

WENDOM, James G.   15 Nov in Christ Church   MORE 27 Nov 1863
MORGAN, Sallie J. (Col. Wyames) "all of St. Louis" Rev. Schuyler
            Poughkeepsie, New York & Chicago pc

WENGLER, O.G., a merchant in Union   Rev. John H. Thompson   MORE 10 Dec 1857
MEALER, Virginia S. (James A.) of Franklin Co.

WENTWORTH, Robert S.   28 Sep in St. Malachi's   Fr. Tobyn   MORE 30 Sep 1865
DUMAINE, Letitia Louise (Lucien)   "all of St. Louis"

WERNECK, Dr. O.H. of Palmyra   22 Dec in Memphis, Rev. Miller of the   PALS 13 Jan 1865
BYWATER, Laura at her father's home   (of Auburn NY?)   /Baptist Ch.

WEST, Erastus H. of Audrain Co.   24 Oct in Ralls Co.   HANT 27 Oct 1855
FINLEY, Mahala (Warren) of Ralls Co.

WEST, William   19 Mar in Clinton   COWS 10 Apr 1857
GORDON, Ellen (Presley) of St. Joseph

WESTLAKE, Leonidas H. of Virginia 12 Apr in St. Louis Fr. Coghlan   MORE 23 Apr 1865
LEE, Kate Marie) only dau/late Col. Stephen of Hannibal

WETMORE, E.F. of Versailles   (23 Jan?)   COWS 23 Feb 1855
BENNETT, Lucy of Lexington KY

WETZELL, Z.F. of St. Louis   15 Feb in Lexington KY   MORE 24 Feb 1853
BELL, Mary H.

WHALEY, Oliver of Marion Co.   20 Jan   HANT 25 Jan 1859
MADDOX, Sue (William) of Ralls Co.

WHEATLEY, Wilkins of St. Louis   28 Nov near Bowling Green KY   MORE 3 Dec 1854
HENRY, Gabrielle Flournoy at the home of W.L. Underwood Rev. Barbour

WHEELER, J.J.   8 Dec in Edina, Knox Co.   PWH 5 Jan 1854
HOLLINGSWORTH, Mary M. (George D.)   Rev. E.K. Miller

WHEELER, William O. of St. Louis   12 Feb, St. Xavier's Church   MORE 19 Feb 1857
HIGGINS, Mary A. of Cincinnati

WHITAKER, Dr. Benjamin   29 Jul   HANT 11 Aug 1857
TODD, Bettie A. (F.C.) "all of Pike Co."

WHITAKER, Charles H., Editor of the Missouri Plaindealer 14 Mar   COWS 29 Mar 1861
SELECMAN, Lizzie (Samuel) "all of Andrew Co."   Rev. S.M. Cope

WHITE, C.E.   20 Feb   Rev. Staples MORE 21 Feb 1861
FULTON, Lizzie (Capt. W.H., at his home)

WHITE, Cornelius D.   22 Dec at Long Prairie   CHAC 6 Jan 1860
RUSSELL, Hester Ann (Joseph T.)   Rev. English

WHITE, Rufus C. of the Trenton Pioneer 4 Jul at St. Aubert   GLWT 14 Jul 1853
ROBIOU, Virginia (L.)   Rev. W.M. Robertson

WHITE, Thomas S.   4 Oct in Potosi   MORE 10 Oct 1855
McILVAINE, Lucinda J. (oldest dau/Gen. J.H.) Rev. John H. Cowan

WHITE, William   21 Sep in Boone Co.   MORE 10 Oct 1854
BALLENGER, Martha (Elijah)   Elder B. Wren

WHITE, William S. of Montgomery Co. 20 Oct near Louisville, Lincoln Co.   LAJ 7 Nov 1863
HAISLIP, Sallie M. (youngest dau/late R.W.)   Elder J.J. Errett

WHITELY, T.J.   10 Jan in St. Louis   MORE 11 Jan 1855
ANDERSON, Sarah B. (Alex M.)   Rev. William G. Elliott

WHITLEDGE, Ralph J. of St. Louis   29 Nov in Exeter IL   MORE 1 Dec 1864
GILLETT, Fannie (Capt. D.O.) of Exeter   Rev. W.B. Davis

WHITMORE, D.R. of St. Louis   2 Nov, 1st Congregational Ch., Quincy   MORE 5 Nov 1865
STOBIE, Mary of Quincy   Rev. S.H. Emery

WHITSON, B.M.   7 Feb in St. Louis Rev. J.N. Gilbreath MORE 9 Feb 1865
OWEN, Elizabeth H. (A.H. and Sarah Ann) of Tipton Co. TN

WHITTLE, Thomas of Columbia   5 Oct by Elder T.M. Allen   COWS 9 Oct 1857
HIDEN, Mary Frances (John A.) of Boone Co.

WIGHTMAN, William of St. Louis at Flisberwick Place Church, Belfast 18 Oct   MORE 8 Nov 1859
SIMPSON, Mary Ann (eldest dau/late James) of Aughenacloy IRE   Rev. Morgan

WILCOX, Lafayette   12 Feb in Bolivar   BOL 18 Feb 1860
HUNTER, Mary E. (William B.)   Rev. Joseph R. Callaway

WILCOXSON, Samuel   6 Jul in Boonville   COWS 11 Jul 1856
PEAKE, Eliza J. (Joseph)   Elder B. Wren

WILEY, Abraham   21 Jan in Henry Co.   COWS 26 Feb 1858
WOOLFOLK, Angeline (C.T.)   Rev. W.P. C. Caldwell

WILFREY, John of Monroe Co.   23 Mar   COWS 10 Apr 1857
SMITH, Minerva (William) of Boone Co.   Elder Doyle

WILHITE, William   30 Jan   M.A. Via   COWS 2 Mar 1855
ELLIOTT, Catherine (Epps) "all of Boone Co."

WILKERSON, Dr. Achilles   18 May   Rev. W.W. Robertson   COWS 26 May 1865
BAKER, Lou (Martin) "all of Callaway Co."

WILKERSON, V.B., late Deputy Sheriff of Buchanan Co. 2? Mar   SJH 25 Mar 1865
MILLER, Mildred A. (Isaac)   Rev. T.W. Barrett

WILKES, Rev. D.B. of Hannibal   SLMD 14 Feb 1854
BRYAN, Rebecca (Lewis) of Palmyra

WILKINSON, Felix K. of St. Louis   17 May at St. Mary of the Barrens   MORE 29 May 1859
SHELBY, Matilda M. (Dr. R.) of Perryville   Rev. Fr. O'Keefe

WILL, Capt. Fred of the State Militia 4 Sep Hopewell Furnace, Washington Co. MORE 13 Sep 1862
THOMPSON, Mrs. Betty S. (John Evans, at his home)   Rev. T.S. Love

WILLIAMS, Alfred of Howard Co.   12 Jun   Elder T.M. Allen   MORE 17 Jun 1855
ROBINSON, Sarah Ann (late George) formerly of Carlyle KY

WILLIAMS, George L.D. of Trenton 9 Sep in Chillicothe   GLWT 22 Sep 1853
GRAHAM, Louisa (J.) of Chillicothe   Rev. Wiley Clark

WILLIAMS, Rev. John T.   15 Jun   PWH 22 Jun 1854
MOORE, Augusta G. (Perry B.)   Elder J.S. Green

WILLIAMS, Rev. J.T.   13 Nov   HANT 22 Nov 1856
CARSON, Maria L. Lafon (Hon. William) "all of Marion Co."

WILLIAMS, Dr. W.C. of Maramec Iron Works at Oakhill near Chillicothe OH   MORE 14 May 1857
DUN, Elizabeth (George W.) of Oakhill

WILLIAMSON, A. of Newton Co.   8 Aug   Rev. William Perkins   MORE 20 Aug 1855
BOWEN, Harriet H. (late Michael Switzler) of Brunswick

WILLIAMSON, E.J.   15 Oct   Rev. E.T. Berkley   SLMD 22 Oct 1861
MORGAN, Maria Louisa (B.T.C.) formerly of Pittsburgh

WILLS, E.A. of Callaway Co.   Elder T.M. Allen   MORE 22 Sep 1854
RIDGWAY, Eliza (John D.) of Boone Co.

WILLS, Edward D. of St. Louis   21 Jun   Rev. S.T. Anderson   MORE 28 Jun 1864
McFARLAND, Cinthia J. (Judge J.S.) of Boonville

WILLIS, Lee Jr.   14 Feb   Rev. A.C. Goodchild   MORE 2 Mar 1859
CAMPBELL, Sarah Thomas (Jidge D.W.) "all of Monroe Co."

WILSON, Andrew J.   12 Feb   LIT 27 Feb 1863
COLLINS, Martha A. (Simeon)   Squire D.J. Adkins

WILSON, B.S.   20 Dec in Cooper Co.   MORE 8 Jan 1856
BAIRD, Harriet (Capt. W.E.)   Rev. H.M. Painter

WILSON, C.J.F. of St. Louis   in Shawneetown IL   MORE 20 Jan 1856
WILSON, Lucy of Union Co. KY   Rev. Ferree of KY

WILSON, D.B. of St. Louis   11 Aug, Christ Church (Episcopal)   MORE 12 Aug 1859
SHEARER, Helen E. (Sextus) of San Francisco   Rev. Schuyler

WILSON, Daniel A. of Holt Co.   9 Feb   Joel Blair Esq.   STGAZ 1 Mar 1854
LEASE, Lyda E. (Jeremiah and Mahala) of Buchanan Co.

WILSON, Henry of St. Louis   18 Jan at Castleton VT   MORE 24 Feb 1861
LANGDON, Elizabeth Champion (B.F.) of Castleton Rev. Willard Child

WILSON, James A., a proprietor of the Columbia Sentinel in Prairieville,   COSE 14 Oct 1852
BARNETT, Mary E. (Wm. B.) of Prairieville / Pike Co. 7 Oct Rev Berryman

WILSON, James F.   30 Sep in Callaway Co.   COSE 28 Oct 1852
CALISON, Sallie (William)   Rev. T. Scott

WILSON, Steward   15 Aug   Rev. S. Scott   COWS 24 Aug 1855
WOODS, Mary Ann (William) "all of Audrain Co."

WILSON, Sylvester   22 Jul   Rev. Page   MORE 26 Jul 1857
McCAUL, Emma (C.W.) "all of St. Louis"

WILSON, Walter W. of Columbia   Tuesday last Rev. T.M. Allen   COSE 27 Jan 1852
JENKINS, Carrie A. (Theodorick) of Boone Co.

WILSON, William B.   6 Aug   GAL 17 Aug 1865
HARDIN, Lavina H. (Rev. J.H.)   John W. Coffy, Esq.

WILSON, William C.   20 Dec, 1st Presbyterian Church   MORE 22 Dec 1855
WEAVER, Mrs. Eliza A. (only dau/James Adams)   Rev. McPheeters

WINCHELL, Joseph R.   2 Sep in Palmyra   HANT 12 Sep 1857
LAFON, Kate A. (Dr. Joseph) "all of Palmyra"

WINENT, William   24 Jan   Theodore Boulware   MORE 12 Feb 1856
WATTS, Anne (Joseph)   "all of Audrain Co."

WINES, Rev. Frederick Howard, former Chaplain at the Springfield MO Post   MORE 3 Apr 1865
HACKNEY, Mary Frances (Mrs. Mary B.) of Springfield
          21 Mar at Norristown PA by Rev. J.G. Ralston

WINN, Thomas C. of Canton   at Locust Ridge 2 Oct   COWS 9 Oct 1857
SEBASTIAN, Meekie (E.C.) of St. Francois Co.

WINN, William R. of Portland MO   MORE 16 Dec 1856
GLOVER, Mary J. of Montgomery Co.

WINSOR, Arnold T. of Colorado Territory 17 Sep at Lexington MO   MORE 22 Sep 1863
WALTON, Mary (Col. W.P.) of Lexington   Rev. McFarland
               Nashville & Baltimore pc

WINSTON, G.B.   8 Sep in Jefferson City   JINQ 17 Sep 1853
HOUGH, Sallie (George W.) "all of Jefferson City" Rev. T.M. Finney, Episc. Ch.

WINTON, Rev. G.M.   17 May   Rev. David Ross   MORE 30 May 1855
LUSK, Mrs. Amanda S. (Col. James Faulkner) "all of Greene Co."

WISELY, Dr. Leonard A.   24 Jun   Rev. O.W. Reck   MORE 28 Jun 1863
BASS, Mary F. (late George P.)   "all of Howard Co."

WISENER, John H. of Greene Co.   5 Dec   MORE 21 Dec 1854
VAUGHN, Mary F. (James) of Taney Co.   Rev. Y.A. Anderson

WISER, P.E.   "at the home of the bride's uncle, A.S. Merritt, on St. Ange"   MORE 4 Jan 1865
MAXFIELD, Belle of Sonora OH   1 Jan   Rev. Cox

WISHON, Frank   "at the residence of Dr. R. Cowan, Edgar Prairie"   MORE 28 Jun 1861
LENOX, Sue B. (only dau/Wilson) of Iberia MO

WITHERS, George W.   29 Oct in Weston   LIT 6 Nov 1857
NEWMAN, Mollie Ella (William A.)   Rev. J.B. Wright

WITHINTON, Charles H.   14 Oct   MORE 15 Nov 1859
KENNEDY, Sallie M. (Henry)   Dr. James H. Brooks

WITTEN, Samuel K.   near Edinburg 6 Aug   MORE 8 Aug 1854
BROWN, Mary Frances (A.D.) of Carroll Co.   Rev. R. Mitchell

WOLF, Thomas   5 Mar   COWS 13 Mar 1857
LAMPTON, Louisa Margaret (James)   Elder Chrisman

WOLLNER, J.F.   26 Mar Elder L.B. Wilkes   HAM 3 Apr 1862
FUQUA, Sue E. (late Nathaniel) "all of Hannibal"   Louisville pc

WONDELL, A.C.   18 Oct   MORE 19 Oct 1854
DOWLER, Margaret (T.)

WOOD, John W.   6 Sep at Linden, Atchison Co.   MORE 13 Sep 1859
HOPKINS, Annie E. (N.C.)   Rev. E. Finley

WOOD, William E. of Commerce MO   17 Jul   MORE 25 Jul 1860
WALKER, Sarah (late Hon. J.C.) of Cape Girardeau   Rev. J.C. Maple

WOOD, W.D., merchant of St. Louis   21 Jan in Otsego NY   MORE 11 Feb 1851
FOLLETT, Mary (eldest dau/James)   Rev. Wakeman

WOODS, D. Waldo of St. Louis at the home of Col. H.H.M. Williams in   MORE 24 Apr 1861
SPEARS, Eliza J. of Pocahontas AR   /Jackson, Cape Girardeau Co.
          by Rev. J.C. Maples

WOODS, David at the home of the bride's father near Fee Fee 5 Jan   MORE 7 Jan 1865
BRUSTER, Eliza A. (Simon) "all of St. Louis"   Rev. Joshua Heckman

WOODS, James   Thursday week   Rev. Wiley Clark   GLWT 8 Jul 1852
HUTCHISON, Sophia Jane (eldest dau/William) "all of Livingston Co."

WOODS, James B., 1st clerk of the Martha Jewett at Buffalo Knobs 18 Nov   GLWT 9 Dec 1852
GOOD, Sarah A. (Maj. John)   (from the Pike Co. Record)

WOODS, Oliver B.   10 Sep   PALS 18 Sep 1863
ANDERSON, Anna Maria (William C.)   Rev. N.G. Berryman

WOODSON, George of Monroe Co.   23 Dec 1855   RANC 10 Jan 1856
JACKSON, Iantha (Capt. Hancock) of Randolph Co.

WOODSON, William B.   24 Jul   Rev. Samuel C. Davis   GLWT 31 Jul 1851
LOCKRIDGE, Martha C. (Capt. William) "all of Randolph Co."

WOODSON, William L. of Platte City 30 Apr   Rev. G.L. Moad   MORE 9 May 1864
WINSTON, Cora A. (Col. John H.) of Platte Co.

WOOLDRIDGE, Powhatan Jr. of St. Louis   28 Nov in Newbern NC   MORE 8 Dec 1860
WASHINGTON, Annie M. (only dau/late William H.)   Rev. Alf Watson

WOOLEY, James H.   27 Mar in Montgomery Co.   MORE 11 Apr 1861
HAMPTON, Malinda M. at her father's home   Rev. S.P. Longhead

WOOLFOLK, James   5 Apr in Cooper Co.   WAVE 14 Apr 1860
LIONBERGER, Belle (Isaac)   Rev. X.X. Buckner

WOOLSEY, George W.   14 Oct in Atchison Co.   SAS 23 Oct 1852
WOOLSEY, Mary Caroline (Gilbert)   Rev. Elias Findly

WORLEY, Caleb Thompson of Cass Co. 4 Dec Elder T.M. Allen   MORE 11 Dec 1855
GARTH, Lizzie (Jefferson) of Fulton

WRIGHT, Allen   9 Jun in Independence   MORE 20 Jun 1856
SHELLEY, Fannie A. (George)   Rev. J.B. Wright

WRIGHT, Hale T.   13 Jun   Elder B. Wren   MORE 25 Jun 1855
LINDSEY, Mary E. (L.L.) "all of Boone Co."

WRIGHT, James W.   11 Sep in Chariton Co.   MORE 1 Oct 1855
AINSWORTH, Elvira (Iren)   Rev. F.A. Savage

WRIGHT, Leonidas E.   30 Nov   Elder T.M. Allen   COWS 8 Dec 1865
TURNER, Catherine E. (Barney) "all of Boone Co."

WRIGHT, Robert H.   2 Mar   MORE 15 Mar 1854
TIMBERLAKE, Mary (William) of Boone Co.   Rev. B.H. Spencer

WRIGHT, Wiley S.   17 Dec   Rev. Boyle   MORE 18 Dec 1863
MALIN, Nannie E. (Capt. John W.) "all of St, Louis"

WYMORE, William   8 Nov   LIT 30 Nov 1860
BAXTER, Ann (John)   President Thompson

XAUPI, E.J. Jr.   25 Jan in Jersey Co. IL   MORE 28 Feb 1863
LURTON, Henrietta L. at her mother's home

YAGER, John G.   Sunday last   LEXC 9 Jul 1856
WITHERS, Mary Kathener (only dau/M.W., Sheriff of Lafayette Co.)

YANCEY, Dr. A.L.   31 Mar   Rev. Mason   COWS 10 Apr 1863
MOSS, Margaret (Russel W.) "all of Shelby Co."

YANCY, Dr. Edward   1 Dec in Providence, Boone Co.   GLWT 15 Dec 1853
PARKER, Hettie W. (John) "both of Boone Co." Rev. P.M. Pinkard

YATES, George   1 Feb in Williamsburg, Callaway Co.   COWS 2 Mar 1855
KIDWELL, Rebecca E. (W.R.)

YINGLING, Washington   16 Mar in Lexington MO   SLMD 24 Mar 1858
TURNER, Isabella (Henry)   Rev. B.M. Hobson

YORE, John E.   7 Jul, Immaculate Conception Ch.   MORE 11 Jul 1858
WALSH, Margaret L. (youngest dau/Joseph G. decd)   Bishop Duggan

YORE, William A.   18 Nov Immaculate Conception Ch.   MORE 22 Nov 1857
WALSH, Mary Frances (late Joseph F.)   Rev. Bannon

YOUNG, Col. Alton of St. Louis   29 Apr   GLWT 13 May 1852
EWING, Maria L. (Hon. R.A.) of Cole Co.   Rev. John G. Fackler

YOUNG, Archibald   14 Oct   Rev. William N. Newland   HAM 30 Oct 1859
HAYDEN, Amanda E. (James) "all of Marion Co."

YOUNG, B.   15 Jun   PWH 29 Jun 1854
BRYAN, M.M. *B.K.)   Rev. N. Ayres

```
YOUNG, Evan of Lafayette Co., late of KY        18 Jan              WAVE 7 Feb 1859
SHELBY, Adelaide (Thomas)                       Elder McGarvey

YOUNG, Lieut. Nelson D.   1 Nov at the home of G.S. Van Wagoner     MORE 6 Nov 1862
COHEN, Mary J. (granddaughter of Thomas)     Rev. Edward F. Berkley

YOUNG, Rufus                        25 Jun                          COWS 26 Jun 1857
BEATTIE, Caroline (William)                     Rev. Glenn

YOUNG, J.H. of St. Louis            4 Sep in Blandford MA           MORE 12 Sep 1853
WRIGHT, M.A. of Blandford                    Rev. Hinedale

YOUNG, John of Lincoln Co.          15 May                         MORE 20 May 1854
DUDLEY, Martha C. (Nicholas)                    Elder Thomas Wright

YOUNG, Thomas J. of Clay Co.        2 Nov in Shelbyville KY         LIT 24 Nov 1854
BEANE, Mrs. Susan of Shelbyville

YOUNGBLOOD, Dr. J.M. of Tennessee  6 Jul Immaculate Conception Church   MORE 10 Jul 1863
XAUPI, Volumnia Orso (E.J. of St. Louis Co.)    Rev. Feehan

YOUNGER, John C.                    26 Feb        Rev. R.P. Holt    COSE 11 Mar 1852
ANGEL, Martha Jane (Robert) "all of Boone Co."


ZEISS, C.C.                         10 Feb                          MORE 12 Feb 1860
DREYER, Helen (G.W.)                            Rev. Wall

ZOLLER, Bernhard                         Sunday                     HANT 1 Dec 1857
BAUM, Lizzie (Henry)      "all of Palmyra"
```

/ - /

ABERNATHY, Zerelda B. - Thomas MANEUL
ADAIR, Eliza - Joseph JAMES
ADAMS, Anna E. - Chauncey J. FILLER
 Hannah A. - Morris COLLINS
 Lizzie - W.F. ULMAN
 Pauline - C. P. RAWLINGS
 Susan J. - John C. THOMPSON
ADKINS, Eliza - William B. EDWARDS
AHERN, Elizabeth - Oliver T. BRAGG
AINSWORTH, Elvira - James W. WRIGHT
ALBRIGHT, Eliza - J. L. DITTO
ALCARN, Celia - Benjamin CHANCY
AKERS, Mary L. - Col. John WARRENSTAFF
ALDEN, Maggie - J. H. HOLMAN
ALEXANDER, Elizabeth - James FORD
 Octavia - Addison HARDCASTLE
ALLEGA, Nancy - William L. BIXBY
ALLEN, Anna - Henry SLACK
 Mary D. - William B. PARKER
 Mary Ann - Franklin W. PHILLIPS
 Nannie - Isaac STURGEON
ALLISON, R.S. - J. M. STEMMONS
ALMAND, Lou W. - William Clem PRICE
ALMOND, Bettie - Thomas PRICE
ALLSMAN, Sarah - Woodruff H. LEE
ANDERSON, Adelaide - Bazil DUKE
 Amanda Jane - Thomas S. EDWARDS
 Anna Maria - Oliver B. WOODS
 Florence - Charles F. VANDERFORD
 Kate - Thomas P. AKERS
 Lizzie - J. H. GIBSON
 Sarah B. - T. J. WHITELY
 Susan - R. S. MANN
ANDREWS, Annie - George R. ROBINSON
 Caroline M. - George M. HARDING
ANGELL, Catherine - Marshall HENDRON
 Martha Jane - John C. YOUNGER
 Julia Anna - James C. FAWKNER
ANTHONY, Fannie L. - George C. KERR
ARDINGER, Carrie D. - Dr. S. T. BASSETT
ARHOLD, Marium - Alexander GREENABAUM
ARMSTRONG, Mary - Charles ARMSTRONG
 Susie J. - F. L. McLEAN
ARNOLD, Minna - Moses BARTH
 Sallie - William P. HOOPER
 Sue - William G. McCAUSLAND
ARNOT, Annie L. - M. J. MURPHY
ARTHUR, Cordelia - D. S. MILLER
ASHBURY, Angeline - Tandy ELKIN
ASHCRAFT, Sallie A. - William P. GLOVER
ASMOND, Esther - H. Clay COCKERILL
ATWOOD, Anna - M. F. FISHER
 Carrie M. - R. S. CAVENDER
AUSTIN, Sally Ann - Johnson ROSE
AXTELL, Addie E. - Oscar P. BALDWIN

BACON, Mary E. - John J. CRUIKSHANK
BADGER, Althea - Dr. Benjamin J. MOORE
BAILY, Anna - John McAFEE
BAIRD, Harriet - B. S. WILSON
BAKER, Betty Ann - Philip HOOPER
 Clarissa Catherine -
  Jonathan ESTELL
 Eliza - A. P. EVANS
 Kitty - J. B. BROWN
 Lou - Dr. Achilles WILKERSON
 Louisa - John F. CREWS
 Martha S. - James MILLER
 Sallie P. - Cyrenius BARNES
BALDWIN, Elizabeth - O. P. GASH
 J. Ann - George CARLTON
 Mrs. Nannie - Thomas T. ARNOLD
 Sarah J. - Isaac N. GIBBONS

BALE, Catherine - John B. BROOKS
BALLENGER, Martha - William WHITE
 Martha - Richard SAPPINGTON
 Sarah A. - James H. RODDY
BANKS, Lizzie - C. M. TRIPLETT
BARCLAY, Fannie - D. A. SPRINKLE
BARLEY, Mary Margaret - L. D. SHORT
BARNES, Alice - William S. PULLINS
 Sarah - Abraham BARNES
BARNETT, Julia - John G. FRAZIER
BARNETT, Mary E. - James A WILSON or
  James A. MILAN
BARR, Cannie J. - F. B. FULENWIDER
 Sallie E. - E. J. STERLING
BARRET, Julia - Charles T. ALEXANDER
BARRETT, Sarah - Jasper J. SEARCY
BARROWS, Mary P. - John H. MOSSE
BARTLEY, Mary A. - S. S. NEWMAN
BASHAM, Hattie E. - Theodore G. MEIER
BASKETT, Elizabeth - George W. SMITH
BASS, Mary - John S. CLARK
 Mary F. - Dr. Leonard A. WISELY
 Sallie - Samuel M. TUTTLE
BASSETT, Mary B. - James H. BIRCH, Jr.
BASSET, Jane R. - Elijah G. BROADUS
BAST, Julia C. - William H. JACOBS
BASYE, Margaret - S. K. MILLER
 Sarah F. - C. J. CORWIN
BATES, Emma C. - Hudson C. CARKENER
 Martha E. - Dr. Edwin J. HAWKINS
 Mary C. - J. T. SHACKELFORD
BATTERTON, F. - J. F. PHILLIPS
 Lizze - William VANLANDINGHAM
BAUM, Lizzie - Bernhard ZOLLER
BAXTER, Ann - William WYMORE
 Elizabeth A. - John L. PICKENS
BAY, Sadie E. - Matthew V. L. McCLELLAND
BAYLESS, Mary Jane - Charles R. FIELD
BAYNE, Sally - Rev. James PENN
BEALE, Clara - Levin N. BAKER
BEANE, Mrs. Susan - Thomas J. YOUNG
BEARDSLEE, Hattie - D. E. GARRISON
BEARDSLEY, Flora Amelia - Charles S. CLARK
BEATTIE, Caroline - Rufus YOUNG
BEATTY, Marie E. - L. W. GANT
BEATUS, Henrietta - M. GOLDMAN
BEDFORD, Sallie - John William ROBINSON
BEEDING, America - Mason T. SUMMERS
BEHRENS, Joanna - Britton A. HILL
BELL, Louisa - Oliver P. GOODALL
 Mary H. - Z. F. WETZELL
 Sarah - John HOPPER
BELLAMY, Mollie E. - N. B. GIVENS
BEMPSON, Martha - Frederick STEEN
BENDLEY, Lydia - Charles DE SPADA
BENEDICT, Mary H. - John T. GALLAHER
BENIGHT, Mary - D. M. LA FORCE
BENNETT, Eliza Jane - Amos B. NICHOLS
 Emma - Leopold BOUVIER
 Lucy - E. F. WETMORE
 N. E. - Jonathan CREST
 Sallie Rollins - Thomas E. TUTT
BENT, Ellen - J. N. HANSON
BENTON, Hattie P. - T. W. STOUTENBURG
BENTZ, Mary H. - Lewis O. KNOTT
BERRY, Catherine - William GARTH
 Elizabeth - L. D. CAMPBELL
 Roxana - Wherry FORTNEY
BETTS, Isabella - Thomas WASH
BILLINGSLEY, M. Belle - Joseph S. NANSON
BINGHAM, Clara F. - Thomas B. KING
 Virginia - Hyman BLOCK

BIRCH, Sarah Catherine -
        Fitzhugh Carter FROST
BIRD, Catherine - Rev. J. C. THORNTON
    Mary - Benjamin F. HUNTER
BISHOP, Missouri - James P. MOORE
BLAIN, Mary Frances - H. S. TONES
BLAISDELL, Mrs. Mary E. - James DOYLE
BLAKEMAN, Kittie - Samuel H. BROWN
BLASDELL, Mary - Edwin W. BARR, M.D.
BLEDSOE, Sarah Frances - Cary TACK, Jr.
BLOCK, Delia M. - Joseph TANNER
    Mary - Mark SAMUELS
BLOID, Ruth Ann - Isaac BRADBURN
BLOOM, Mrs. Sarah - Arthur W. ELLIOTT
BLUE, Lizzie - Granville D. KENNEDY
BLUMENTHAL, Caroline E. - Ferdinand BROCH
    Dora - William G. PLASS
BODLEY, Euphemia B. H. - William T. ESSEX
BODTON, Mrs. Sarah - Addison REESE
BOGGS, Ann E. - William THACKSTON
    Fannie L. - C. Lester HAMM
    Mattie R. - Thomas K. McCUTCHAN
BOGY, Celeste - Eugene KARST
BOLTON, Josie - P. O'CONNOR
    Mollie - Lt. Rufus CHAMPION
BONIFACE, Hattie F. - William P. NASH
BONNER, Carah Catherine - Dr. James W. ROSS
BOON, Ann - Carter ADAMS
BOONE, Susan - Reason A. MOSS
BORDERBY, Bettie - Samuel J. COALE
BORRON, Florence Williford - William DOUGLAS
BOSS, Lizzie - Chauncey C. MAUPIN
BOSTWICK, Elizabeth B. - Dr. E. EASTERLY
BOSWELL, Josephine - Edward TICKNOR
BOULWARE, Elizabeth J. - Richard S. RUCKER
    Fannie - James COCKERILL
BOWEN, Harriet H. - A. WILLIAMSON
BOWER, Annie M. - Allen W. HAWKINS
    Laura S. - P. T. BOONE
    Sue M. - Thomas S. MILLER
BOWLES, Kate - Dr. William H. JOPES
BOWLIN, Jennie S. - M. C. JENKINS
BOWMAN, Anna Reed - John Kirk EARICKSON
BOYCE, Catherine - William L. ALLEN
BOYD, Anna B. - W. A. CUNNINGHAM
    Evaline - James RENOE
BOYLAN, Anna W. - W. H. HAGGERTY
BRADFORD, Kittie E. - Edwin W. PRICE
BRADLEY, Fannie - E. C. ST. CLAIR
    Lucretia A. - James S. STONE
BRAGG, Mary - Nathaniel RICHARDSON
BRANCH, Eliza - Joseph CROOKS
BRAND, Emily Austin - Arthur CLARKSON
BRANHAM, Laura - Anthony WALKER
    Mary W. - James W. CHORN
BRANNAN, Mary V. - J. E. JEWELL
BRASHEARS, Zarilda - George L. DICKSON
BRASHER, Mollie - M. G. TAYLOR
BRATTON, Sallie - Tiliman T. S. KEMPER
BRENNAN, Mary Ann - Thomas GRACE
BRENNEISEN, Louisa - Julius SOMBART
BRENT, Rosalie V. - Louis KUMM
BRERETON, Janie - John G. FOWLER
BRESH, Mrs. L. M. - Augustin MULLINS
BREWINGTON, Mary B. - Thomas B. COONTZ
BREWSTER, Susan - Charles COOK
BRIAN, Maria L. - O. W. LINDSEY
BRIDGES, Mary E. - Julian BAGBY
    Mary L. - William ALLEN
BRIGHT, Maggie A. - William T. BISHOP
    Mollie - William F. B. GRIGSBY
    Sarah - Dr. T. L. STEPHENS
BRISON, Mary Ellen - Edward MORTIMER

BROADDUS, Helen L. - Dr. James P. BECK
    Mary A. - Lewis C. HAGGARD
    Mary Ann - William C. JAMES
BROOKING, Julia - W. T. TAYLOR
BROOKS, Emma E. - Andrew HARVEY
    Josephine - Josiah FOGG
    Mary Miller - David MICKY
BROUGHTON, Adelia - John W. KIMBROUGH
BROWN, Miss - L. D. LINDSAY
    Alice - B. Frank McCORD
    Annie E. - G. W. WADE
    Christiana - Ezra CASTARPHEN
    Clarinda - James BRASHEARS
    Harriet - Oliver D. MATTHEWS
    Harriet S. - Thomas T. TURNER
    Ida R. - William J. GAMBRELL
    Isidora Ritter - John WATSON
    Lucinda Jane - Easton EARLEY
    Mary - Jesse L. HART
    Mary - Dr. James H. STIVERS
    Mary C. - James DENNIS
    Mary E. - Jacob B. MORROW
    Mary Frances - Samuel K. WITTEN
    Mollie H. - George H. VAUGHAN
    Rosa - Richard WALLACH
    S. E. - R. A. McCLURE
    Selina - Kenzie HEYDON
BROWNELL, Harriet L. - Joseph S. MULFORD
BROWNEWELL, Emma - Edwin P. DIEHL
BROWNLEE, Sarah J. - A. A. AUSTIN
BRUCE, Mollie - M. M. MARMADUKE, Jr.
BRUMBAUGH, Marietta - Charles FINK
BRUMFIELD, Caroline - Richard DOZIER
BRUSTER, Eliza A. - David WOODS
BRUTON, Sarah J. - James R. STEPHENSON
BRYAN, Annie - David H. HICKMAN
    M. M. - B. YOUNG
    Maria - J. H. OBEAR
    Mary - Sterling J. PRICE
    Rebecca - Rev. D. B. WILKES
    Sallie - William BAXTER
BRYANT, Lizzie L. - Samuel R. DYER
    Mary - Dr. Matthew W. CARTWRIGHT
BUCHANAN, E. Fannie - Alexander VILIE
    Julia - Henry T. CROSBY
    Nancy - Dr. Francis M. REYNOLDS
BUCK, Hannah - Horace SAUNDERS
BUCKINGHAM, Lizzie M. - George W. PURNELL
BUCKINS (BUCKIUS?), Annie - James S. ADAMS
BUCKLAND, Juliaette C. - Joseph W. CONE
    Mattie - William GUMM
BUCKNER, Pinkie - Claggett (Cleggett) OFFUT
    Sallie - Thomas P. BOTELER
    Sallie T. - William H. FINNEY
BULL, Julia - William BARTON
BULLARD, Eliza Jane - W. L. FRENCH
BULLITT, Ada - Dexter S. CROSBY
BULLOCK, Nannie M. - William P. HARRISON
    Sue M. - Rev. W. L. T. Evans
BUNTING, Elizabeth - Robert Stewart
BUNYIN, Mrs. Augusta B. - Benjamin H. TWOMBLEY
BURCH, Harriet - Absalom STEPHENS
BURDSALL, Mary E. - I. H. GEST
BUREN, Sallie E. (P. H.) - Charles G. WARNE
BURK, Mollie M. - Thomas M. SMITH
BURKE, Maggie L. - William D. DOUGHERTY
BURNHAM, Louise - James N. MORRIS
BURNES, Victoria - Charles L. ROGERS
BURTS, Martha Ann - George CROSS
BUSH, Nancy - Col. Walter L. LOVELACE
BUSHNELL, O. M. - A. H. McDANALD
BUTLER, Martha V. - William TURNER
BYRD, Mary Bruce - Jefferson RUSSELL

BYWATER, Laura - Dr. O. H. WERNECK
CALDWELL, Julia - Harrison HOWARD
      M. E. - James M. SMITH
CALISON, Sallie - James F. WILSON
CALLAGHAN, Catherine - Franz Alexander
                DRUESDAN
CALVERT, Locia H. - Lambert L. DOYLE
      Mary Belle - George L. SEAVER
CALVIN, Sarah - William H. CRAIN
CAMDEN, Sallie Ann - Dr. George S. CASE
CAMPBELL, Emily - W. J. BONEY
      Maggie K. - Joseph G. HICKMAN
      Mary Ann - Jackson THOMAS
      R. P. - William A. McPHAIL
      Sarah Thomas - Lee WILLIS, Jr.
CAPEN (COOPER?), Flavia C. - Albert E. HALL
CAPLINGER, Mary - Harvey HANCE
CARBIS, Maggie - Henry T. KERLIN
CARDWELL, Sue A. - Thomas DEPEW
CAREY, Mary Jane - Garrison PATRICK
CARPENTER, Anna E. - H. J. GALBRAITH
      Mary - Rev. Gary HICKMAN
CARRINGTON, Julian - Richard F. DAVIS
      Martha J. - E. J. BEARD
CARSON, Maria L. Lafon - Rev. J. T.
                WILLIAMS
      Sarah A. - Noah SIVIRHER
      Mary A. - Rev. William MODISET
CARTER, Catherine - N. FIELD
      Lizzie - John A. CASTLEMAN
      Mary C. - Greenberry JOHNSON
      Mary Ann Elizabeth - James M. CARTER
CARUTHERS, Margaret - John R. RICHARDS
CASH, Susan E. - James A. McMILLEN
CASON, Susan - Clifton TOOLEY
CASTERLINE, Ann Eliza - Alexander G. GREEK
CASTLEMAN, Catherine - Dr. John B. BELL
CATES, Edmonia H. - Dr. Thomas KENNARD
CATHRAE, Bettie McDowell - Col. T. P. BELL
CATT, Sarah - Charles BARLOW
CAUTHORN, Martha L. - Joseph D. MORRIS
CAVE, Susan - S. R. TRABUE
CHADWICK, Mary - Leander J. SHARP
CHAMBERLIN, Mrs. Ann Eliza - B. W. SHARP
      Flora B. - Lucius ABBOTT
CHAMBERLAIN, Maria L. - Lesley GARNETT
CHAMBERS, Lizzie - Edward Brodie HULL
      Mary - Arthur Oakland BANKHEAD
CHANDLER, Maria Louisa - Henry McPHERSON
CHANEY, Nary Ann - James Columbus POWER
CHAPMAN, Catherine - Joseph M. HARLOW
      Mrs. Mercy B. - Thomas MASON
CHAPPELL, Mary Susan - John MOORE
CHENIE, Julia - J. S? CABANNE
CHILDS, Isabel - Jonathan SHORTRIDGE
CHILES, Emma A. - Thomas B. KING
CHILTON, Mary Ella - John G. THORNTON
CHINN, Anna - Shelby KIRTLEY
      Malinda M. - Charles T. MURDOCK
      Mary - Christopher MULLER
CHITTENDEN, Julia M. - Charles D. AFFLECK
CHRISMAN, A. E. - G. R. KEILL
CHRISTIAN, Sarah E. - John F. DARR
CHRISTOPHER, Ellen J. - Alex C. CRAIG
CHURCH, Sue - James B. GOFF
CLAGETT, Mary - William PAYNE
      Russie - William J. JACKSON
CLAPP, Helen - Frank H. FLETCHER
CLARK, Annie - Joseph W. BRANCH
      Betty - J. H. GARNETT
      Elizabeth Jane - James C. JONES
      Hattie C. - Frederick HEARSUM

CLARK, Mary D. - L. BARNUM
      Mary E. - John H. RAMSEY
      Sophia - Fred H. HEARSUM
      Sue - Benjamin TOMPKINS
CLARKE, Mrs. C. M. - J. C. BARLOW
      Sarah J. - Thaddeus B. HATCHER
CLARKSON, Margaret - John R. LIONBERGER
CLATTERBUCK, Mary Elizabeth -
              Thomas F. GUTHRIE
      Nancy - A. LEOPARD
CLAY, Mildred - Capt. R. FISHER
CLENDENIN, Julia - W. C. BUTLER
CLEMENS, Pamela A. - William A. MOFFETT
CLEVELAND, Juliet M. - Dr. J. H. HERNDON
CLINTON, Esther - Michael J. MURPHY
      Maggie - William J. CANTWELL
CLOSE, Christina L. - Charles H. BURKLIN
CLUFF, Mrs. Martha J. - Rev. James S. GREEN
CLUSKEY, Mary E. - Stephen A. CROMWELL
COATES, Sarah - John ROBERTS
COATS, Catherine - Madison PAYNE
COBB, Mary W. - Rev. G. K. DUNLAP
COCHRAN, Amanda - William Elliott
      Amanda J. - G. N. SEARCY
      Anna - A. L. CUMMINGS
      Eliza - Ben WARFIELD
      Mary D. - W. H. McDANNOLD
      Medor - W. J. TURNER
COFFMAN, Kate - Lewis F. WALDEN
      Sarah - H. H. EVANS
COGSWELL, Anna M. - John COLLIER
      Isabela - Dr. Thomas MACKINNIS
COHEN, Mary J. - Lt. Nelson D. YOUNG
COLHOUN, Mary K. - William B. JOHNSON
COLLINS, Annette Isabel - Louis BROCKMAN
      Lida A. - Joseph HOBLITZELL
      Martha A. - Andrew J. WILSON
COLTON, Julia M. - William W. COMSTOCK
COLVIN, Nancy - John C. SAPP
CONDUIT, Virginia - Walter F. CHAPMAN
CONGER, Margaret E. - Henry C. BOGUE
CONLEY, Elizabeth - Reuben T. HUME
CONNELLY, Mary Ann - William B. HUNT
CONNER, Annie - Dr. J. N. COONS
CONRADT, Emily - J. B. DEAN
CONRAN, Julia - Capt. Richardson MONTGOMERY
CONSTABLE, Isabelle - Truman SKINNER
      Jennie - John W. GODFERY (sic)
CONWAY, Sarah Magdalen Gayle - John BRENNAN
COOK, Elizabeth L. - Samuel McDOWELL or
                McGOWEN
COONS, Mary A. - George H. DERBY
COOPER (CAPEN?), Flavia - Albert E. HALL
COOPER, Sallie - F. E. BRENT
      Lizzie - James F. TOWSON
COPHIER, Adelia Helen - Robert D. WALTON
COPPER, Mrs. (nee BISHOP) - H. S. BENEPE
CORDELL, Christine - James HARDING
      LLewella - Edward HARDIN
COREY, Mary Elle - Edward R. BATES
CORSE, Mattie - John W. MATTHEWS
COTIER, Ellen - J. B. RICORDS
COTTER, Mrs. Clarence E. - George PARTRIDGE
COTTON, Catherine - John DICKENSON
COUZINS, Adeline - Austin A. OWEN
COWDEN, Mag E. - G. W. TOALSON
COX, Mrs. Emma - Robert T. GAMBREL
COZENS, Lue - Joseph A. HULL
CRAIG, Mrs. - Thomas BRADLEY
      Clara - Samuel A. GARTH
      Pollie Ann - John P. MOSELEY
CRAWFORD, Catherine - Lee B. MANNING
CREARY, Mrs. Ann S. - P. B. FROST

CREWS, Mrs. Susan E. - James LONG
CROSSWHITE, Lucy Ann - George M. CASEY
CRIDER, S. C. - F. L. SHINKLE
CROW, Emma Conn - Edwin C. CUSHMAN
    Lizzie - Samuel RAWLINGS
    Mary Isabella - Robert W. EMMONS
CROWSON, Louise Jane - Harrison FLESHMAN
CROZIER, Jennie - John A. HOGDMAN
CRUMBAUGH, Mollie - J. V. C. KARNES
CRUMP, Mary S. - Col. William H. OTTER
CRUSE, Mary F. - Peter McCREA
CRUTCHER, Mattie - Dr. Robert T. LARUE
    Sallie - W. CRUTCHER
CRUNETT, Miranda - Walker G. REID
CURD, Die - William H. SMITH
CURRIE, Margaret - T. M. L. BEDSWORTH
    Mary E. - Reinhard BAKER
CUSTER, Emma - J. F. S. BURLINGAME
    Lou M. - Dr. J. L. THOMAS
    Mollie J. - Lord W. SALISBURRY
CUTTER, Mary W. - Hugh McKITTRICK

DADE, Julia - S. C. VAUGHN
DAIGRE, Mary E. - Henry VON PHUL, Jr.
DAILEY, Malissa J. - B. W. BENIGHT
DAKE, Julia E. - Edward F. CASTERLINE
DANIELS, Ann - Joseph PEARSON
DARBY, Margaret - Allen MAYHEW
DARNES, Ella - Edwin SWON
DARROW, Millie - John R. MOORE
DARST, Clara E. - John R. HAMILTON
DAUGHERTY, Lou - William HOOKER
DAVENPORT, Susan - Thomas BARNS
DAVIDSON, Angeline B. - James W. ENGLISH
    Ann M. - Dr. A. M. POWELL
    Eliza Jane - Dr. W. MOORE
DAVIS, Adda V. - H. T. CROMWELL
    Betsy J. - John T. GARTWRIGHT
    Charlotte - Charles G. MAURO
    Delila Ann - William H. CHILES
    Dolthera P. - Thomas McLAUGHLIN
    Ellen M. - Henry KELSEY
    Eliza J. - T. E. CLAYTON
    Eliza S. - Will C. LINDELL
    Jane - Dwight DURKEE
    Jennie M. - George HART
    Joella - R. H. OBER
    Lottie - C. B. ROBBINS
    Margaret - George W. HUTTS
    Mary A. - J. J. DEAN
    Mary L. - Washington TODD
    Mollie D. - J. P. HAMILTON
    Nancy E. - Housan HUNN
    Sallie - Capt. Warren Woodson HARRIS
    Sallie - A. FOSTER
    Sue C. - Thomas M. SMITH
DAWSON, Barsheba - James PROWELL
DEAN, Cornelia V. - Capt. J. G. TILFORD
DEARTH, T. A. - Charles E. CHAPMAN
DeHODIAMONT, Josephine - Henry LINHOFF
De La VEGA, Donna Lula - John G. SHELTON, Jr.
DeMOSS, Sophrona Ann - Caleb HURD
DENISON, Lucy Wetmore - H. B. KETCHAM
DENNY, Rachel Eliza - Thomas B. REED
DERBY, Cornelia - Elon G. SMITH
DERINGE, Elizabeth - John H. SELTNER
DeSPADA, Elizabeth - John A. JOHNSON
DETCHEMENDY, Mary - E. F. CRAFT
DEVIN, Emily Jane - William H. STILWELL
DIFFENDORFER, Salome - Dr. Montgomery JOHNS
DINGALE, Susan Ella - John T. DAVIS
DIXON, Nancy - Gen. J. M. BASSETT
DOERBAU, Margaret - Julius KESSLER

DOGGETT, Mary L. - Frank SHAPLEIGH
DONAHO, Louisa - Charles A. McNAIR
DONAHOE, Mrs. Kate - William A. ALBRIGHT
DONALDSON, Lizzie H. - Sherman SPENCER
DONELLY, Alice - William J. WARD
DONERLY, Serelda Ann - Joseph GRADY
DONNELL, Mary Virginia - Henry HUDSON
DONNELLY, Margaret - D. M. SEXTON
DOOLITTLE, Alice L. - Rev. Theodore HOPKINS
DORRIS, Martha - Joseph A. BROWNING
DOTY, Miss - N. R. STONE
DOUBLEDAY, Mrs. Anna M. - Rev. S. S. LAWS
DOUGLAS, Jennie - John L. Leahey
DOUGLASS, Maria - Clay COGSWELL
DOVENER, Charlotte - Samuel PETEFISH
DOUTHITT, Martha Gleim - George P. PLANT
DOW, Lucy A. - Charles SHEPPARD
DOWNING, Sallie Ann - Robertson C. EWING
DOWLER, Margaret - A. C. WONDELL
DOZIER, Elvira - Jo. W. STONE
DRAKE, Ella B. - J. Clarence CRESSON
    M. S. - Thomas McBRIDE
DRAPER, Maria - George H. JONES
DREYER, Helen - C. C. ZEISS
DROUGHT, Annie Frances - Thomas FORRESTER
DRY, Elizabeth - Valentine McCULLY
DRYDEN, Lizzie - N. D. GORDON
DU BOIS, Sarah - Isaac M. VEITCH
DUDGEON, Martha - John D. SETTLE
DUDLEY, Eliza - James W. PATTON
    Martha C. - John YOUNG
DUMAINE, Letitia Louise- Robert S. WENTWORTH
DUN, Elizabeth - Dr. W. C. WILLIAMS
DUNCAN, Caroline J. - William L. MUDDOCK
    E. T. - E. BIXBY
    Lucie E. - Dr. G. W. FIELD
    Margaret A. - T. T. ALLEN
    Pamelia - Calvin J. AUSTIN
    Sarah C. - Richard A. STONE
DUNLAP, Mary J. - F. G. FARRELL
DUNN, Charlotte Cecelia - Henry F. HARRINGTON
    Sarah E. - E. Combs MUSIC
* DUNNIES, Sallie K. - Dr. Samuel M. HORTON
DUNYER, Fannie - J. Clark WAY
DUPUY, Sarah L. - V. C. PEERS
DURHAM, Mary A. - Daniel NEWSOM
DYE, Sallie E. - George W. KILE
DYER, Emily H. - Henry C. WELLS
DYSART, Mollie F. - Frank COLE
    S. A. - W. M. DAMERON
DUVAL, M. E. - J. H. McALPIN

EADS, Genevieve - John A. UBSDELL, Jr.
EAGER, Sarah J. McBride - T. STRINGER
EAKIN, Julia - Vincent MARMADUKE
E-ANS(EVANS?), ___ - George W. GORDON
EARICKSON, Martha - Henry CASON
    Sarah - Richard EARICKSON
    Susan E. - William SPEAR
EATON, Mary Ann - James B. F. DUNCAN
ECK, Annie H. - John M. HUNTER
EDGAR, Fannie B. - Edward P. RICE
EDMONSTONE, Lou - Rev. Thomas FINNEY
EDRINGTON, Virginia S. - John REEL
EDWARDS, Eliza - William SEAY
    Eliza J. - Bernard PRATTE
    Harriet - D. D. SAPPINGTON
    Laura P. - Richard E. BLAND
    Malinda - Joseph C. ADKINS
ELBERT, Mary - Capt. John S. SHAW
ELDER, Eliza Key - Pierre F. CHATARD
ELGIN, Sarah Catherine - William COBB
ELLIOTT, Catherine - William WILHITE

*DUNNICA, not
Dunnies

ELLIOTT, Fanny - John W. THURSTON
   Jane - Samuel M. SPENCER
   Sarah - Henry NEILL
ELLIS, Amanda F. - Thomas M. FILED
   Martha E. - William H. BIGGS
   Rosanna - Isaac N. PRATHER, Jr.
ELLISON, Isabelle - George W. DAVIS
ELLISTON, Sallie Ann - J. A. BARRON
EMERSON, Olive - Dr. Charles M. FORBES
ENGLISH, Helen T. - Benjamin C. T. PRATT
   Louise - James EDWARDS
ERWIN, Ann M. - James H. URZ
   Caroline C. - John SCOTT
ESTES, Catherine E. - Reuben HUME
EUSTACHE, Caraline - John HOARSMAN
EVANS, Annie A. - John W. CARLILE
   Lucy A. - Mason S. BONNEL
   Martha E. - Dr. William W. HENDERSON
   Theresa - James L. BUSKETT
EVENS, Mary - Charles T. MANTER
EVERETTE, Beatrice G. - Theodore B. MALONE
EVERHART, Margaret - James H. TUREMAN
EWING, Annie - Maj. Ben J. NEWSOM
   Lavinie - Jesse HOLLOWAY
   Margaret - William N. MOORE
   Maria L. - Col. Alton YOUNG
   Mary B. - William Cyrus WALLACE

FAGIN, Abbie B. - J. E. CARPENTER
FALES, Carlotta Nestue - William S. GLASGOW
   Sarah - William LOUCK
FALL, Hettie O. - Henry BOVER Jr.
FANT, Hattie A. - William H. CURTIS
FARNAM, Mrs. Renetta Wilcox - Dr. STICKLES
FARRICE, Mary Jane - John C. WALKER
FAULKNER, Amanda S. (Mrs. LUSK) -
      Rev. G. M. WINTON
FENBY, Jennie - William D. MITCHELL
FERGUSON, Anna E. - Charles W. SAMUEL
   Mrs. Eliza - Carey B. H. DAVIS
FIELD, Carrie W. - J. A. QUARLES
   Rebecca - Joel A. MAUPIN
FIELDS, Lizzy L. - W. D. McGUIRE
FILLEY, Ellen - T. T. RICHARDS
FINE, Sophronia - Robinson F. STROUD
FINGLAND, Maggie - Dr. F. R. GALLAGHER
FINKBURGH, Ella T. - Harrison J. PAINTER
FINKS, Anna - James KINNEY
   Louisa - Alonzo H. DONAHOE
FINLEY, Mahala - Erastus H. WEST
   Mary - George VOORHIES
FINNEY, Mary - Maj. John P. McGRATH
FISHBACK, Lizzie - Richard HOLME
FISHER, Eliza E. - John E. DEY
   Mrs. Elizabeth D. - John K. WELCH
   Annie or Fannie - John C. ADKINS
   Sarah M. - John CHAMBERLAIN
FITZGERALD, Jeannie - Charles J. HOLME
FITZPATRICK, Kate - Peter O. D. BYRNE
FLEMING, Lizzie M. - Dr. J. Bowen CLARDY
FLETCHER, Eliza I. - James S. HILL
   Lucinda S. - Thomas S. ROGERS
FLOURNOY, Nannie C. - Milford JENNING
FLOWERIE, Mollie - Nehemiah HOLMES
FOLLETT, Mary - W. D. WOOD
FORBES, Nannie - Edwin H. IRVINE
FORBIS, Elizabeth - William M. ROBERTS
   Nancy - Erastus BURNHAM
FOREE, Miriam F. - E. D. ALLEN
FORMAN, Amanda - James GENTRY
   Lizzie - James A. CORDER
FORSHEY, Nannie - William W. VIA
FORTUNE, Mary Adelaide - Lt. Col.
      William G. HEATH

FOSTER, Mary Ann F. - James KELLY
FOURDIGNIERS, Josephine - Modeste PAULIS
FOUNTAIN, Hannah - James H. ANGELL
FOURDRIGNIERS, Jeannette - Francis DUPONT
FOWLER, Mary Jane - Richard McMURTREY
   Telitha - Hayden BROWN
FOX, Malvina A. - Thomas L. FOX
FRANCIS, Diana B. - Capt. William S. NELSON
FRANCISCO, Sophia - Dr. J. W. ROSS
FRARY, Ellen M. - John H. BARNARD
FRAZIER, Ann H. - H. W. BROUGHTON
FREAKS, Ellen - Tilden REED
FREEMAN, Malvy Ann - William RENFROW
   Sarah Ann - Napoleon BAKER
FRIDAY, Fanny - Morris OBERMAYER
FRIES, Carrie V. - Johnson M. TUCKER
FRISTOE, Elizabeth M. - Andrew J. MARTIN
FROST, Mrs. Elizabeth (nee CARTER) -
      James H. BIRCH
FUBRODT, Mrs. Anna Maria - John BESEL
FULKERSON, Amanda - A. F. FAWCETT
   Rebecca - C. C. HEADMAN
FULLER, Mrs. Mary S. - Maj. George MATHEWS
FULTON, Lizzie - C. E. WHITE
FUQUA, Lizzie A. - Luther COLLIER
   Sarah - Wray BROWN
   Sue E. - J. F. WOLLNER
FYLER, Louisa - Charles D. LAKE

GALBRAITH, Nannie - H. HANSBROUGH or
      HORNSBERGER
GALLAHER, Julia O. - S. SPARKS
GALLATIN, Cornelia - John K. DOBBINS
GAMBLE, Jennie R. - Thomas P. BARBOUR
   Mary E. - Dr. James C. PAGE
   Mary Coalter - Edgar MILLER
GAMEWELL, M. Anna - F. G. GRIFFITH
GANDEE, Virginia - A. W. KING
GANT, Anna J. - John P. HUDGINS
GANTIE, Emily - Dr. Charles V. F. LUDWIG
GARAGHTY, Eliza D. - Charles B. MACK
GARDINER, Mary J. - G. Chapman ALEXANDER
GARDNER, Elizabeth - John FOLEY
GARNETT, Mariah - David DEAN
GARRISON, Anna - John G. WELLS
   Cordelia - Samuel BONNER
GARTH, Alice E. - William P. SHRYOCK
   Lizzie - Caleb Thompson WORTHY
GARTIN, Sarah - John A. FUNK
GASH, Lucinda - Richard JEANS
GASPER, Josephine - Robert CHEYNE
GATRIGHT, Mary - Justinian CAVE
GENTRY, Ann Eliza - Porter BUSH
   Mrs. Julia - Richard GENTRY
   Mary - Robert CLARK
   Sarah - Thomas HART
GERSHON, Maria - A. S. MYERS
GIBBONS, Mollie E. - Capt. T. K. VOORHEES
GIBBS, Russella - John S. JAMES
GIBSON, Elizabeth E. - Thomas PHILLIPS
   Mary D. - Zebulon T. STEELE
GILHAM, Lizzie - S. P. SEELY
   Mary C. - P. W. CHICK
GILL, Mary B. - John CAMPBELL
   Sarah Jane - H. C. HOWARD
GILLETT, Fannie - Ralph J. WHITLEDGE
GILLIAM, Bettie - E. T. GUERIN
GINGRY, Helen - Dr. J. A. CHAMBERS
GIST, Harriet A. - W. H. ADAMS
GIVENS, Rhoda E. - James A. FERREL
GLASCOCK, Maria Louisa - Charles MARTIN
   Maria Louisa - James E. ROBINSON
GLASGOW, Susan C. - D. W. BARNES
GLOVER, Mary J. - William R. WINN

GLYCKHERR, Albertine - James Milton LORING
GODWIN, Adeline - Robert M. GROOMES
GOLDSOLL, Nattie - Dr. SPIER
GOOD, Sarah A. - James B. WOODS
GOODE, Frances M. - David E. HUMPHREYS
GOODFELLOW, Mrs. Madama - James L. GRAHAM
    (nee WILES)
GOODLIVE, Sarah - George HILDERBRANDT
GOODMAN, Laura R. - Dr. J. J. McELWEE
GORDON, Catherine S. - Urias GORDON
    Ellen - William WEST
    Lucy - Milton EWING
    Mary - James M. CLAY
    Mary - Charles THOMPSON
    Julia - H. A. ALTHOUSE
GORGAS, Caroline - S. M. MOORE
GOSLIN, Charlotte - James H. COOK
GRADY, Mary - Stephen LEMONS
GRAHAM, Louisa - George L. D. WILLIAMS
GRANT, Matilda - R. G. SALMON
GRAVES, F. Ellen - James A. CRAIG
    Harriet - J. D. OSBORNE
    Lucy Ellen - Eli G. ROWLAND
    Lucy C. - Samuel S. NOWLIN
    Nancy Jane - John P. NAILOR
GREEN, C. E. - F. M. TREVATHAN
GREENE, Cora Willey - T. A. MORRIS
    Edith E. - J. W. McLANAHAN
GREENWOOD, Amanda - Capt. John C. HINDS
GREGORY, Mrs. Martha - William MORROW
GRIFFIN, Elizabeth - William THOMAS
GRIFFIN (GRIFFITH), Lucinda H. - John F. SEE
    Sallie Ann - Robert GRIFFIN
    Susan - Sardis HICKAM
GRIFFITH, Mrs. (widow of Noah) _
           John GRIFFITH
    Mrs. Margaret - Gilman SMITH
    Sallie - Francis T. H. RAGLAND
GRIMSHAW, Lillie - George L. FAULHABER
    Margaret - William A. GRIMSHAW
GROVE, Binnie C. - Henry C. HAYDEN
GROVER, Kibbie M. - J. L. BACON
GUITAR, Lizzie - James V. ROGERS
GUNN, Ellen Eliza Griggs -
         Joseph Thomas BROWN
GUTHRIE, Jennie A. - John H. GOLDSMITH
    Sarah - William H. HOLEMAN
GUY, Lizzie - P. H. LAMB
GWINN, Fannie - George W. BALLENGER

HAAS, Ellen - Henry HELFRICH
HACKMAN, Mary E. - William Henry JOHNSON
HACKNEY, Mary Frances - Rev. Frederick
         Howard WINES
HAENISCH, Natalie - Frederick ROEVER
HAILMAN, Jane - William C. JAMISON, Jr.
HAINES, Annie - Frank H. TUCKER
    Carrie A. - George SCHRATER
    Ellen - William BARNHILL
HAISLIP, Sallie M. - William S. WHITE
HALBERT, Julia - Harrison N. GOURLEY
HALE, Judith P. - R. S. PORTER
HALEY, Mattie J. - R. POINDEXTER
HALL, A. - Thomas LYNCH
    Addie - Samuel HARDWICK
    Jane - Fielding HUGGINS
    Julia C. - James D. LEONARD
    Mrs. Mary A. - H. M. GREENE
    Penelope P. - Dr. William C. PHILLIPS
    Sarah - John H. MOSEBY
HALLEY, Arzela E. - James M. STEPHENSON
    Lizzie - Dr. J. M. HAYS
    Susan L. - J. R. COLLINS

HAM, Georgetta Jacqueline - Rudolph ULRICI
HAMBLETON, Robyna - Reuben SMART
HAMILTON, Angeline Ann - Thomas FORBUS
    N. P. - Rev. W. G. MILLER
HAMPTON, Malinda M. - James H. WOOLEY
HAND, Mollie T. - G. H. HITCH
HANLEY, Harriet - John METCALF
HANNA, Louisa - Rev. James SHARP
HANSON, Margaret Ann - William JOHNSON
HARDIN, Ann - John EATON
    Lavina H. - William B. WILSON
    Nannie - H. C. LACKLAND
HARMON, Martha Ann - Josiah CRUMP
HARRINGTON, Sophia - A. G. PAYNE
HARRIS, Ann Eliza - John S. ROBINSON
    Bettie - William H. KIMBROUGH
    Cornelia - James BENNETT
    Marcus Ellen - Robert R. McBAIN
    Martha - A. S. CAZE
    Mary - G. M. BURROUGHS
    Mary E. - Dr. S. W. HOLT
    Rebecca A. - R. SHIFER
    Sarah Jane - D. S. MERRY
HARRISON, Amanda J. - Frederick WEED
    Annie - Edward T. PITTMAN
    Cynthia E. - James LYONS
    Dora - Dr. J. G. W. STEEDMAN
    Mat M. - B. L. FLOYD
    Mattie J. - R. S. BUCHANAN
    Sarah - Thomas SHACKELFORD
    Sarah A. - David CASTLEMAN
    Sarah B. - John D. LONG
    Virginia - Daniel PATTERSON
HARRY, Augusta - Lt. Col. R. F. DUNN
HARSH, Rosa May - Moses FRALEY
HARSHAW, Josephine - Ben M. McCOLLOCK
HART, Elizabeth - William STARKEY
    Elizabeth - J. C. STREET
    Maria Church - James BROWN
    Rachel - Moses MORRIS
HARVEY, Estella Anna - George SHEPHERD
    Mary C. - Thomas H. BOTTS
HASTON, M. A. - Dr. J. H. BARNES
HAUK, Lizzie - John C. BURNESON
HAWKINS, Amanda A. - James L. APPLEGATE
    Mattie Ann - William K. BIGGS
    Thetis C. - W. H. HATCH
HAYDEN, Amanda E. - Archibald YOUNG
    Delila - George TERRILL
    Margaret - John W. CARTER
HAYS, Marvann - F. W. BROWN
    Rebecca - James H. TRUMBLE
HEAD, Clara Elizabeth - Dr. J. Wellington
    Texie A. - S. T. MOREHEAD   / GRAY
HEATON, Lizzie G. - Dr. W. C. HILL
HEELEY, Sarah E. - John F. JONES
HEINEGEN, Mrs. Sarah - C. SCHOFFLER
HELFENSTEIN, Anna M. - Stephen W. GORE
HELLEN, Josephine - Hamilton G. FANT
HELM, Fannie - Thomas D. DAY
HENDERSON, Mary J. - James C. MAYNARD
HENRY, A. B. - E. H. WARE
    Gabrielle Flournoy - Wilkins
          WHEATLEY
HENSLEY. Amanda - William ARCHER
HENTON, Rebecca C. - John F. CORDER
HERBERT, Nancy A. - Oliver J. CANDY
HERMON, Elizabeth Frances - William T.
          NEVENS
HERNDON, Harriet - David GUITAR
HEULEN, Mrs. Mary - Francis M. ROBERTS
    / Nee ARMSTRONG
HIBBARD, Mrs. Mary A. - Apexander MITCHELL

HICKAM, Mariam - Thomas DODD
      Samira Ann - Lafayette HUME
HICKMAN, Irene - William H. BASS
HICKS, Elizabeth - Samuel J. BURTON
      Kate - M.(or H.) Harrison SLOAN
HIDEN, Mary Frances - Thomas WHITTLE
HIGGINS, Mary A. - William O. WHEELER
HILL, Sallie M. - William C. WEIR
      Susan M. - Henry GARNETT
      Zarilda A. - Robert H. GUERRANT
HILTIBIDAL, Harriet E. - Franklin SMITHLAND
HINDS, Kate - William H. SCUDDER
HOBAN or Mary Jane - Samuel G. BERRY
* HULEN,
HOCKADAY, Eva - R. B. PRICE
HOCKERSMITH, Emma - B. F. SHORTRIDGE
HODGES, Mary - William A. WAUGH
      Mrs. R. A. (nee GRISWOLD) -
          Dr. M. J. LEONARD
HOGAN, Sophia - Simon L. BOOGHER
HOGEN, Susan M. - Truman J. HOMER
HOLLAND, Eliza Ann - Benjamin BISHOP
HOLLINGSWORTH, Mary M. - J. J. WHEELER
HOLME, Annie - John HOLLISTER
HOLMES, Nelly - Col. N. P. CHIPMAN
HOLT, Elvira - Lt. John L. STANTON
HOLTOM, Eliza Jane - Elias Newton NICHOLS
HONEYMAN, Lavenia P. - James J. PORTER
HOOTEN, Elizabeth - James GARRET
HOPE, Mattie - Edward G. WALKER
HOPKINS, Annie E. - John W. WOOD
      Martha A. - George F. ELLIOTT
HOPPER, Mollie - William N. TURNER
HORINE, Sue M. - William L. RILEY
HORNBECK, Lucie L. - William H. McMAHAN
HOUGH, Laura - Capt. John P. KEISER
      Sallie - G. B. WINSTON
HOUGHTON, R. J. - Rev. C. D. SIMPSON
HOW, Eliza - David W. BRYANT
HOWARD, Anna Maria - Rev. J. W. DUNN
      Annie - Charles H. THORNTON
HOWE, Susan W. - David KEITH
HOY, Therese M. - W. E. MEAD
HOYLAND, Mrs. Mary Ann - George HILES
HUBBARD, Emma - Herndon LINDSEY
      Mary Jane - Thomas S. BIDWELL
      Fannie - Daniel GANO
HUCKSTEP, Sallie - William McDANIEL
HUDGENS, Jennie - Dr. James G. B. FURGUSON
HUDSON, Sarah Ann - Mathias KIMES
HUGHES, Alvina - James N. McCLELLAN
      Kate - Calvin F. BURNES
      Laura - A. H. BUCHANAN, M.D.
      Lou M. - W. Renfro ROTHWELL
*   Lucy A. - Prof. Benjamin T. GILKEY
HULEN, Nannie - Robert HODGE
HULL, Eliza - William F. RUSSELL
      Lou B. - Cornelius VOORHIES
HUME, Mrs. Sue (nee LONG) - J. D. EGBERT
      Susan - William HAYS
HUNT, Ann - R. R. POWELL
      Helen L. - John J. CANTWELL
      Lizzie - David DYER
      Mary - L. K. BRADLEY
HUNTER, Bettie - M. G. MARTIN
      Lucy - William J. SCOTT
      Martha E. - A. J. TISDALE
      Mary A. - Blind DAVIDSON
      Mary E. - Lafayette WILCOX
      Mary M. - James PARROT
HUTCHINSON, Margaret - Enoch STILLWELL
      Sophia Jane - James WOODS
HUTT, Valeria B. - Col. Charles W. PARKER

HYATT, Mary E. - W. H. R. BECKER
ICENHOWER, Eliza Jane - George S. FULLER
INGE, Fannie - Henry C. NORTH
ISBELL, Susan - Robert ELLIOTT
ISRAEL, Mattie M. - Clark J. MORTON

JACKMAN, Hannah - Newman T. MITCHELL
JACKS, Mary E. - J. E. HARVEY
JACKSON, Ann - John CANDLER
      Eve R. - David J. PIKE
      Iantha - George WOODSON
      Luda J. - Dr. Charles L. LAMB
      Margaret - Dr. Louis A. DELIME
      Mary C. - John THOMPSON
      Rebecca - Julius L. MOSES
JACOBS, Louisa F. - William G. H. BECKER
      Mary - John V. LEAR
      Pauline - Alex BARTH
JAMES, Elizabeth W. - John W. HOGGE
      Kate - James M. HENDERSON
JAMESON, Susie - John R. FERRIL
JAMISON, Mary Ellen - Robert BAILEY
      Sallie - John F. CARTER
JANUARY, Priscie - James Hamilton HARDEN
** JENKINS, Carrie A. - Walter W. WILSON
      Margaret - Walter T. BROWN
JARVIS, Mrs. E. A. - F. R. CONWAY
JEFFRIES, Virginia - Thomas B. CREWS
** JENKINS, Mary - Christopher KING
      Mary J. - Boyd BARR
JENNINGS, Lizzie W. - Harry CAPEN
JOHN, Mary M. - James C. HIGGINS
JOHNSON, Anna M. - Thomas HOOPER, Jr.
      Bettie B. - Charles W. SPENCER
      Delilah P. - James L. McNAIR
      Eusebia C. - E. William FOX
      H. G. P. - H. F. CLARK
      Henrietta - Henry SORIA
      Kate - Frank BAILEY
      Philena - W. W. WELLER
      Rebecca - David McREYNOLDS
      S. A. - F. M. POSEGATE
JOHNSTON Moriah - Louis K. WATERS
      Sallie - J. W. KEENE
      Sarah - Israel D. WATERS
      Virginia - John P. POWELL
JOHNSTONE, Emily M. - W. C. DAVIS
      Jane Ann - Moses STUART
JONES, Emily M. - W. W. CARTER
      Hattie - James R. CLAYTON
      Jane - H. T. HUNT
      Kate - Melvin GUTHRIDGE
      Mary Emily - David G. CANTRELL
      Mary S. - T. P. SAUNDERS
      Matilda G. A. - John C. LANE
      Sarah A. - W. D. MUIR
      Sarah E. - Jackson EWING
JORDAN, Mrs. M. L. - Thomas H. NUGEN
JOSLIN, Elvira - George LEADER
JUDSON, Maggie - Alfred MACKAY
JULIAN, Ophelia F. - James F. REGAN

KEANE, Rachel - William McCLINTOCK
KEEBAUGH, Addie - Thomas D. PRICE
KEEGAN, Elizabeth J. C. - Wm. W. KETCHUM
KEEN, Elizabeth - James E. HICKS
      Harriet Isabella - Edward W. STEPHENS
KEENE, Eliza - James McDOWELL
      Marium - Samuel HANNA
KEHOE, Lizzie A. - George H. JUDY
KEISTER, Caroline C. - W. A. MARKS
KEITH, Bell - John B. TAYLOR
KELLER, Mary Eliza - James G. NORISS
      Pauline - Jefferson HARPER

KELLERHALS, H. L. - John HILDEBRAND
KELLY, Helen - W. W. FORMAN
   Lucy J. - John POOL
   Mary Ann - G. W. JONSON
   Sarah Ann - Andrew D. CRONK
KELTNER, Sarah E. - Thomas BROWN
KELTON, Anna - H. L. PEARCE
KENAN, M. Fanny - Dr. T. J. HARDIN
KENDALL, Olly - Horace M. PARKER
   Mrs. Susa (nee HALL) -
       James M. DICKSON
KENNEDY, Sallie M. - Charles H. WITHINTON
KENNY, Martha - John GEORGE
KESSLER, Barbara - Philip TROEB
KETHLINE, Mrs. Annie - Herman EPERLEIN
KEY, Martha - Alonzo CRAIG
KEYES, Annie M. - C. F. KNIGHT
   Mary Frances - B. COLMAN
KIDWELL, Rebecca E. - George YATES
KIENLEN, Adaline - James A. BILLINGS
KILGOUR, Margaret - John MEEK
KING, Anna H. - C. Waldo MARSH
   Bettie - James MOORE
   Ellen - Dr. James E. GIBSON
   Lizzie C. - Robert M. SANDERSON
   Martha Ann - James THORPE
   Nancy E. - Joshua M. ROWLAND
KIRBY, Sallie - Thomas M. SMITH
KIRGAN, Mary Ann Crowell - James MORTON
KIRTLEY, Eliza - John C. ROYLE
KLAUSER, Carolene - Dom. URBAN
KLINEFELTER, Josephine - Daniel ADAMS
KNAPP, Mary - William HAND
KRING, Mary A. - Charles GIVENS
KRISEL, Mrs. Lucinda - John S. BIGBEE

LACK, Anna M. - I. W. BOULWARE
LACKLAND, Augusta - Norman LACKLAND
LADD, Alice K. - James A. COMSTOCK
   Carrie M. - Dr. William GILFILLAN
LAFFOON, Mary E. - Joseph CHRISMAN Jr.
LAFON, Kate A. - Joseph R. WINCHELL
   Susan - Rev. Thomas H. TATLOW
LAIL, Mollie - John W. ARNOLD
LAMB, Mrs. Sarah R. - R. W. BLAKELY
LAMPTON, Louisa Margaret - Thomas WOLF
   Martha Jane - Robert SMITH
LAND, Harriet H. - Joseph B. SMITH
LANDER, Mollie - John J. STEELE
LANDSBERRY, Matilda - John C. DAVIDSON
LANGDON, Elizabeth Champion - Henry WILSON
LANGWELL, Mariah L. - William P. GORD
LANHAM, Nancy - Lincoln R. MARTIN
LANSING, Fannie G. - R. H. BILLINGSLEY
LARD, Lizzie - Elder Richard D. SHANNON
LARKIN, Mary C. - Dr. D. L. MAGRUDER
LASALTER, Ida Binda - Walter J. HORSLEY
LATZ, Nathalie - S. MEYER
LAUGHLIN, Nancy - James T. MOONEY
LAUMAN, Emilia - Louis SPELBRINK
LAWRENCE, Helen L. - David R. GRANT
LAWS, Gertrude F. - James PRITCHARD
LAWTON, Angie - John GOTT
LEACH, Eliza Jane Perry - J. HAMILL
LEAGUE, Mary Jane - Dr. I. Byron BRITTINGHAM
LEAR, Jane V. - James W. BRADLEY
LEARNED, Clara - E. Dunham HENRY
   Mary E. - D. J. HANCOCK
LEARY, Mrs. Virginia - Henry BLAKESLEY
LEASE, Lyda E. - Daniel A. WILSON
LEE, Christina - Joseph JACOB
   Kate Marie - Leonidas H. WESTLAKE
   Sue - William P. DUTY

LEER, Ella G. - William L. EATON
LEFFINGWELL, Sophie - F. A. QUINETT
LENNON, Margaret O John Alexander MAGINN
LENOX, Sue B. - Frank WISHON
LEONARD, Ada - Rev. C. S. HAWKS
LESLIE, Mary S. - Dr. Charles KNOWER
LETT, Nessy - Charles CASEY
LEVI, Lizzie - T. G. BLACK
LEWIS, Mildred S. - James P. STROTHER
   Rachel - Michael ABRAHAMS
   Sallie B. - Capt. Theodore W. DUNNICA
   Sarah - Robinson HENNINGER
   Sarah - John Ellis
LINCOLN, Julia - John McMICHAEL
LINDELL, Ann Eliza - Robert C. GORDON
LINDSEY, Mary E. - Hale T. WRIGHT
LINK, Lou J. - Drury UNDERWOOD
LIONBERGER, Belle - James WOOLFOLK
LIPP, Caroline - Joseph R. BIGGERS
LIST, Dorrie V. - Samuel HILDRETH
LITTLE, Marion B. - Isaac H. STONE
LLOYD, Elizabeth Jane - Wm. L. GILLESPIE
LOCK, Elizabeth A. - John A. DAUGHERTY
LOCKRIDGE, Martha C. - William B. WOODSON
LONG, C. V. - Gen. Thomas L. PRICE
   Maggie L. - John J. MATTHEWS
   Permelia Jane - J. BILLINGTON
LOOK, Emma Amanda - Rev. R. H. WELLER
LOURY, Mary Benton - William NELSON
LOUTHAN, Sarah - Peter B. CLUFF
LOVE, Harriet - Griff P. THEOBALD
LOWRY, Gilly - Thomas G. TUTTLE
   Kate - William HALE
   Mary - Dr. W. W. VASSE
   Rebecca - David A. BIGGERS
LUCKEY, Bettie - John M. GORDON
LURTON, Henrietta L. - E. J. XAUPI Jr.
LUTZ, Marie - Auguste VUCHER
LYMAN, Ada - Horis HOSTATER
LYNCH, Kate - Dr. Fayette CLAPP
   Mary E. - Hubert PRIMM
LYNES, Elizabeth - William L. HUBBARD
LYON, Maria - A. GERSHON
   Mary Evelyn - David W. BRINKERHOFF
LYTES, Albina - John W. SHEELEY

McAFEE, Mary R. - Marvin R. BANKS
   Rebecca J. - Maj. Joseph H. McAMEY
McBRIDE, Mary - James HURT
   Mary E. - J. H. McVEIGH
McCALESTER, Kate - Benjamin LEONARD
McCALL, Martha Susan - M. B. ESKRIDGE
McCANBY, Martha M. - James BRADLEY
McCARTHY, Ellen - Patrick FLETCHER
McCARTY, Elizabeth - Maj. John BATTLE
McCAUL, Emma - Sylvester WILSON
McCLINTOCK, Martha - Henry A. GOADBY
McCLURE, Annie - J. W. HARRIS
   Cynthia - Patrick BALLARD
McCLURG, Mary Emma - Marshall W. JOHNSON
McCONATHY, Alice T. - Richard E. BEAZLEY
McCOUN, Amelia - Capt. William JACQUES or
         JACOBS
McCOY, Juliet - Robert L. BASS
McCREA, Elizabeth Jane - James DOWNEY
McCUBBIN, Ann - Patrick BURNS
McDANIEL, Mary Harriet - Henly J. MADDUX
   Sallie - James P. THOMAS
McDERMOTT, Mary A. - John DURKAN
McDONALD, Mrs. M. E. (nee ARNOLD) -
        T. J. LAMAR
   Mary Jane - Thomas LYNCH
   W. - Charles B. FRANCE

McDUMOTT, Rosa M. - Henry A. DEAN
McENTIRE, Margaret - John H. SHANNON
     Mary E. Wells - Eustace W. COWEN
McFARLAND, Cinthia J. - Edward D. WILLS
McGEE, Cassie A. - James R. FARRELL
     Hannah - John GOUGH
     Mary A. - Robert H. SIMPSON
     Mary E. F. - Octavius A. GLANVILLE
McGREADY, Lucy - Robert BUST
McGREGOR, Julia O. - Charles F. CODY
McGUFFIN, Mollie E. - Anthony BURBACH
McGUIRE, Ann E. - George W. NORTHCUTT
McGUNNEGLE, Lizzie S. - Capt. Benjamin WALKER
McHATTON, Annie - Alfred M. BRITTON
     Sallie A. - Cornelius CHINN
McILHANEY, Bettie - Dr. George R. MILTON
McILVAINE, Lucinda J. - Thomas S. WHITE
     Sallie B. - Capt. Thomas B.
          CASTLEMAN
McKELLOPS, Grace - William N. MacQUEEN
McKINNEY, America - Dr. G. D. HANSBROUGH
McKISSICK, Martha Ann - H. R. DAVIS
McKNIGHT, Louise E. - John D. SCOTT
McLIN, Maggie - R. D. BOVARD
McMURTRY, Nancy - William H. MORRIS
McPHERSON, Sally - J. P. HOPKINS
McQUITTY, Harriet - James T. CHILTON
     Hattie - Dr. G. W. ELLIOTT
McROBERTS, Lizzie R. - Jacob T. CHILD
McSHERRY, Kate - Charles W. McCORD
McVEIGH, Ada M. - William R. PRICE
McWILLIAMS, Elizabeth L. - William M. GORDON

MACDONALD, M. C. D. - I. W. HUTCHINSON
MACHETTE, M. E. - William H. HARLAN
MACK, Adelia M. - Charles DRAKE
     Etta R. - Thomas L. ELIOT
MACKAY, Charlotte - Ben I. BOGY
MADDOX, Ann Elizabeth - W.H.H. CUNDIFF
     Sue - Oliver Whaley
     Mary P. - Francis KELLAR
MAGRAW, Jennie E. - T. J. HIGGINS
MAGUIRE, Eulalie - Charles W. FRANCIS
MAGWIRE, Mary P. - Maj. Gen. Eugene A. CARR
MAHONEY, Mary Jane - Edward G. ELLY
MAJORS, Sarah - James R. GARDENHIRE
MALIN, Nannie E. - Wiley S. WRIGHT
MANEFEE(?), Mary S. - E. H. HOPKINS
MAPPIN, Ann Eliza - Edward LONG
MARKLAND, Nancy - J. W. BROWN
MARMADUKE, Jennie C. - George W. SHARP
MARSHALL, Sallie R. - Henry B. LOUDERMAN
MARTAIN, Elizabeth - George W. TURNER
MARTELL, Melina - Henry OTTERMAN
MARTIN, Agnes A. - William B. SWITZLER
     Anna W.E. - Edmond K. NORRIS
     Charlotte Rebecca - James K. CANNON
     Cora - Wesley FALLON
     Emily D. - Col. J. H. McILVANE
     Jennie A.E. - F. D? SHAFFER
     Martha E. - Hyram NOEL
     Mary F. - Edwin A. HAWK
     Nannie - John T. McMILLIN
     Sarah A. - Joseph B. DAVIS
     Sarah G. - Paul VEMER
MARTYR, Fannie - Oscar HAWKINS
MASON, Helen - William P. HANCOCK
MASSEY, Nina - Warwick HOUGH
MATHEWS, Elizabeth - Augustus LEWIS
MATHIS, Dona - James M. SEARS
MATTHEWS, Mary - James B. HANNA M.D.
     Roxana - J. E. CARTER
MAUPIN, Mary Frances - Thomas H. MAUPIN
MAXWELL, Mary - James H. LOWRY

MAUGHAS, Jennie - T. D. BOGIE
     Eliza P. - Joseph CHRISTIAN
MAUPIN, S. J. - Dr. Thomas PEEVY
MAXFIELD, Belle - P. E. WISER
MEALER, Virginia S. - O. G. WENGLER
MELONE, Fannie - William T. REYNOLDS
MENEFEE, Mary Tabitha - Robert STEEN
MERCILLIOTT, Elizabeth - John F.
             CHAMBERLAIN
MICHAEL, Esther Mary - James McARTHUR
     Julia - Charles W. TOWNSLEY
     Mary Louise - George W. SIMPSON
MILLER, Elizabeth - Theodore COON
     Georgianna - Thomas J. HARRIS
     Lila A. - Dr. J. T. GREEN
     Lizzie - George W. WELLS
     Louisa A. - George D. HALL or
          HALE
     Mary - Richard B. HUBBARD
     Mrs. Mary A. - Fountain McKENZIE
     Mildred A. - V. B. WILKERSON
     Nancy - Byrd SMITH
     Sarah - G. C. JONES
MILLS, Eliza A. - Franklin McCLUNG
     Matilda - Judge M. S. STITH
MILSTEAD, Emily G. - Isadore PREVATT
MINTER, George Ann - Charles W. BUSTER
MITCHELL, Fannie B. - Henry CLARK
     Lizzie H. - Nat. ROFF
     Mary S. - E. R. HUTCHINSON
MITTNACHT, Amelia - J. B. VAN COURT
MOBERLY, Josephine - Capt. G. W.
             CUNNINGHAM
MOBLEY, Mary - Henry Dalton LITTLETON
MODIE, Sallie - Richard LEACH
MOFFETT, Mary E. - William A. DIVINE
MONROE, Mary Ann Soule - Rev. William T.
             ELLINGTON
MONTGOMERY, Elizabeth - Richard PHILLIBER
     Jessie F. - William H. GRAVES
     Lottie - Hugh ROGERS
     Maria - George H. HANSON
     Mary E. - James A. KING
MONTMOLLIN, Sallie P. - E. R. SPOTSWOOD
MOORE, Augusta G. - Rev. John T. WILLIAMS
     Delilah - Henry SCHOULTON
     Lizzie - Lyne S. BROTHERTON
     Mary Ann - William H. SIMPKINS
     Matilda C. - Stephen T. ELLIOTT
     Rebecca B. - John KING
     Sarah Elizabeth - Samuel GREENE
MOREHEAD, Fannie - Gilleve BELLES
MOREHED, Ann Amanda - Simeon SISK
MORGAN, Kittie G. - Calvin E. McCLURG
     Maria Louisa - E.J. WILLIAMSON
     Sallie J. - James G. WENDOM
     Sarah - George T. PARISH
     Sophia A. - John F. LAY
MORRIS, Cynthia - William DIGGS
     E. O. - R. R. ARNOLD
     Lou - Jacob MADDOX
     Mary J. - William F. PENNY
MORRISON, Helen - Dr. J.W. SOUTHWORTH Jr.
     Sallie - Wm. B. DONALDSON
MORROW, Mary J. - William H. NORTHCUT
MORTON, Fulvia - Thomas P. ROSS
     Matilda - Philip C. GIBBS
MOSEBY, Mrs. Emeline (nee TILLERY) -
           George DRESSLER
     Mildred - Dr. J. A. CHAPMAN
MOSELEY, Amanda - Peter ELLIS
     Kate E. - J. N. DINWIDDIE
MOSS, Margaret - Dr. A. L. YANCEY
     Mary - Robert LAKENAN

MOTTRAM, Alice - Robert DUNHAM
MOURNING, Emily Jane - Robert WADE
MUDGE, Annie - J. C. REYNOLDS
MULHERIN, Mary E. - Francis M. STRAWBE
MUNDAY, Ella A. - Thomas F. LEVEL
MUNDY, Rebecca - Ezra MUNDY
MURPHY, Almarinda - Joseph DENNIS
        Mary - Daniel WARREN
        Sarah A. - Peter Sowers BANTZ
        Theresa - George W. BREWSTER
MURRAY, Magg Clara - William H. FISHER
MUSGRIVE, Jane W. - John B. CAMDEN
MUSGROVE, Ann M. - Ethan ALLEN
        Fannie - J. J. REABURN
MUSICK, Amanda - John CORBY
        Cornelia - Ferdinand HENDERSON
MUSSER, Lizzie - A. S. HARRIS
        Mrs. Martha - David HORNER
MYERS, Mary E. - F. C. CARE
        Mrs. Nancy A. - John DITTMORE

NANCE, Sarah Frances - Joseph GOSSADGE
NASH, Mary - John HUBBARD
        Mary - David H. FORBES
NEET, Lizzie R. - T. E. BRAWNER
NEILLE, Kate - S. HINSON
NELSON, Mrs. Eliza Ann (nee CLARK) -
                Robert W. SINCLAIR
        M. A. - William A. ROBIRDS
        Mittie - Dr. H. G. GIBSON
NESBIT, Mary J. - Charles W. RUBEY
NEWKIRK, Sallie E. - Henry C. ROGERS
NEWMAN, Mary S. - William A. OBER
        Mollie Ella - George W. WITHERS
NICHOLAS, Matilda - J. R. BARRET
NICHOLS, Fannie T. - John H. CRUMP
        Georgella - William H. BUFFINGTON
        Mary - Dr. J. T. BAILEY
        Sarah R. - Francis M. GRANT
        Susan - Samuel B. COLLIER
NICHOLSON, Lutie G. - John M. EAGEN
        Matilda - W. Ben HALE
NIFONG, Bettie - Sam FLEMING
NISBET, Mary Spottswood - Leonard MATTHEWS
NIXON, Dora - Dr. W. A. COLLINS
NOE, Bettie - S. H. GARNHART
        Jennie C. - Judge Wm. F. FERGUSON
        Mary E. - William E. JAMISON
NOEL, Sarah Frances - William H. NOEL
NOLAND, Elizabeth - Charles E. FISHER
NOONAN, Gussie - George C. HADLEY
NORAY, Catherine S.J. - John BLACK
NORMAN, Nevada Jane - A. J. McILVAIN
NORRIS, Ann E. - James Miller STOCKWELL
NORTH, Elizabeth Agnes - Samuel T. ADAMS
NORTON, Sarah Ann - Johnson SMITH
NOYES, Caroline I. - F. B. KIRBY
NULL, Henriette - F. BARNES
NYE, Amelia H. - Macklot THOMPSON
        Harriet J. - Lemuel W. PATTERSON

O'BANNON, Virginia - James R. BERRYMAN
O'FALLEN, Ellen - Francis J. SMITH
OFFATT, E. C. L. - Dr. M. M. MAUGHAS
OFFUT, Jemima - James JENKINS
OFFUTT, Frances A. - George H. CHASE
        Lou M. - E. T. SCOTT, M.D.
OGLE, Emily - William H. CARVER
        France C. - George H. HAZZARD
OLDHAM, Mary E. - William B. TIPTON
OLIVER, Ann - Presley BROWN
        Georgie E. - W. C. HORNBEAK
        Mittie J. - J. R. NEAL
OREAR, Elizabeth - Inskeep QUISENBERRY

OREAR, Julia - E. J. OREAR
O'REGAN, Kate M. - Capt. H. HARKINS
ORME, Olivia - John L. FERGUSON
ORNDORFF, Lizzie C. - John R. COLEMAN
OSBORN, Sarah J. - Hiram H. DRYER
O'TOOLE, Mary E. - I. C. PARKER
OWEN, Annie - John T. TILLAY
        Elizabeth H. - B. M. WHITSON
OWENS, Annie - P. J. COLLINS
        Mary A. - James R. CALDWELL
OWINGS, Marietta E. - Joseph FOLBRACHT

PAIGE, Frank L. - A. A. CHILD
PALLER, Permelia - John S. ROBINSON
PALMER, Kate - W. T. EDGAR
        Mary - T. W. STEWART
        Tabitha - James B. PALMER
PALTON, Sallie - Lewis M. FRAZIER
PARK, Ann Eliza - James F. KEMPER
PARKER, Estelle - Charles P. JOHNSON
        Hettie W. - Dr. Edward YANCY
        Susan - Edward D. HENRY
PARKS, Sarah Ann - Henry HIGGINS
PARR, Eliza J. - Cyrus R. SHOLL
PARSONS, Arabella - H. W. CRANE
        Betty Clark - J. H. GARRETT
        Julia M. - E. E. TRICKEY
        Mrs. Miriam (nee BENTLEY) -
                William Hamilton HAYSE
        Sarah - Dr. H. D. LINN
PASLOW, Mrs. Anna B. - James MING
PATRICK, Elizabeth - John T. NANSON
PARTRIDGE, Emily F. - Lucien EATON
PASHAW, Annie R. - J. P. LAMPTON
PATTERSON, Adaline M. - Granville ATKINS
        Bettie H. - Dr. Thomas B. HEAD
        Mrs. Helen E. - Abner HITCHCOCK
        Jennie M. - John Christy WATSON
        Kate A. - J. W. BUNNELL
PATTON, Sarah A.D. - Franklin DAVIS
PAYNE, Anna - William W. BLAND
        Martha Jane - James W. ROBINSON
        Sarah - Ben Woolley PAYNE, M.D.
        Mrs. Sarah A. (nee ROSE) -
                Ira ALEXANDER
PEAK, Mary A. M. - Winfield J. MARSHALL
PEAKE, Eliza J. - Samuel WILCOXSON
PEBLEY, Sarah - Moss EASLEY
PECK, Mary Ann - John GERTHER
PEEBLES, Allie M. - Frank G. FLOURNOY
PEERS, Julia - Thomas J. LaBARGE
PELTON, Julia - J. G. BEAUMONT
PEMBERTON, Ann Eliza - William TRUITT
        Georgia - J. T. ANDREWS Jr.
        Lucy R. - Dr. W. A. REESE
        Talitha - Lemuel NORTHCUTT
PENCE, Tetie - William KING
PENDLETON, Mag - George DOUGLASS
        Mary E. - J. C. DOWNING
PENN, Virginia - Dr. C. E. SMITH
PERKINS, Abby L. - George E. BEARD
        Mary - Jphn McHOME
PERRY, Mrs. Ann S. - George B. FRENCH
        Fannie - Richard PERRY Jr.
        Hannah - I. T. UTTERBACK
PERSINGER, Delia Ann - Jesse F. EARLE
PETERS, Martha A. - Simpson PARKS
PETERSON, Susan Jane - Thomas JONES
PETTIBONE, Mattie L. - Frank BURNETT
PETTUS, Martha - George W. SUTTON
PEYTON, Ella S. - William R. TRASK
PHELPS, Nancy Jane - John DOZIER
PHILIBERT, Mary Elizabeth - George T. LEWIS

PHILLIPS, Harriet - B. F. TARR
  Mattie - Dr. _. W. McCLELLAND
  Velona A. - Robert D. PATTERSON
  Zerelda - William P. HULETT
PHIPPS, Melissa A. - Richard R. GOODING
PIEPER, Therese - Milton C. GETTY
PIERCE, Josephine - R. A. BENEDICT
PITTS, Mattie McDowell - Alex Finley DENNY
  Susan - John S. GRANT
PIM, Lizzie - D. C. HORNSBY
PIXLEE, Caroline J. - A. W. MATSON
POCKMAN, Lucy Ann - J. H. P. LAMPTON
POMEROY, Gracia - Ed. A. SEAY
POOR, Ella - D. A. CLARK
PORTER, Andromache - Rev. John R. TAYLOR
  Ella - A. R. LEVERING
  Mary E. - Elder Henry H. HALEY
POST, Frances H. - J. VAN NOSTRAND
POSTAL, Theda - George P. COCHRAN
POTTS, Sallie A. - John KARNES
POWELL, Julia A. - John J. HUNTER
PRATT, Alice - Francis LOGAN
PRESTON, Caroline - Thomas M. GLENN
PREWITT, Mrs. Carrie M. (nee SHAW) -
     Alexander PROCTOR
  Clara - Rev. X. X. BUCKNER
  Mattie - John M. BATES
PRICE, Annie E. - William M. POWELL
  Eleonora Jane - John B. COLLINS
  Mrs. M. E. (nee WOODS) -
     Waide A. PARKS
  Mary E. - Archie P. GRIFFITH
  Sarah J. - William F. PIXLEE
  Talitha - Charles O. GRIMES
PRIEST, Ann E. - George W. HAWKINS
  Maddie M. - A. L. SHORTRIDGE
PRITCHARD, Fannie - Dr. William T. HELMUTH
PROCTOR, Clara A. - Owen J. LEWIS
PROUTS, Anna - James H. JONES
PRYOR, Mary - William S. McNEILL
  Virginia M. - George T. LINCOLN
PULIN (POLIN?), Mary A. -
    Constantine MAGUIRE
PULLIS, Sallie - John DANIEL
PURCELL, Frances - M. W. ACKERLY
PURSEY, Miss - John HOOD

QUAIL, Mary C. - William P. HUBBELL
QUIREY, Ann Eliza - Zachariah F. MARTIN
QUISENBERY, Molie (sic) E. -
    Edward G. CAMPLIN

RAINS, Mary Ann - George PAINTER
RALSTON, Rowena - Ezra R. HICKMAN
RAMSEY, Annie E. - John W. PECK
  Mary J. - J. W. PECK
RANDOLPH, Kate - Dr. J. W. BARTLETT
  Kate - Oliver H. GRISWOLD
  Mollie - J. M. LOCKWOOD
RAWLINGS, Annie - Joseph GAMBLE
REDD, Annie E. - Edward F. BRIGHT
REDMAN, Mrs. Evalina - Jacob L. SHARP
  Helen J. - Capt. Thos. Howard OLIVER
REED, Frances - John Wesley BUTLER
  Irene F. - John K. DPUGHERTY
  Mary B. - Eugene W. DIX
  Mollie - Samuel W. ANDERSON
REID, Amy Jane - N. A. HARVEY
RELF, Gertrude S. - H. W. HOUSE
RHODES, Mary C. - Stewart CARTER
RICE, Mrs. E. G. - Rollin RICHMOND
  Elizabeth - Andrew P. JONES
  Mary - John VANLANDINGHAM
  Mary Ellen - John ADAMS

RICHARDS, Priscilla - John Watson LITTLE
RICHARDSON, Emma - Capt. Richard B.
     LINVILLE
  Mrs. N. P. - G.T. CHAMBERLAIN
RIDDLE, Martha C. - Edmond F. ROBIDOUX
RIDGWAY, Eliza - E. A. WILLS
RIGS, Mrs. Sophia - James HAVENS
RILEY, Alley - William McCARTY
  J. Amanna - Henry P. DUHRING
RINGO, Florence - William A. HALL
  M. Louisa - Dr. William B. TEBBS
RITTER, Emma Matilda - Alexander DRYSDALE
ROBARDS, Jennie E. - Elder J. R. ROGERS
ROBERTS, Elvira - Tandy Q. RUSH
  Frances A. - John TATE
  Martha A. - Aquilla ROBERTS
  Mary - Benjamin SHARP
  Mary - Peter NICHOLSON
  Mary E. - Rev. G. ANDERSON
  Nancy Elizabeth Jane -
     Robert GALLOP
ROBERTSON, Ariadne H.M. - James K. McKENNA
  Laura A. - Eugene ESTILL
  Mattie A. - Peter TILTON
ROBINSON, Bettie - P. Mars GEESTERANUS
  Charlotte - Richard COADY
  Dorothy F. - Dr. Adams PEABODY
  Eliza - John WALKER
  Eliza M. - James R. BRADFORD
  Mary A. - Dr. Samuel OVERALL
  Mary Ellen - Andrew R. GIBSON
  Sarah Ann - Alfred WILLIAMS
ROBIOU, Frances V. - George L. TOWNER
  Virginia - Rufus C. WHITE
ROBIRDS, Isabella - George F. CARVELL
ROCHE, Emily J. - George M. LEWIS (LEVIS?)
ROCHFORD, Bedelia - William H. SINCLAIR
RODES, Sarah - James R. DUDLEY
ROGERS, Judith - James E. JOHNSON
  Lottie A. - John J. EDWARDS
  Mary Cornelia - Dr. J. French JUDGE
  S. A. - J. T. CAMPBELL
  Virginia - Charles SCUDDER
ROPER, Anna E. - Charles H. LEWIS
  Edmonia J. - Theodore BARTHOLOW
  Olive - Thomas GRANT
ROSE, Sarah R. - John H. FARRAR
ROSEWELL, Sarah A. - James S. GRIFFITH
ROTHWELL, Sallie C. - Dr. W. A. ROTHWELL
ROUSE, Mary Frances - James CLARKSON
ROUSSIN, Sophia P. - Lawrence W. CASEY
ROUTH, Ann - William MORRIS
ROWE, Mary Willie - Robert BUCHANAN
ROWLAND, Frances E. - William T. GOSLIN
ROYALL, Virginia - James A. HENDERSON
RUBY, Lavenia M. - A. G. MASON Jr.
RUCKER, Sallie J. - J. H. BOSWELL
RUNYAN, Mary R. - William J. BURGESS
RUSSELL, Fannie E. - Fitzhugh ALEXANDER
RUTH, Lizzie - John S. HOOD
RUSSELL, Hester Ann - Cornelius D. WHITE
RUTHERFORD, Mary Isabella - H.W.G. CLEMENTS
RYAN, Kate Fitzgerald - George W. THOMAS
RYLAND, Clintona - Dr. ERR

ST. VRAIN, Mary Louisa - John P. SKELLY
SALER, Augusta - Sylvester FREEMAUN
SALISBURY, Julia E. - Thomas F. DOXEY
  M. M. _ Thomas STEVENS
SAMUEL, Alice - John H. BROWN
SAPPINGTON, Catherine - Samuel FUNK
  Jennie - Darwin W. MARMADUKE
  Mary Emily - William BAXTER
SAYERS, Laura Agnes - James M. BROWN

84

SAYERS, Susan - James W. HART
SCHAEFER, Jennie - W. B. CALHOUN
SCANLAN, Maggie - William PRICE
      Susan - Rev. A. A. MORRISON
SCHAUFFELBERGER, Kate - P. H. GROPPEL
      Lena - H. B. BRINKMEYER
SCHAUMBERG, Nannie - William R. JOUETT
SCHIPP, Henriette - Aaron KAHN
SCHULTE, Gertrude - Daniel NICKLAS
SCHWEINECK, Sophia - Ernst NEUENDEUTEL
SCOTT, Alice - Emmet R. HAYDEN
     Margaret Isabella - John W. SPOTSWOOD
     Martha Jane - Dr. P. O. HARVEY
     Sue - Daniel D. JENKINS
SCRUGGS, Anna E. - Joseph T. McLEOD
SEARS, Elizabeth - John G. TREDWAY
SEBASTIAN, Mary Catherine -
          John Hendrick TOWNSEND
     Meekie - Thomas C. WINN
SEBREE, Lucy - William TURNER
BEDAM, Carrie G. - Charles C. GREENE
SEE, Catherine - Daniel NUMELLY
SEIF, Eliza J. - Nicholas MARTIN
SELECMAN, Jennie - Thomas W. CLASBY
     Lizzie - Charles H. WHITAKER
SEVERSON, Margaret - Dr. Samuel SPROUL
SHACKELFORD, Bettie - Charles L. THOMPSON
     Lizzie - Capt. J. B. DEXTER
     Mattie H. - D. P. ROWLAND
SHAFER, Nancy - John A. PERDEE
SHAMOUS, Margaret Ellen - Richard HUDSON
SHANKS, Eliza G. - Rev. Samuel McPHEETERS
     Helen P. - William W. PARK
SHARK, Amanda - John OVERSTREET
SHARP, Lizzie - H. C. WALLACE
     Mary E. - Josiah McCLELLAN
SHAW, Eliza - Alvin M. LONG
SHEAFFE, Margarette H. - John M. TAYLOR
SHEARER, Helen E. - D. B. WILSON
SHEBLE, Miriam - Leon J. DeLISLE
SHEETS, Annie M. - Daniel M. McNEIL
SHEETZ, Susan - Peter McCLAIN
SHELBY, Adelaide - Evan YOUNG
     Mary Pindell - Wm. B. NAPTON Jr.
     Matilda M. - Felix K. WILKINSON
SHELLEY, Fannie A. - Allen WRIGHT
SHELTON, Gillie - Dr. F. L. RIVES
     Martha - Thomas WELLS
SHEPARD, Martha Ann - A. D. LOCKRIDGE
SHERIFF, Rosanna - Richard MILES
SHIELDS, Mississippi - James K. HARDY
     Sophia - Mark BYRNE
SHIRLEY, Mary - George S. SEXTON
     Scottie - Robert M. MENEFEE
SHOCK, Rebecca - Amos G. SULLINS
SHOOT, Kitty - Charles P. HEYWOOD Jr.
SHORT, Minerva - John F. PATTERSON
SHRYOCK, Lucy - Samuel C. EDWARDS
SHULL, Sarah - Clarence WALLACE
SHULZE, Susan Mary - Samuel ROLAND
SHUMATE, Ginnie A. - Gabe LONG
SIDLE, Caroline - Fred A. HUBENSMITH
SIGERSON, Laura - William N. McDEARMON
SILVER, Eliza - J. W. LEWIS
SIMONDS, Laura - J. G. BELL
SIMPSON, Lizzie A. - R. S. KING
     Mary Ann - William WIGHTMAN
     Mary H. - James T. THORNTON
SINCLAIR, Eliza - John ADAIR
SKINNER, Ann Eliza - Dr. John W. ROBERTS
     Elizabeth P. - Jackson SINGLETON
     Emily - William CROYSDALE
SLACK, Kittie - Newman T. MITCHELL

SLAUGHTER, Mollie -John B. TILDEN
SLAVEN, Susan O. - Allen OREAR
SMALLWOOD, Agnes S. - J.B.L. STEPHENS
SMEAD, Mrs. Eliza J. (nee LANCASTER) -
         Stephen G. HAWKINS
SMITH, Annie - George A. BRADFORD
     Annie - Dr. Thomas C. POOR
     Anna M. - James D. VANDERFORD
     Bettie - James MARTIN
     C. Annie D. - Maj. Jure C. CRAVENS
     Cynthia - Sebastian FERGE
     Drucilla Frances - Francis CLARK
     Jane E. D. - J. D. MANNY
     Jessie C. - D. G. TUTT
     Julia - Henry SHERMAN
     Kate - Joseph TUCKER
     Kate - James RUCKER
     Lissie - Charlie THAW
     Lizzie C. - Samuel M. STONE
     Lucy A. - J. J. SUTER
     Lurinda - James GEORGE
     Martha - Robert S. HUDSON
     Martha A. - Dr. C. M. JOHNSON
     Mary A. - William TRAVIS
     Mary Ann - John D. BROWN
     Mary E. - William B. MAXWELL
     Mary M. - William Y. SISK
     Mary S. - James HOOD
     Michal Francis - Luther P. GOOCH
     Minerva - John WILFREY
     Permelia - John THATCHER
     Phebe Ellen - James BURGESS
     Sallie - John C. McFAUL
SMIZER, Eliza H. - Charles L. JOHNSON
SMOOT, Hattie - Eben CORBY
SNELL, Mrs. (nee DICKEN) - Cyrus HUTCHINSON
     Amanda - Prof. L. S. HEAD
     Eliza - John W. MITCHELL
     Eliza J. - A. R. TOMPKINS
SNELSON, Susan - Clark H. GREEN
SNODDY, Mary Ann - Alexander DENNY
SOLOMON, Susan Emily - Charles SHUTTER
SOWERS, Mary A. - Henry MORTON
SPARKS, Margaret A. - Thomas B. STASEY
SPARR, Sarah Louise - Charles F. HILLS
SPEARS, Eliza J. - D. Waldo WOODS
SPIES, Mrs. Catherine - Newton RANKIN
SPRAGUE, Laura T. - Thomas J. BARTHALOW
SPRINKLE, Jane - James CONLEY
SQUIRE, Sarah J. - Charles J. STEBBINS
STAMPS, Cordelia A. - C. RANNELS
STAPLES, Fannie - John W. WATSON
STARKE, Ann E. - William H. RUSSELL
     Priscilla - Robert C. DYSON
STEDMAN, Henrietta - Dr. J.S.D. ALLEYNE
STEENBERGER, Mollie - Zadoc HOOK
STEPHENS, E. A. - William ROHRER
STEPHENSON, Marietta - P. H. JONES
     Mary - J. S. STEPHENSON
STERN, Henrietta - Isaac O. STRIKER
STETTINIUS, Bertha - John WANN
     Julia - Robert P. MORRISON
STEVENS, Annie - John A. PICKEN
     Charlotte E. - James A. CUMMINGS
     Jennie - Charles BOARDMAN
STEWART, Annie - Charles KEARNY
     Elizabeth J. - G. P. PEPPER
     Elizabeth - John STEWART
     Helen - Edward APPLETON
     Julia - Gen. Daniel M. DRAPER
     Kate - T. B. HILL
     Margaret - Clinton P. CROW
     Virginia - Finis M. McLEAN

STEWES, Lavinia - Edward ROZIER
STICKNEY, Josephine - Ransom R. CABLE
      Susan - Orange W. CHILD
STILWELL, Mary E. - John N. BOFINGER
STOBIE, Mary - D. R. WHITMORE
STOCKTON, Elizabeth - J. William CANNON, M.D.
STOKES, Henrietta A. - Benjamin M. LOVEJOY
      Mrs. Malley - Jerome MILLINGTON
STONE, Cecelia W. - James JOHNSON
      Martha R. - D. D. MILLER
      Nannie - George W. HANCOCK
      Nannie - Dr. Stephen RITCHEY
STORK, Amanda - Ephraim MINOR
STOUT, Leontine - Philip C. TAYLOR
STRATFORD, Helen M. - Charles A. HOLTON
STRATTON, Jeannie P. - Aaron B. LEVERING
STREET, Mary - James M. ROBINSON
      Sarah Eleanor - George A. BAKER
STRICKLIN, Zilphia Jane - Wm. R. KIRKPATRICK
STRODE, Nannie M. - A. J. RUSSELL
STROVE, Hinetta - Thomas E. DOZIER
STUART, Anna - Henry M. BUTLER
      Maggie E. - James PRICE
STURGES, Kate - William H. BENTON
STYLES, Caroline - George L. SOHCALING
SUBLETTE, Margaret - George A. CHANSLOR
SUGGETT, Eliza P. - Henry C. BRADLEY
SULLIVAN, Frances C. - J. Milton THATCHER
SUTTON, Sarah P. - Camillus C. DURKEE or
                            DURKER
SWALES, Sallie - F. G. HENESY
SWARINGEN, Isabelle D. - Andrew B. McCREERY
SWERINGEN, Annie E. - Arthur B. BARRET
SWINDELL, Emily M. - Benjamin L. QUARLES
SWINK, Sarah A. - George M. McNUTT
SWINNEY, Mary E. - James J. EMORY
SWITZER, Martha - Dr. F. M. SCROGGINS
SWITZLER, Frances Jane - William WALLACE
SYMINGTON, Mya W. - Gen. Samuel D. LUCAS

TAFT, Eliza A. - Christian SCHAEFERMEYER
TALBOT, Alice - Thomas WARD
      Mrs. Cordelia A. - Dr. S. P. CUTLER
      Elizabeth - George R. GREEN
      Mary Brent - A. S. MITCHELL
      Sallie E. - William E. BARD
TALBOTT, Kate - Joseph SPENCE
TAMM, Bertha - Charles EVERTS
TANNEYHILL, Rebecca - B. F. HOLLAND
TATLOW, Anna Mary - Dr. S. H. ANDERSON
TATUM, Sophie - Frank T. CASEY
TAYLOR, Ellen A. - Edward A. BERNOUDY
      Elizabeth N. - Philip T. WASH
      Fannie L. - James Wilmer STITH
      Helen M. - Walter T. H. MILLER
      Mary C. - Caernarven L. RICHARDS
      Rachel A. - Rev. I. M. O'FLYNG
      Rebecca - William KIDWELL
      Sarah - Alonzo THORP, M.D.
TERRILL, Louisa - George S. PALMER
      Sarah - John ROBERTS
TERRY, Emily - George W. BUCHANAN
TEST, Mrs. E. L. - T. T. ASHBY
THALSON, Elizabeth - Alfred D. MURRY
THIXTON, James Ann - George PHIPPS
THOMAS, Flora - Rev. E. A. TERRY
      Isabella - Reese PAYNTER
      Julia Ann - John W. THOMAS
      Lydia A. - Thomas F. BAKER
      Mary J. - Richard A. BYRNES
      Mollie B. - James M. PIPER
      Nancy S. - B. D. PHILLIPS
      Sallie F. - George W. BELLAMA

THOMPSON, Amelia - William J. ROWLAND
      Ann E. - George W. HURST
      Mrs. Betty S. (nee EVANS) -
              Capt. Fred WILL
      Caroline - Joseph PARKER
      Cornelia - Rufus ANDERSON
      Elizabeth - Samuel HORNER
      Lou F. - J. P. RICHARDS
      Minerva - Henry GANT
      R. M. - James H. McGEE
      Virginia A. - William F. BRIGHT
THOMSON, Leona V. - William B. BROWN
THORNTON, Mattie - H. C. SUMMERS
      Theodosia - Leonidas LAWSON
THROCKMORTON, Annie - George A. NOLEN
THURMAN, Rachel Ann - James W. FAIR
TILLERY, Martha Ann - George W. JONES
TIPTON, Sarah - Jamuel BALDWIN
TIMBERLAKE, Mary - Robert H. WRIGHT
TISDALE, Mrs. Nancy (nee PREWITT) -
             Daniel HOSKINS
TOALSON, Mary Ann - Andrew J. RUMMANS
      Polly - John E. WALLER
TODD, Bettie A. - Dr. Benjamin WHITAKER
      Letitia - Edward C. BRECK
      Mollie W. - W.K. (or W. E.) FALCONER
TOMPKINS, Lucy Mildred - Levi DAWKINS Jr.
TOONEY, Mrs. Elizabeth Jane - P. S. BURNETT
TORRILL, Frances - James LOAN
TOURNEY, Mina - Emile KARST
TOWNER, Timorah - Levi LINGO
TRABUE, Mary E. - William H. BARKSDALE
TRACEY, Mrs. Ella M. (nee MARTIN) -
             Dr. M. MARTIN
TRACY, Eliza R. - Howard SHAW
TRIGG, Jose H. - John T. PIGOTT
      Julia - William N. JOHNSON
      Lizzie - Thomas W. SHIELDS
      Sallie - Lewis MILLER
TRIPLET, Mary Angeline - Christopher COCKERILL
TRUSLOW, Amanda - B. M. STIGALL
TUCKER, Elmira - DeMarcus PALMER
      Frances - Samuel D. TURNER
TUNSTALL, Mary - H. S. ROBBINS
TUPPER, Mary Frances - James C. SLOSS
TURLEY, M. C. - John A. MILLER
TURNBULL, Elizabeth C. - Leonidas D. WALKER
TURNER, Abbie - J. T. UTTERBACK
      Blanche - William M. McKOWEN
      Catherine E. - Leonidas E. WRIGHT
      Mrs. Cynthia - W. T. GIBBS
      Eleanor - B. W. LEWIS
      Elizabeth E. - Charles B. SAWYER
      Isabella - Washington YINGLING
      Rebecca - William J. LEWIS
      Rhoda Ann - Henry Harrison GARTH
TURNHAM, Louisa - Joseph DOWNING
TUTT, Mrs. Elizabeth (nee JACKMAN) -
             John C. McKINNEY
TUTTLE, Arena M. - Abner MARTIN
      Elizabeth M. - George W. HAYNES
      Mary E. - P. H. ABRAMS
      Sarah C. - Robert A. RODDY
TWYMAN, Elizabeth C. - Rev. James W. MORROW
      Emma - Benjamin J. EDDINS
      Nannie - St. Clair PAGE
TYLER, Emma - Henry W. BARRETT
      Mary Lawrence - Charles F. JOHNSON

VALIANT, Roselaire - Preston MATHEWS
VALLE, Blanche - John A. DILLON
VANCE, Mrs. C. C. - George F. ROOTES
VANDIVER, Elmira - Joseph HAGENS

VANDIVER, Missouri J. - James SELBY
VANLANDINGHAM, Elenore - John JACOBS
VAN NESS, Harriet - Francis Maury LUDLOW
VAN RENSSELAER, Mary E. - Samuel GARDINER
VASQUES, Rosalie Mignault - Eleazer BLANCHARD
VAUGHN, Mary F. - John H. WISENER
VICKERS, Laura - Dr. P. H. JENNINGS
VIVION, Hallie - Thomas S. GHORHAM
                    OR
            Sallie - Thomas S. GRAHAM
VOELKER, Maria - Charles A. SNELL

WADDELL, Sarah Elizabeth - J. F. HARRELL
WADDLE, Lucy F. - Reuben R. GEARY
WADE, Fereby - Cyrus HUTCHENS
WADLEY, G. E. (or J.E.) - James J. TREVOR
WAGNER, Natalie - Frederick KUEMMEL
WAITE, Mary M. - Ad C. CAUGHLIN
WALKER, Ella - John L. HICKMAN
            Mary H. - Elijah CHILES
            Sarah - William E. WOOD
            Susan - William H. PARKS
            Virginia - James TAYLOR
WALL, Elizabeth - Jackson CORDER
WALLACE, Jennie - George Mifflin HARKER
            Maria Ann - John M. DAVIS
            Martha P.E. - Andrew J. AUSTIN
            Mollie A. - Irvin C. VIVION
            Sarah A. - C.W. MAJOR
WALLER, Margaret - Henry MORRIS
WALLINGFORD, Sue E. - William SELBY
WALLS, Sarah - John W. HOWE
WALSH, Margaret L. - John E. YORE
            Marie C. - B. Maziere CHAMBERS
            Mary Frances - William A. YORE
            Mary J. - Francis MAGUIRE
WALTERS, Sallie - William J. HOUGH
WALTON, Mary - Arnold T. WINSOR
            Mat A. - James F. CREWS
WARDLAW, Annie F. - Thomas S. MILLER
            Virginia - Rev. A. P. FOREMAN
WARDWELL, Georgie M. - James CARROLL
WARFIELD, Debbie J. - A. N. CROWDER
WARNE, Sallie - Oscar F. STEBBINS
WARREN, Anne E. - Dr. J. S. WARREN
            Elizabeth A. - Thomas H. NELSON
WASH, Elizabeth - John Y. PAGE
WASHBURN, Georgia Augusta - Jonathan CLAYCOMB
WASHINGTON, Annie M. - Powhatan WOOLDRIDGE Jr.
            Mrs. Caroline M. -
                    Francis WEBSTER
WATERS, Lizzie - John H. ASHBURY
WATERSIN, Nannie - Rufus R. EDWARDS
WATKINS, Elvira E. - Lemuel F. GATCHELL
            Mary J. - J. Bailey SMITH
WATSON, Davilla A. - F. Kirtley LYNCH
            Emma - L. H. BARNARD
            Josephine - Samuel JACKSON
            Laura Kate - Charles W. BUCHANAN
            Lucy Missouri - Eli HARMAN
            Mary Jane - Samuel SAPP
            Russilla - Willis C. WALKER
            Sallie Virginia - D. Robert BARCLAY
WATT, Harriet - Lee A. HALL
WATTS, Anne - William WINENT
WAUGH, Mary - Thomas M. SHAW
WAYLAND, Ann R. - William B. MILLER
WEAR, Mildred Y. - Charles BRYAN
WEARALL, Minerva - Andrew BLANKS
WEAVER, Mrs. Eliza A. - William C. WILSON
            /NEE ADAMS
WEBSTER, Emma - John C. POWELL
            Emma A. - George DENISON
            Hattie A. - Fred A. LUNARD

WEBSTER, Mary - J. M. LOUGHBOROUGH
WEIZENECKER, Minnie - C. H. ROEDLER (or O.H.)
WELCH, Hadge Jane - William H. JENNINGS
            Mat - Dr. R. GANO
WELLING, Mary J. - Z. M. SAPPIERE
WELLS, Mary E. - Henry C. LEWIS
            Rachel M. - Henry M. REID
WEST, Ann - T. J. BAKER
            Annie H. - William FAGON
            Augusta A. - Conrad R. STINDS
            Martha E. - Walter E. SELL
            Mary W. - Edward Thomas ESTES
            Sallie - George E. MILLAN
            Sarah L. - Rev. Samuel J.M. BEEBEE
WETHERGREEN, Mrs. Nina (nee HIRSCH) -
                    Thomas E. BASSETT
WETZEL, Sallie - John H. HOWARD
WHALEY, S. Augusta - Alonzo D. PRICE
WHIPPLE, Fannie A. - Alfred A. PARKER
WHITAKER, Emma F. - Benjamin LACY
            Jane - John ROGERS
            Sarah Ann - William HAMPSON
WHITE, Fannie A. - William L. GATEWOOD
            Georgeanna - John W. JAMISON
            Mrs. J.C. (nee FIFE) -
                    H. HOLTZCLAW
            Laura - J. C. MOORE
            Lizzia - John TUCKER
            Lucy C. - Stephen SCOBEE
            Margaret - Lysander HICKAM
            Maria C. - Richard T. JACKSON
            Mary Ann - John SCUDDER
            Mattie - Lt. J. G. STRODE
WHITESIDES, Mary - James SULLIVAN
WHITING, Florida - P. M. KENNEDY
WHITSETT, Martha - Henry McLAUGHLIN
WHITTLESBY, Mary Frances - Thomas
                    Jefferson FLETCHER
WICKLIFFE, Annie E. - R. BEARDSLEE
WIGGINTON, Mary C. - W. P. KARNES
WIGGS, Mary Jefferson - John W. RUSSELL
WILCOX, Lizzie A. - John B.C. THOMAS
WILCOXSON, Tabitha - Berryman SAPP
WILDE, Amelia - Thomas S. HAYES
WILDER, Harriet E. - A. ARNOT
WILEY, Mary E. - Joshua BOTTS
WILHITE, Eliza Harl - O. C. HARRIS (O.G.)
            (Mrs. HARR, nee WILHITE)
WILKERSON, Milly Amm - James C. CONNELLY
WILLIAMS, Amanda - M. S. ALLGAIER
            Annie - B. L. McGEE
            Jannie C. - S. A. McPHEETERS
            Kate - William L. UPTON
            Mag. - J. S. DORSEY
            Mary - M. P. POOL
            Rachel - John S. J. MILLER
            Sarah Jane - James C. BEARD
            Sarah Louisa - Jordan GRAVES
WILLING, Sallie - James E. DOWNEY
WILLIS, Mildred M. - Repps O. DUFFER
WILSON, Annie - Howard BROTHER
            Caroline - G. W. EVERETT
            Elizabeth H. C. - J. SCHOONOVER
            Emma - F. G. STICHTER
            Henrietta - Reuben HUME
            Kate - J. B. GROVE
            Lucy - C. J. F. WILSON
            Mary E. - Dr. N. C. TATE
            Mrs. Mary E. - Capt. John COBB
            Nannie - Fleming BATES
WINFREY, Sallie - John S. PITTS
WING, Sarah E. - Robert J. McMAHAN
WINN, Elizabeth Jane - Dr. Bennett H. CLARK

WINN, Mollie - W. W. BATTERTON
    Virginia - Hon. D. D. BURNES
WINSTON, Cora A. - William L. WOODSON
WISE, Margaret - James NORRIS
WISHON, Josie E. - Joshua C. MICHEL
WITHERS, Mary Kathener - John G. YAGER
WITT, Sallie - Thomas BEASLEY
WOLF, Mary Ann - Henry SMELSER
WOLFE, Louisiana - Benjamin UNDERWOOD
WOLFSKILL, Martha - Irving BALLEW
WOOD, Amanda - Overton M. HARRIS
    Eliza H. - William A. SMITH
    Josephine - Arch K. NISBET
    Kate - W. C. SIPPLE
WOODRUFF, Helen S. - Edgar R. MOFFATT
WOODS, Annie - Dr. Charles Quarles CHANDLER
    Clemency - Robert M. SNODDY
    Lou - Henry RONEY
    Mary Ann - Steward WILSON
    Mary Pauline - John L. O'TOOLE
    Sarah J. - Garland D. MAUPIN
WOODSON, Anne E. - James ANDERSON
    Olevia A. - Prof. George H. MATTHEWS
WOODWARD, Emma C. - P. A. LADUE
    Emily - William JONES
WOOLEY, Lizzie - E. B. OVERSTREET
WOOLFORK, Angeline - Abraham WILEY
    Bettie - J. F. WALL
    Sallie - James W. AVERY
WOOLSEY, Mary Caroline - George W. WOOLSEY
WOOLVERTON, Rachel - Edward G. BROOKE
WORD, Sophie - D. A. CONSTABLE
WORTHINGTON, Ariadna - Joseph D. LAWNIN
WREN, Elizabeth - Anderson CRUMP Jr.
    Martha Frances - George DAVENPORT
    Tinetta - Daniel DUNHAM
WRIGHT, Amanda - John J. EDWARDS
    Mrs. Carrie E. (nee ELLIS) -
                 P. Dick CORDELL
    Julia - John B. BEAUVAIS
    Lizzie - T. P. McMURRY
    M. A. - J. H. YOUNG
    Maria Elizabeth - W. V. N. BAY
    Melinda Frances - Upton Lawrence BOYCE
WYANT, Sarah E. - P. B. HEELAN
WYCKOFF, Mary A. - Dr. L. H. ROBBINS
WYMORE, Lottie D. - C. H. HALL
    Mary - Prof. J. B. BRADLEY

YANCY, Elizabeth - John O. BURTON
YANTIS, Kate - John BEAN
YARNALL, Lida - Dr. T. J. PAPIN
YATES, Sarah - George HUNT
YOUNG, Mary C. - E. G. MURPHY
    Matilda - Andrew ROBINSON
    Mollie - Charles C. BIRCH

XAUPI, Volumnia Orso - Dr. J. M. YOUNGBLOOD

ZIMMERMAN, Augusta - John A. STURGES